Chaucer Reads 'The Divine Comedy'

KARLA TAYLOR

CHAUCER READS 'THE DIVINE COMEDY'

STANFORD UNIVERSITY PRESS, STANFORD, CALIFORNIA

Stanford University Press, Stanford, California
© 1989 by the Board of Trustees of the Leland Stanford Junior University
Printed in the United States of America

CIP data appear at the end of the book

Published with the assistance of the Frederick W. Hilles Publication Fund of Yale University
and a special grant from the Stanford University Faculty Publication Fund to help support non-
faculty work originating at Stanford

Acknowledgments

It gives me great pleasure to thank those whose intellectual and material help have made this book possible. My first and lasting gratitude is to Alfred David, who introduced me to Chaucer. John Freccero, Elizabeth Closs Traugott, Joseph Harris, and Stephen Barney read all or parts of earlier versions of this study; their criticism and encouragement made my dissertation a far better piece of work, and have guided my thinking since. Marie Borroff and John M. Ganim read the entire manuscript with great care and acuity; I am grateful to each of them for their criticisms and for more. My editor, Helen Tartar, has been indispensable, for her patience and for her perception—better than my own—of what I was trying to say. I thank Karen Brown Davison for her careful preparation of the manuscript.

This study has been generously supported by the Whiting Foundation, with a Whiting Fellowship in 1980–81; and by Yale University, with a Morse Fellowship in 1985–86. It has been published with the assistance of the Frederick W. Hilles Publication Fund of Yale University.

Much of the material in Chapter 2 originally appeared in *Comparative Literature*, 35 (1983): 1–20. I thank the editors for their permission to use it in revised form. I have also revised the material on proverbs in Chapter 4, first published in *Chaucer's Troilus: Essays in Criticism*, edited by Stephen A. Barney (Hamden, Conn., 1980).

In March 1987, as I was finishing the draft of this book for Stanford University Press, Donald R. Howard died. I am profoundly grateful for the privilege of studying with him, and I sorely miss his shrewd intelligence. He directed the dissertation out of which this grew, and I profited then and profit still from his perceptive, acute criticism. If the reader I imagined as I wrote has a face, it is his.

K.T.

Contents

Note to the Reader

The following abbreviations for Chaucer's works are used in the text and the Notes:

BD	*The Book of the Duchess*	LGW	*The Legend of Good Women*
CT	*The Canterbury Tales*	PF	*The Parlement of Foules*
HF	*The House of Fame*	TC	*Troilus and Criseyde*

Quotations from Chaucer are from *The Riverside Chaucer*, 3d rev. ed., edited by Larry D. Benson et al. (Boston, 1987).

Quotations and translations of the *Commedia* are from *The Divine Comedy*, edited and translated, with a commentary, by Charles S. Singleton, 3 vols., 6 pts. (Princeton, N.J., 1970–75).

Biblical quotations in Latin are from *Biblia sacra iuxta vulgatam Clementinam*, 6th ed. (Madrid, 1977). English translations are from *The Holy Bible, Translated from the Latin Vulgate*, translated by the English College at Rheims, 1582–1609 (New York, 1844).

Chaucer Reads 'The Divine Comedy'

Introduction

No one doubts that Chaucer read Dante's *Commedia*. Since the early part of this century, the task has been not to establish the fact of Dante's influence on Chaucer, but rather how to interpret it. The fundamental questions about canonical works of literature seem to be asked and answered anew by each generation of critics, and in recent years the Dante-Chaucer relationship has again attracted a good deal of attention. Despite the renewed interest, however, the two basic positions on Dante's importance to Chaucer remain the same. Either one believes that Chaucer's numerous Dantean borrowings reflect little more than aesthetic appreciation for a turn of phrase or a striking story—Ugolino, in the Monk's Tale, is the only generally recognized instance of the latter—or one sees Chaucer as "Daunt in Inglissh," indebted to Dante not only for words and images but also for poetic and philosophical aims.[1] What is missing from both views is the notion that Chaucer's Dantean borrowings arose out of an intellectual engagement both deep and deeply critical. Dante clearly sharpened Chaucer's sense of what poetry could do, and in this sense the influence is very great indeed.[2] But it would be a mistake to forget how different the two poets are, how difficult it is simultaneously to believe both poets' constructions of the world. Chaucer's most pervasive use of Dante, I suggest, was as a spur and a background against which he defined his own, very different poetic and moral vision.

Poetic influence operates not only in local imitations of phrasing and technique, but also in the considerably more elusive realm of form. A good example of how Chaucer defined his

poetic world in contrast to Dante's is *The Canterbury Tales*, like
the *Commedia* a journey seen in retrospect.³ In *The Canterbury
Tales*, Chaucer portrays the human community by reporting the
words of the pilgrim's fellow travelers on the road to Canterbury, just as Dante reported the words of the souls he encountered on his way. Despite this structural influence, Chaucer's
vision of the world differs enormously from Dante's. Dante sees
the world eschatologically, under the aspect of death and judgment. He moves through eternal realms peopled by souls whose
permanent habitations have already been assigned according to
their moral states at the time of death. They are all flatly saved
or flatly damned. And, except in the *Purgatorio*, they are all beyond change. Even the souls in purgatory change only in limited ways, for they have already been saved. The world of *The
Canterbury Tales*, though, embraces neither heaven nor hell. Its
inhabitants live within the world and time, and hence can
change right up to the moment of death. Because of this mutability, Chaucer utters no final judgments. Even the Pardoner,
whom George Lyman Kittredge called the "one lost soul" on
the Canterbury pilgrimage, could in theory still repent.⁴

The temporality of *The Canterbury Tales* defines the crucial
difference between its vision of the world and that of the *Commedia*. The Parson's Prologue leaves us on a hill overlooking the
pilgrimage's goal; at four o'clock in the afternoon, day is fad-
ing, but the final hour has not yet arrived. At this point the Parson replaces "fables and swich wrecchednesse" with his "myrie
tale in prose" on penance, and redefines the goal of the journey
as the otherworldly "Jerusalem celestial" (ll. 34, 46, 51). Neither destination is reached within the work, however. When the
Parson is finished, Chaucer withdraws to a vantage outside the
work, looking forward to last things, and in a disembodied
voice distinct from that of the remembering narrator, speaks a
Retraction distinct from the remembered journey. The tales
that precede the Parson's penitential treatise and the Retraction
are allowed to exist only as long as this perspective is not invoked. Whereas Dante had written a divine comedy, Chaucer

writes an earthly comedy about people still in the process of becoming.

As Donald R. Howard suggests,⁵ Chaucer had promised this
other sort of comedy at the end of *Troilus and Criseyde*:

> Go, litel bok, go, litel myn tragedye,
> Ther God thi makere yet, er that he dye,
> So sende myght to make in som comedye!
> But litel book, no makyng thow n'envie,
> But subgit be to alle poesye;
> And kis the steppes where as thow seest pace
> Virgile, Ovide, Omer, Lucan, and Stace.   (*TC*, v.1786–92)

This stanza has been something of a crux in *Troilus* criticism,
for it contains the only generic label Chaucer gives his poem.⁶ I
will not add my voice to the controversy; instead, I suggest that
Chaucer's reference here is specific rather than general. He calls
the *Troilus* a tragedy in order to dissociate it from Dante's comedy. But why identify the poem in relation to the *Commedia* at
all? His primary source was Boccaccio's *Il Filostrato*, which he
does not mention even obliquely. No generic label adequately
captures the whole poem, with its play of distance and intimacy, laughter and sorrow;⁷ "tragedye" points rather to a critical engagement with Dante's poem. It links Chaucer's poem of
ancient Troy to the Virgilian historicism of the *Aeneid* (for history in both poems is secular, though the *Troilus* lacks the
Aeneid's providentiality) rather than to the Christian historicism of the *Commedia*.⁸ The *Commedia* lies behind the *Troilus* as
a second and more elusive text, influencing not only the shape
Chaucer gives to Boccaccio's story, but also his concern with the
more abstract issues of the poet's craft: truth, fiction, representation, and authenticity.

The notion that the *Troilus* depends on the *Commedia* for
more than scattered images and lyrical ornamentation crops up
frequently, although usually as a provocative suggestion rather
than a focus of rigorous argument.⁹ However, two recent studies
demonstrate the rewards of pursuing Chaucer's use of Dante in

greater detail. R. A. Shoaf argues that the images of coining in the *Troilus* are derived from those of the *Commedia*, and on the basis of this influence, concludes that referentiality in Chaucer works much as it does in Dante.[10] In a less theoretical vein, Winthrop Wetherbee shows the extent to which Chaucer's use of the classics was molded by Dante, and finds in the consummation scene "a complex structure of allusions to Dante, a sustained ironic paralleling of Troilus's experience with that of Dante in the *Commedia*."[11] The central sequence—in which Criseyde accuses Troilus of false suspicions, he swoons, and she forgives him—parodies the accusation, swoon, confession, and forgiveness of the confession sequence at the top of purgatory. The pattern of animal imagery also corresponds ironically to the allegorical pageant of the Church beset by evil in *Purgatorio* XXXII. Wetherbee concludes that

the primary function [of this elaborate borrowing from the *Commedia*] is to provide a setting in which to consider the love of Troilus for itself, and the identification of these lesser characters with evil archetypes becomes meaningful only to the extent that we see Troilus's vision of love as comparable to Dante's. Chaucer has appropriated the resources of the greatest Christian poet to show us through Troilus's experience what human love is in itself and what, being only human, it cannot be; what rich spiritual capacities are implied by its aspirations and how inevitable it is that any worldly attachment, taken too seriously, will betray these aspirations.[12]

This, I think, is essentially the right approach to Dante's influence on Chaucer in *Troilus and Criseyde*. Yet it needs to be qualified. First, it does not accord enough integrity to the enormously different surfaces of the two poems; had Chaucer intended the *Troilus* to be so nearly parallel to the *Commedia* he would not have chosen to embed his treatment of love in a pagan fiction. Second, there is an alternative, or rather additional, explanation of Chaucer's elaborate Dantean borrowings, one which directs the irony Wetherbee so skillfully traces not only at Troilus and his vision of love, but also at Dante and his. These two objections are closely connected, for it is the historical embeddedness of a story set in the ancient, pagan past that enables Chaucer to treat love so differently from Dante even while borrowing from him so heavily. Like the *Commedia*—though in an utterly and characteristically different way—*Troilus and Criseyde* is a poem made of time. Time is a prime constituent of the relations among Chaucer's narrator, his material, and his audience. Chaucer's Troy is separated from and joined to himself and his fourteenth-century England as much by the interventions of history (the coming of Christ, the *translatio imperii*) as by place. And this is no more than just, for the *Troilus* is (among many other things) Chaucer's major contribution to the writing of historical poetry. In it he explores the shape of history itself—the temporal bounds that define human experience, general and particular, and especially the central human experience of love—and the meaning the past might hold for those who hear or read the poem in their own historical present.

In trying to understand the influence Dante exerted on the *Troilus*, I have sought always to account for my sense that, though both it and the *Commedia* are self-consciously historical poems, they do not record the same world. The threads of this study—the truth of fiction, authentication, the nature of the narrators, and the figurative representation of the world—can all be traced back to this sense. The historical poetry of the Middle Ages raises the problem of truth—either phenomenal or a more elusive kind—and hence, with these self-conscious works, the problem of the authenticity of their versions of the world. In addition, in the *Commedia* and the *Troilus* the quality of the narrative voice—its relation to subject and to audience—is a crucial aspect of each poem's argument about the world. To explore these issues, I turned my attention to the fine details of language that, in locating the narrator temporally, spatially, and modally with respect to story and audience, create perspective and a "universe of discourse."[13] My exploration, that is, focused initially on deixis and the subjective and objective systems within language. Although I have tried, insofar as possible, to make my discussions of the *Troilus* and the *Commedia* accessible to readers unfamiliar with the work of Ann Banfield, Emile Benveniste, Gérard Genette, Käte Hamburger, Harald Weinrich, and the other linguists and narrative theorists who have guided my own understanding, I think there is some use in explaining the underpinnings of my thinking more thoroughly here. What follows, then, is a brief discussion of the terms and methods that lie at the root of my understanding of "point of view" and its relation to narrative authentication.

Benveniste was the first linguist to describe two complementary subsystems within language, *l'énonciation du discours* and *l'énonciation de l'histoire*, which designate, respectively, subjective and objective ways of interpreting the world.[14] (Despite the awkwardness, I have retained Benveniste's original terms in order to distinguish the modes to which they refer from other possible meanings of "discourse," "history," and "story" in English.) These modes are defined by their different uses of person, verb tense, and in general the temporal, personal, and spatial references that together make up language's "pointing function," or deixis.[15] An utterance is deictic if it can be understood only by knowing something about its speaker. A well-known example illustrates the concept: someone finds a bottle washed up on a beach, containing a note that tells him "Meet me here tomorrow at noon and bring a stick about this big."[16] In order to understand, the finder must know who wrote the note (*me*), when (the day before *tomorrow*) and where (*here*) it was written, and what size *about this big* is. *Bring*, also a deictic, meshes with *here* and tells us that the addressee must *come to* here *from* a place farther away from the speaker. (Thus pairs like *come–go*, *bring–take*, *to–from*, and determiners like *this–that* also manifest deixis.) Without this information the finder cannot respond to the invitation. Taken together, the three aspects of deixis—personal, spatial, and temporal—contrast a complex *I–here–now* to a more distant complex *he–there–then*, to create a frame of reference in which the speaker locates the object of his discourse.[17] *Discours*, the subjective mode of language, has a built-in point of view oriented to the speaker and the context in which he speaks. *Histoire*, the objective mode, lacks this speaker-oriented frame of reference. Consequently, we need know nothing about the speaker or his context in order to understand what is said in histoire.

In practice, of course, discours is an inevitable element of language in use; in all utterances, someone says something to someone else for a purpose, which may be a direct or a more covert appeal.[18] Since words are not value free, pure objectivity is impossible. Thus discours and histoire are not entirely separable; rather, they are poles toward which utterances tend. Discours focuses more heavily on the speaker, his perspective and concerns, and the context in which he speaks. Histoire focuses on the content of the utterance, and minimizes the importance of the subjective elements so crucial to discours.

Each mode achieves its focus primarily through its characteristic combination of personal pronouns and verb tenses.[19] In discours, the *I–you* relationship between speaker and addressee is always implicit, often explicit. In histoire, which seeks to minimize this fundamental communicative situation and render the questions "who speaks?" and "who sees?" irrelevant, these pronouns are absent. Instead, the mode uses the third person, which Benveniste calls a "non-personne" because it does not participate in the relationship between speaker and addressee.[20] In moving from *I* to *you* and *he*, we start very close to the speaker and become progressively more distant from him.[21]

Similarly, verb tenses measure distance from the speaker. Only the present tense can express close proximity to the speaker and his moment of enunciation; all others are temporally or modally removed.[22] However, some tenses indicate greater distance than others. In this regard, the distinction between discours and histoire is particularly helpful, for it allows us to resolve the array of verb tenses into two different ways of expressing the temporal sequence of past, present, and future.[23] The tenses of discours are always anchored in the speaker; the point of departure is the moment of enunciation, expressed in the present tense. When the speaker looks forward in time, he generally does so in the future tense; immediate future can also take the deictically closer form of "I am going to . . ." When he looks back in time, he does so with the *passé composé* in French, the *passato prossimo* in Italian, or the *Perfekt* in German. In English, he does so with either the preterite or the present perfect. Like the retrospective tenses of discours in French, Italian, and German, the English present perfect stresses "present relevance" over the pastness of the event. In any case, the temporal sequence of discours is, broadly speaking, anchored in the speaker's perspective, concerns, and knowledge, in the present moment of communication.

Temporal sequencing in histoire, however, is accomplished by a different set of tenses oriented around the events to which the speaker's utterance refers. The morphologically past forms characteristic of histoire establish a deictic distance from the speaker. The dominant tenses of histoire are the *passé simple* in French, the *passato remoto* in Italian, and the preterite in German and (again) in English. Retrospection from this point of departure is expressed with the pluperfects of these languages, prospection with the various conditionals. All of these tenses can also appear in discours, where they express time and mode relative to the speaker. But the characteristic tenses of discours—present perfect, present, and future—do not appear in histoire, because of their orientation to the speaker. The two systems of temporal sequencing are illustrated by the following examples, of which the first set focuses on the speaker's temporal location, while the second set does not:

I am walking my dog now. (present progressive)
I have already walked my dog. (present perfect)
I walked my dog yesterday. (preterite)
I am going to walk my dog again. (present progressive)
I will walk my dog tomorrow. (present and modal [future])

She walked her dog that day. (preterite)
She had walked her dog the day before. (past perfect)
She would walk her dog again the next day. (past and modal
    [subjunctive])

The conjunction of person, tense, and adverbial reference determines whether these sentences maximize or minimize the importance of the speaker's perspective or temporal location; hence in the second set, *the day before* and *the next day* have no necessary relation to the speaker's *yesterday* and *tomorrow* in the first set.

Verbs with interior or exterior perspectives also establish the personal frame of reference of discours. Some verbs vary modally according to their person. I can say "I feel angry" and presumably report in the indicative, so to speak—though I might be lying, or trying to manipulate you. But if I say "You feel angry" or "He feels angry," I am supposing, interpreting facial expressions, or recalling something "you" or "he" told me. All of these modalities fall away from the certainty that is at least possible in the first-person statement. The same restrictions apply to all verbs of "inner action," which have an interior focus. One can really know only one's own inner action. However they are used, these verbs indicate a built-in perspective on the event they report. They arise from within the speaker's perspective in the first person, and from the speaker's various subjective modalities of supposing in the other persons. Other verbs have an exterior focus. "He feels angry" very often means "He seems angry"; the second statement brings the modal uncertainty inherent in speaking about the inner action of others to the surface. But if I say "I seem angry," it sounds odd. I am either surmising that I seem angry to you, or fragmenting myself into a part that feels and a part that observes myself feeling as if from without.[24] If a verb has either interior or exterior focus, it depends on the perspective of the speaker and so is limited to the subjective mode of discours.

Various genres of discourse, literary and otherwise, are also limited primarily to discours because they depend on the speaker's participation, active or perspectival, in the content of his utterance. Benveniste and Weinrich list didactic works, essay, commentary of all kinds, ritual, and performative speech among the genres of discours.[25] Comparisons as well are part of discours.[26] They stem from the speaker's perception of similar-

ity between vehicle and tenor, and from his desire to communicate better to his addressee, rather than from the nature of the
tenor itself. And autobiography, because of the constant presence of an *I* out of whom everything arises and to whom the
narrative is subordinated, also belongs to discours.[27]

The two modes of discours and histoire, as different ways of
apprehending the world in language, also have different authenticating strategies. Because discours focuses on the speaker
and his context, his character and reliability are crucial to our
assent. If he gives us no reason to believe him, we might think
him either ignorant or a liar. Authentication in discours seeks
to support the claim "This is true because I saw (did, experienced) it. I know it intimately; therefore you can trust me." In
histoire, the focus is shifted away from the speaker and onto the
content of the utterance itself. Because the speaker is only min-
imally present, authenticity must arise from the presentation of
the story as true to the world. Authentication in histoire implicitly urges, "This is true because I had no effect on what I
report. I did not participate, and I do not distort the events for
personal reasons. The events speak for themselves."

As Genette notes, linguists took their time in recognizing
the subjectivity of language, and narrative theorists have been
equally slow to formulate analogous terms for narrative.[28] Until
recently, most discussions of narrative form have stressed point
of view—omniscient, focalized, or objective—and person,
without fully recognizing that these are more than stylistic
choices. But Benveniste's modes of discours and histoire have
now gained increasing importance in narrative theory, and this
has resulted in greater attention to the relationship between the
"what" of the story (histoire) and the "who, where, when" of
its generating act (discours). This relationship leaves its traces
in the same clues of person, tense, and deictic references we
have seen above. Genette does not consider person important in
narrative, and indeed he is correct to point out that any narrator, whether he intrudes into his narrative or not, can speak
only in the first person. Genette then argues that the real dis-

tinction is whether or not the narrator is a character in the story.[29] However, because he is less troubled by fictionality than are many fictional narratives themselves, he does not discuss strategies of authentication. I think it is partially for this reason that he argues against the importance of person in narrative. For authentication, the relation between "who speaks?" and "who sees?" is crucial.[30] Our standards of authenticity in a narrative depend in large measure on the particular mixture of the subjective qualities associated with an *I* and his discourse, and the otherwise more distanced features of the narrative.

Narrative theorists have always distinguished between first- and third-person points of view, and within each broad group, among a number of subcategories.[31] In "objective" third-person narratives,[32] the narrator does not participate in the story he tells from an external, objective, distanced stance; the participants are referred to in the third person. The focus of these objective narratives is on what is shown; the distanced style seeks to render the questions "who speaks?" and "who sees?" irrelevant. Hemingway's "The Killers" exemplifies objective narration; in this story the narrator does not even seem to exert an ordering force on his material.[33] He shows uninterpreted reality rather than filtering it through his interpreting perspective. The intervention of the narrator (as Genette says, in the first person) would ruin the narrative, for the fiction is that he does not exist in any significant way. Since objective narrative focuses so overwhelmingly on the story,[34] we ask that what is shown seem real. The actions need not be true in the sense of having happened, but they need to resemble real actions very strongly. If the narrative achieves this plausibility, then the authenticating strategy that imitates objective narration of fact works. Again, the fictionality resides partly in the suppression of discours, but primarily in the fact that the story, which is presented so realistically and objectively, and which is the locus of authentication, is a product of precisely the subjective imagination that its style seems to exclude. The absence of subjectivity is thus both the fiction and the authenticating strategy. By suppressing the speaker's importance, the objective third-person style exemplifies the quality of authority to which histoire aspires.

In other, more unabashedly fictional, third-person narratives, the narrator adapts points of view manifestly not his own.[35] The primary fiction here lies in the separation of "who speaks?" from "who sees?" and "what is shown?," which are far more important in this narrative than the speaker. Yet works in this category retain elements of discours mixed into their basic histoire, and the mixture is indeed how we recognize their open fictionality. These elements, the basis of the separation between "who speaks?" and "who sees?," include combining verb tense with temporal deictics (tomorrow with a verb in the preterite, for example) and verbs of inner action with person in a way that would be anomalous for a real speaker.[36] Hence Banfield's "unspeakable sentences."[37]

In the subcategory of omniscient narration, the narrator not only says more than any of his characters knows, but also dips at will into their minds, seeing things from their points of view. When he does this, he reports the inner action of these characters as if from within, and yet in the third person—an anomalous conjunction of verbs with a built-in perspective and the "wrong" person. Since the narrator's insinuation into perspectives other than his own is obviously fictional, authentication in omniscient narration arises from the plausibility of the events (as in objective narratives), the sheer detail and completeness of the narrator's knowledge—often in its social realism—and from the plausibility of the consciousnesses into which the narrator dips. Does their manner of seeing and interpreting correspond to what we know of our own? If so, the narrative will be realistic, and it will succeed in drawing attention away from the basic fictionality of the narrator's way of speaking and knowing.

In the subcategory of focalized narratives, the plausibility of the "seer" is even more important. We see events as the focal characters see them, and we know what they know about them. If a narrative filters its information through the consciousness

of one of its characters, it must make that consciousness realistic. This does not necessarily mean that the character's perspective is accurate; Emma Woodhouse and Isabel Archer are
frequently wrong. Indeed, the drama of such narratives often
arises out of the changes in interpretation forced upon these focal characers by the weight of events. Nonetheless, the question
of reliability is shifted from the narrator (who speaks) to the
point of view through which we see. This point of view is the
locus of fictionality, and also the locus of authentication.
Whether it is reliable or not matters less than whether it is presented realistically. To authenticate psychological realism, various styles have been used in focalized narratives to present
point of view: Henry James's "lucid reflector," with whom the
narrator sees and knows; free indirect style (*erlebte Rede*), as in
Mrs. Dalloway; and interior monologue, as in Molly Bloom's
concluding section in *Ulysses*.[38] These styles illustrate progressively more immediate ways of "showing" the inner consciousness of the character from whose perspective we see, with progressively fewer marks of "telling," the traces (in person and
tense) that a narrator nonetheless mediates between us and this
character, until we get what appears to be completely immediate mimesis in interior monologue.[39] These are all techniques
to achieve greater realism, and yet, as Genette says, the closest
we can get to "showing" in narrative is only "telling as if showing"; since all narrative is "telling," greater immediacy in point
of view is not only psychologically more realistic but also more
fictive.[40] In all focalized narratives, the narrative is distanced
from its real speaker and his point of view;[41] and the authenticating realism of the fictive perspective distracts our attention
from its fundamental fictionality.

In fictional first-person narratives, the narrator is an "I" who
tells a story in which he participated, either as the main character or as an observer; his participation in events distinguishes
him from the "I" that can always potentially intrude in third-
person narratives.[42] The primary fiction of these narratives lies
in equating "who speaks?" with "who sees?," equating, that is,

the "I" from whose perspective we see with the author of the narrative. We know this proposition—in essence the creation of a fictional discours—to be fictional because Ishmael is not the same as Melville, in name or in life history. To get us to assent to this fiction as "real," the point of view through which events are seen must again correspond to our own experience of seeing and knowing. If the narrator sees with all the ordinary limitations an "I" faces, and with a realistic personal frame of reference created by speaker-anchored deictics, then this "I" works as an authenticating device. His realistic point of view guarantees the truth of events that may be realistic or fantastic; though no one would argue that Ahab or the white whale is exactly realistic, they are presented as the realistic experiences of Ishmael. The question of reliability of this "I" is important: is he ignorant? a liar? competent? trustworthy? Our belief in what is shown depends on these factors, but even if the "I" is not entirely reliable (Zeitblom in Mann's *Doktor Faustus*) we can sometimes arrive at the truth of events through interpreting his characteristic distorting quirks. Thus the authentication of this category of narrative lies in its resemblance to the ordinary communication of discours, in which we believe a reliable speaker no matter how exotic his report, and make mental corrections for a conversational partner whom we know (or suspect) to be unreliable. But since the "I" in these first-person narratives is not the author, the primary fiction lies in the creation of the imaginary *I–you* relationship of discours.

Because none of the anomalies that mark omniscient and focalized third-person narratives appear in fictional first-person narratives, they are grammatically indistinguishable from those other first-person narratives told by an "I" who really is identical to the author. To this category belong autobiographies, memoirs—and Dante's *Commedia*. We expect not just realism from these narratives, but also truth. The possibility of the life story that is not merely realistic but also true furnishes the fundamental authentication for the fictional first-person narratives that do not identify the narrator with the author.

The truth we expect of autobiography is not the objective truth of histoire, as in objective third-person narration, but the subjective truth of discours. It depends primarily on the narrator, his perspective and interpretations, and his act of communicating. Since the content of the narrative is always filtered through him—and in some cases would be unavailable from any other source—he is subject to the same limitations found in the point of view of fictional first-person narrators. His combinations of deictics, tense, person, and perspectival verbs must be restricted in the same way as in anyone's subjective perspective. The better the correspondence, the more authentic the narrator's point of view will seem, for the "I" is the primary authenticating device of first-person narrative. Indeed, we read the autobiographies of eminent public figures not so much for the events reported as for the autobiographer's personal perspective on them; an inconsistent point of view would arouse our skepticism. Similarly, too much focus on public events reported as if objectively would undermine the premises of autobiography; the author might as well have written a more impersonal history. The more private the material, the more exclusively the narrative focuses through the "I." In the most extreme cases—spiritual autobiography, for example—the truth of the narrative consists almost entirely of the narrator's inner action and subjective interpretations.

Autobiography, especially where comparatively little outside substantiation is possible, raises an authenticating problem deeper and more elusive than any that can be solved by simple consistency of the narrator's subjective perspective. This is the problem of self-justification. A narrative may be nonfictional and yet arouse skepticism rather than belief if the narrator's self-justification is not located in the right place. We become skeptical if we ever sense that the narrator's efforts to prove himself a trustworthy authority are focused too much in the past. If the "I" seems primarily apologetic (in the sense of a defense) for his past behavior, thoughts, and perceptions, we doubt his authority. He seems nostalgic; or perhaps he lacks

self-knowledge; or perhaps he has learned nothing of significance, from or since the events he narrates, that would give him
sufficient reason to burden us with his therefore flawed, inauthentic autobiography. Distrusting the narrator, we also distrust the events he reports. Conversely, if an autobiographer
elides the change his narrative supposedly records—for instance, by attributing to the past an understanding achieved
only later—his self-justification is equally dislocated. The autobiographical narrator must keep his times straight, especially
the time of insight. Otherwise the autobiographical past is an
invented one, and the narrator a self-made fiction.

Yet our aim, if we continue reading, is still subjective truth,
though it may bear little resemblance to what the author intended to communicate. We read not for the truth of events,
but for the truth of the teller—a truth that might well appall
him were he to recognize it. We encounter this revealing inauthenticity sometimes in the writings of politicians who have
been harried from office. Fascinating though these cases may
be, they nonetheless have little to do with authorial authenticating strategies; they merely indicate the strength with which
we expect truth from such narratives.

The authenticating strategy by which autobiographies usually counter the problem of self-justification is a scission between what Eugene Vance has called the "I-as-subject" and the
"I-as-object."[43] As E. B. Vitz writes in her study of the *Roman
de la rose*'s narrator, "the *me* to whom this *I* refers is indeed
someone who no longer exists, a past self."[44] The split in the
"I," then and now, subjective and objective, is accomplished by
the presence of both tense systems, that of histoire and that of
discours. Benveniste and Hamburger rightly classify autobiography as discours because all the tenses originate in the "I";
temporal references are to the narrator's time.[45] Still, the use of
histoire's dominant passé simple or passato remoto transfers the
relative objectivity of that mode to those parts of the narrative
in which they appear, thus distancing and depersonalizing what
we ordinarily think of as the most personal kind of writing.

The justification of the narrator as an authority worth believing is focused on the "I" here and now, addressing us in our shared present, rather than on the "I" there and then. The present "I" has learned more, perhaps even the Truth, and thus treats his less knowledgeable past self more or less ironically. The narrator shows throughout that he is capable of sometimes merciless objectivity about himself as he was, and thus gives us good reason to trust him as he now is. But because the personalized forms of discours—time, space, and person all relative to the narrator—invade and control even the distanced parts of the narrative, they blur the distinction between subjectivity and objectivity.

The tense system of Chaucer's Middle English presents certain problems for an approach to *Troilus and Criseyde* so heavily reliant on deixis; there aren't as many tenses in English, then or now, and they aren't as neatly separable into subjective and objective modes as in Dante's Italian.[46] Still, Chaucer is as consistent as Dante in creating exactly the temporal, spatial, and modal relations he desires among narrator, story, and audience. Although in the *Commedia* one can sometimes reason from the stylistic choice of tense alone, in the *Troilus*, with its mixture of first- and third-person narrative, one must rely on person and the distinction between interior and exterior focus of verbs to supplement the poem's fundamental distinction between the narrator's time (anchored by the present tense) and the story's time (anchored by the preterite tense). With these, it is almost always possible to tell the difference between the "world of the story" and the "world of commentary."*[47]

Although *Troilus and Criseyde*, as Chaucer's fullest response to Dante, is the focus of this study, I approach the poem indirectly. An account of Chaucer's use of Dante in the *Troilus* ought to preserve the line of continuity with his initial re-

---

*There is one crucial exception: the line at the end of Troilus's vision from the eighth sphere, which reads, "And sholden al oure herte on heven caste" (v. 1825). It is not clear whether this is the world of Troilus's story or the world of the narrator's commentary; I will discuss this problem in the last chapter.

sponse, recorded in the restless octosyllables of *The House of Fame*. A better introduction to the Dante-Chaucer relation than any I could devise, *The House of Fame* is itself Chaucer's meditation on poetic influence. So to it I turn first. Chapter 1 seeks both to establish the nature of Chaucer's first response to Dante and to define the terms on which Chaucer later, in the *Troilus*, responded to the *Commedia* as authentic history.

Chief among the points of access granted by *The House of Fame* is Chaucer's new concern with the problems of authentication. This concern is the source of my strong sense that one cannot simultaneously accept both the *Commedia* and the *Troilus* as true, or believe in the versions of the world for which Dante and Chaucer argue in their poems. I will have more to say about authentication after discussing *The House of Fame*. Chapter 2 shows the pivotal role of *Inferno* v in the *Troilus*. The major borrowing of *Inferno* v, with its intertwining of reading and romance, locates Chaucer's new concern with authentication as a response to Dante in particular. The remainder of the study returns to authentication in order to flesh out the way Chaucer reacts against Dante in the *Troilus*.

To do this, I have distinguished between primary and secondary authentication. Primary authentication, the chief device by which the two poets establish their authority, is the voice that addresses us directly, in the first person, and tells us the story: the narrator. The intimate reading relationship engendered by first-person narration requires that, in order to assent to the truth of the text, we learn to trust the speaking voice. Otherwise, we think the narrator a liar, the narrative a lie rather than a fiction. We must also trust the speaker's competence, his ability to report not only truthfully (a matter of intentions) but also accurately. These issues occupy Chapter 3.

By secondary authentication, treated in Chapter 4, I mean the credibility of the invented world. In order to believe in this world, of course, we must trust the truthfulness and competence of the narrator. But the version of the world, if it is credible, also inspires trust in the narrator. Hence both kinds of authentication are intertwined. In the *Troilus*, Chaucer represents a version of the world differing from that of the *Commedia*, perhaps not substantially but certainly epistemologically. The proverbs and conventional literary love language of the *Troilus* constitute a strategy of analogical language that, in responding to the similes and allegory of the *Commedia*, argues for the separate truth of the world Chaucer creates. By exploring the Dante-Chaucer relationship through authentication, we can see the reason for Chaucer's use of Dante: *Troilus and Criseyde* should be read as a moral retraction of Dante's moral fiction, with regard to both the place of love in the world and the place of fiction in the world.

1. First Readings: 'The House of Fame'

he House of Fame is the first work in which Chaucer shows familiarity with Dante.[1] Unfinished and more than a little enigmatic, it is not the best place to look for a final, considered response to the *Commedia*. But it may owe its vigor and imaginative energy to the exhilaration of discovering what Dante had done in another vulgar tongue; and as a first response, it raises issues of authority and truth in fiction that may guide us to a better understanding of the *Troilus*. In addition, *The House of Fame* is Chaucer's "art poetical,"[2] a sustained examination of his craft of poetry and an enthralling statement about the nature of poetic influence.[3] With Wetherbee,[4] I am convinced that it was Dante who spurred Chaucer to consider what goes into the making of literature.

The setting of *The House of Fame* is the mental world of books.[5] From the Temple of Venus in Book I, with its visual illustrations from the *Aeneid*, to Fame's palace in Book III, with its vaulted roof supported by the poets who memorialized the famous "matters" of the Western literary tradition, nearly everything in the poem comes from other poems. It used to be thought that *The House of Fame* recorded Chaucer's move from his early reliance on written authority to a new vision based on direct, fresh experience of life, unmediated by literature.[6] But even the eagle—the guide who wrests the dreamer Geffrey from his stuffy library and carries him to Fame's aery realm, and who is the poem's chief proponent of empirical observation—comes from another book. The eagle is the most memorable of the many traces Dante has left on *The House of Fame*.[7] He is a witty borrowing and something more. In a very real sense, the poem tells the story of how the eagle came to be here.

Until he speaks, the eagle remains relatively faithful to his origins. Chaucer took him chiefly from the dream in *Purgatorio* IX, in which an eagle seizes Dante, as Jupiter had seized Ganymede, and carries him aloft:

> in sogno mi parea veder sospesa
>   un'aguglia nel ciel con penne d'oro,
>   con l'ali aperte e a calare intesa;
> ed esser mi parea là dove fuoro
>   abbandonati i suoi da Ganimede,
>   quando fu ratto al sommo consistoro.
> Fra me pensava: "Forse questa fiede
>   pur qui per uso, e forse d'altro loco
>   disdegna di portarne suso in piede."
> Poi mi parea che, poi rotata un poco,
>   terribil come folgor discendesse,
>   e me rapisse suso infino al foco.
> Ivi parea che ella e io ardesse;
>   e sì lo 'ncendio imaginato cosse,
>   che convenne che 'l sonno si rompesse.   (*Purg.* IX, 19–33)

(I seemed to see, in a dream, an eagle poised in the sky, with feathers of gold, its wings outspread, and prepared to swoop. And I seemed to be in the place where Ganymede abandoned his own company, when he was caught up to the supreme consistory; and I thought within myself, "Perhaps it is wont to strike only here, and perhaps disdains to carry anyone upward in its claws from any other place." Then it seemed to me that, having wheeled a while, it descended terrible as a thunderbolt and snatched me upwards as far as the fire: there it seemed that it and I burned; and the imagined fire so scorched me that perforce my sleep was broken.)

The House of Fame echoes several details from this dream, including the feathers of gold (*HF*, 503, 530) and the eagle's descent like a thunderbolt (*HF*, 534–38). That the dream is Chaucer's primary source for the eagle is confirmed when Geffrey, again borrowing from Dante to wonder whether he is being "stellyfyed," includes "the goddys botiller" Ganymede among those chosen few whom he does not resemble:

> "O God," thoughte I, "that madest kynde,
> Shal I noon other weyes dye?
> Wher Joves wol me stellyfye,
> Or what thing may this sygnifye?
> I neyther am Ennok, ne Elye,
> Ne Romulus, ne Ganymede,
> That was ybore up, as men rede,
> To hevene with daun Jupiter,
> And mad the goddys botiller."
> Loo, this was thoo my fantasye.   (*HF*, 584–93)

But Chaucer complicates his eagle by combining elements drawn from elsewhere in the *Commedia* as well. The splendor of Dante's ascent into the heavens (*Par.* 1, 61–63) amplifies the description of the eagle's plumage, so bright that it seems "the heven had ywonne / Al newe of gold another sonne" (*HF*, 505–6). Less apparent but more important, Chaucer also appropriates the heavenly version of Dante's dream eagle, the sign of empire and justice in the Heaven of Jupiter.[8] From the sixth heaven (*Par.* XVIII–XX), Chaucer borrows not words, but an image and the process by which it is formed.

Dante's eagle of justice is a remarkable event of artistic creation. First, Dante sees the resplendent souls of the sixth heaven "segnare a li occhi miei nostra favella" (trace out our speech to my eyes; *Par.* XVIII, 72), forming the opening words of the Book of Wisdom: "Diligite iustitiam, qui iudicatis terram" (Love justice, you who judge the earth; Wisdom 1:1 and *Par.* XVIII, 91–93). The final M of the sentence changes into a lily, and then into the eagle that illumines the theme of divine justice in the next two cantos. The souls that form letters, lily, and eagle are guided by God's artistry: "Quei che dipinge lì, non ha chi 'l guidi; / ma esso guida" (He who there paints has none to guide Him, but He Himself does guide; *Par.* XVIII, 109–10).

The eagle, thus born of words, is the heavenly archetype of the Jovian eagle in Dante's earlier dream. The process by which the heavenly eagle is created matches the divine artistry described in the terrace of pride, the place Dante attains immediately after (and symbolically by means of) his dream. In the first terrace (*Purg.* X–XII), Dante encounters two sets of carvings depicting counterpointed images of humility and pride. Of the first set, Dante states that "non pur Policleto, / ma la natura lì avrebbe scorno" (not only Polycletus but Nature herself would there be put to shame; *Purg.* X, 32–33). The product of neither human nor natural creativity, the bas-reliefs were made by "lo fabbro" (the craftsman; *Purg.* X, 99), *Deus artifex* himself. Dante marvels at the images of Mary, David, and Trajan, so perfectly expressive that they speak to all his senses at once. He smells incense and hears singing, he thinks, and sees the fluttering ensigns of the Roman Empire: "l'aguglie ne l'oro / sovr' essi in vista al vento si movieno" (above them the eagles in gold moved visibly in the wind; *Purg.* X, 80–81). Dante's verbs also reflect the synesthesia. The scenes are not only "intagliato" and "effigiata" (carved and figured; *Purg.* X, 55, 67), denoting the artist's action on the material stone, but also "imaginata" and "impressa" (imaged and impressed; *Purg.* X, 41, 43). The common metaphor of impressing further suggests the inward effect of the carvings on the mind of the beholder. Each scene is a "storia" (story or history; *Purg.* X, 52), not uncommon in the language of painting and plastic arts; but the last, of Trajan, seems actually to *tell* a story. Full of dialogue and movement, it is "storiata" (*Purg.* X, 73), historiated or narrated. The word captures the delicate blurring of verbal and visual arts that pervades the entire passage. To conclude his description, Dante asserts openly what he had earlier implied, that the craftsman responsible for such perfect art is divine:

> Colui che mai non vide cosa nova
> produsse esto visibile parlare,
> novello a noi perché qui non si trova. (*Purg.* X, 94–96)

(He who never beheld any new thing wrought this visible speech, new to us because here it is not found.)

The key term here is *visibile parlare*, visible speech. It binds the divine artistry of these bas-reliefs to the more literal *visibile parlare* of the heavenly eagle, the speaking image formed from letters.[9] Dante's mimesis of the speaking reliefs forms a cornerstone of his imitation of God's Book—his role as *scriba Dei*—in the *Commedia*.[10] It inverts the usual hierarchy in which the human artist imitates nature imitating God (hence the Platonic disparagement of poetry as the shadow of a shadow). In describing the reliefs with his own kind of *visibile parlare*, writing, Dante circumvents the mediacy of ordinary human creativity and instead imitates God directly with the material most conformed to God's own principle of creation, the Word.

With the second set of carvings, Dante seals the link between *visibile parlare* and his art, and strengthens his claim to the authority and truth with which the role of *scriba Dei* invests the poet. The apostrophe to the proud in *Purgatorio* XII contains an acrostic in which the first letters of twelve successive *terzine*, four for each letter, spell out the word VOM (*uomo*, or man). VOM is then recapitulated in the three initial letters of the apostrophe's final *terzina* (*Purg.* XII, 25–63). The acrostic—which is matched only by one spoken by the heavenly eagle in *Paradiso* XIX[11]—works both verbally and visually, horizontally and vertically, for the poet has arranged his words in such a way that, without referring directly to man, they nonetheless form the visual sign for man. With this acrostic, quite literally *visibile parlare*, Dante approaches as nearly as any human artist can God's manner of writing in Scriptures.[12] There, not only words, but also the events to which they refer, signify other events in providential history. The words of the acrostic passage also function both as normal signs referring to the proud course of human history and, like the events of the Old Testament, as traces of a higher message. Although the initial letters are meaningless in themselves, when read vertically they collapse the ordinary

temporal experience of reading horizontally, and mime the
eternal present of God's perspective. They thus reveal the hidden spiritual significance of the apostrophe. Pride defines *uomo*,
mankind, and the destructive sweep of its history.

There is no evidence to suggest that Chaucer thought anything about the acrostics. But he must have been struck by the
concept of visible speech, for he uses it to put forth an idea of
poetry quite at odds with Dante's. From the images of the
Aeneid in Book I to the eagle and "tydyinges" in the rest of the
poem, Chaucer adapts Dante's visible speech to portray a problematic poetry of the imagination.[13]

Although the plot of Chaucer's cobbled-together story of
Dido and Aeneas comes from Virgil and Ovid, the manner in
which he represents it is drawn from both the bas-reliefs of *Purgatorio* X and the genesis of the heavenly eagle in *Paradiso* XVIII.
The dreamer first sees the opening words of the *Aeneid* carved
in brass (l. 142); he then describes what appears to be a series
of wall-paintings or bas-reliefs depicting scenes from Virgil's
work.[14] Although the repeated phrase "Ther sawgh I" (or "Ther
sawgh I graven") suggests visual art, the exclusively literary
techniques of *amplificatio* and *occupatio* imply a direct narrative
source for Chaucer's retelling.[15] The diversity of opinion about
the images—painted or written?—arises because Chaucer has
deliberately obscured the boundaries between the two kinds of
representation.[16] If words can be engraved in brass, so can visual
scenes; and if walls can be painted, so can words—although our
poet suggests the analogy only to distance himself from it:

> What shulde I speke more queynte,
> Or peyne me my wordes peynte
> To speke of love? Hyt wol not be;
> I kan not of that faculte.   (*HF*, 245–48)

Chaucer blurs the distinction between words and visual images because he means to present the story of Dido and Aeneas
as a mental experience. For it is in the mind that words and images work together to produce understanding. Chaucer does

not merely retell the story; he tells what it is like to read it. The dreamer responds to the *Aeneid* by imagining vivid pictorial scenes of the poem's action. Like the heavenly eagle, the images he sees are born of words. The cooperation of words and images is complicated, from our point of view, because the dreamer is also a poet. Hence at the same time that Virgil's words become scenes in the dreamer's imagination, the poet (separated from the dreamer only by time) describes the images in his mind's eye with new words that convey his understanding of what he has read. The nature of representation in the Temple of Venus is confusing because the mental processes work in both directions: inward, as it were, during reading, and back outward during writing. In this manner, Chaucer achieves an artificial simultaneity of the mental acts involved in reading and writing that mimes the simultaneity of memory itself.

With the oddly indeterminate medium of representation in Book I, Chaucer thus captures the peculiarities of the written word as Augustine had described them, and as Dante had already exploited them in the passages Chaucer drew on for his own visible speech. Two passages will suffice to illustrate the Augustinian interplay of words and images. The first, from the commentary on the gospel of John, contrasts visual and verbal representation because of the greater demand words make on the imagination of the perceiver:

> Picturam cum videris, hoc est totum vidisse, laudasse: litteras cum videris, non hoc est totum; quoniam commoneris et legere. Etenim dicis, cum videris litteras si forte non eas nosti legere, Quid putamus esse quod hic scriptum est? Interrogas quid sit, cum jam videas aliquid.[17]

> (When you are shown a picture, it is everything to have seen and praised [the artist]. When you are shown writing, it is not everything, because you are also put in mind to read. For truly, when you are shown writing, which you perhaps do not know how to read, you say, "What do we think has been written [here]?" Surely you ask what it might be [mean], when you see something [written].)

Words require the reader to construct his own picture, as is also
clear from the second passage, from the *Confessions*:

> quamquam praeterita cum vera narrantur, ex memoria profe-
> runtur non res ipsae, quae praeterierunt, sed verba concepta ex
> imaginibus earum, quae in animo velut vestigia per sensus
> praetereundo fixerunt.[18]

> (When past events are truly narrated, out of the memory are
> drawn forth, not the things that occurred in the past them-
> selves, but words conceived from the images of those events—
> images that the events, in passing through the senses, have im-
> pressed in the mind like footprints.)

This complex sentence amounts to a general theory of verbal
cognition that remained important throughout the Middle
Ages.[19] All memory is verbal, and the inner words of memory
(*verba concepta*) are themselves based on mental images, the
traces left in the mind by sensory impressions and captured, in
this passage, by the strongly visual comparison to footprints
(*vestigia*). These images and the inner words they engender can
represent the events they relate directly, from experience, or indirectly, from other words, as implied by the narration that
spurs memory here. In this passage Augustine again stresses the
large role assigned to the recipient of verbal representation; in
addition, we can see a clear distinction between events per se
and their essentially verbal afterlife in the human mind. This
distinction between event and tiding becomes the axis on which
The House of Fame turns.

If the scenes in the Temple were controlled entirely by the
authority of Virgil's words, the dreamer's reimagined *Aeneid*
would not differ from the original. But something happens
when the story enters the mental world of the dreamer, and we
know it as soon as the famous opening lines appear rendered in
nearly faithful English translation:[20]

> "I wol now synge, yif I kan,
> The armes, and also the man
> That first cam, thurgh his destinee,

Fugityf of Troy contree,
In Itayle, with ful moche pyne
Unto the strondes of Lavyne."   (*HF*, 143–48)

The interpolation "yif I kan" is distinctly un-Virgilian; indeed
it is characteristically Chaucerian. From the beginning, then,
the dreamer's recreation of the *Aeneid* differs from the original
in a way that is almost a personal signature of new authorship.
As the story of Dido and Aeneas unfolds, it resembles less and
less the story Virgil told. The proportions are shifted so that the
last eight books receive a scant 30 lines, and "pius" Aeneas and
his high civic duty seem mere afterthoughts to the real center
of interest, the love story of *Aeneid* IV. Even here, the more vividly and fully the dreamer imagines the story, the more he veers
away from his source. Aeneas becomes a cad interested only in
selfish dalliance and the "magnyfyinge of hys name" (l. 306);
Dido becomes the teary victim of male untruth, betrayed by
her trust in Aeneas's self-serving tale of his adventures—how
far we are from the *Aeneid*![21]—and fearful for her reputation,
enshrined now in a monument as perdurable as brass:

"O wel-awey that I was born!
For thorgh yow is my name lorn,
And alle myn actes red and songe
Over al thys lond, on every tonge."   (*HF*, 345–48)

The dreamer's reading, then, tells Dido's side of the story. In
reconstructing her perspective, Chaucer follows Ovid, who had
countered Virgil in the *Heroides*.[22] It is not clear whether Chaucer knew that, in Dido, he had such a perfect example of the
difference between event and report. The "real" Dido, also
known as Elissa, was thought to have lived well after the fall of
Troy and Aeneas's subsequent landfall in Carthage. Moreover,
she did not die a suicide for love, but in order to preserve her
faith to her dead husband Sichaeus. Ovid's version of her
story—which Chaucer follows in *The Legend of Good Women*, as
Boccaccio had done in *De mulieribus claris*—thus owes more to
Virgil than to the historical record as it was understood in the

Middle Ages know the real the Dido, tis Dido of Virgil's

Boccaccie

Middle Ages. Awareness of how Dido had been traduced in order to heighten the difficulty of Aeneas's heroic piety is not uncommon. Jerome, who celebrated her widowhood, knew that Virgil had altered Dido's history.[23] Much later, Ranulf Higden also knew that the famous love story was poetic invention.[24] Boccaccio returned repeatedly to Dido's fate at the hands of the poets. He proves the chronological impossibility of the love affair in his comments on *Inferno* V;[25] his chapter on her in *De mulieribus claris* does not even mention Virgil's Dido in its paean of praise for the real woman's chastity, honor, and civic spirit.[26] In the *De genealogie*, he cites her case to show the power of literature: Virgil's eloquence is so great, he writes, that it persuades us of what we know to be false, that Dido broke faith with the ashes of Sichaeus and killed herself for the love of Aeneas.[27] It is perhaps due to its cogency as an example of this power that Boccaccio returned to Dido's story so often.

In any case, in *The House of Fame* Chaucer does not merely rewrite Virgil into Ovid. He adds new material: Dido's piteous lament, for which, he says, "non other auctour alegge I" (l. 314). More important, he does not attempt to reconcile his sources, but instead stitches them together with such obvious seams that they are shown to be irreconcilable.[28] The uneasy juxtaposition of versions suggests that all the material, old and new, is equally fictive, imagined from the original history in the same way Chaucer imagines his version from the words he reads in Virgil.

Thus the imagination of Book I is not only the image-receiving faculty, to which medieval epistemologies assigned the essential function of mediating between sense perception and the intellect, but also the image-creating faculty.[29] In its partial independence from the authority of Virgil's words, Chaucer's visible speech of the imagination differs from Dante's *visibile parlare*. Because Dante's description of the bas-reliefs is an important part of his claim to imitate divine artistry, he so subordinates his own creative powers that God seems to fashion not only the images in stone but also those in the pilgrim's mind. The power of his imagination to create images neither

adds to nor subtracts from the carvings themselves; the poet is
a transparent medium through which God's perfect expressive-
ness shines. The genesis of the heavenly eagle from words, an
even clearer instance of God's artistry, suggests retrospectively
that the visible speech of *Purgatorio* is not a product of the fal-
lible human imagination but a feature of the universe as Dante
found it. The eagle written in the heavens confirms the authenticity of Dante's construction of the world and asserts the validity of his claim to the personal authority of a *scriba Dei*. The
fallibility of the imagination, however, is precisely the point of
Chaucer's visible speech. It is difficult to tell where image receiving leaves off and image making begins in the Temple of
Venus. The result is a broad questioning of the authenticity of
any human version of the world or history, whether it be Virgil's, Ovid's, or Chaucer's own.

The difficulty of ascertaining truth in the products of the
imagination—a common problem in interpreting dreams as
well—is extremely unsettling to the dreamer. It lies behind his
sense of dislocation at the end of Book I, when, as he leaves the
Temple of Venus, he wonders who made its wonderful images:

> "A, Lord," thoughte I, "that madest us,
> Yet sawgh I never such noblesse
> Of ymages, ne such richesse,
> As I saugh graven in this chirche;
> But not wot I whoo did hem wirche . . ."   (*HF*, 470–74)

The bleakness of the desert into which he then wanders suggests the importance of the question; suddenly he has left the
familiar world of the *Aeneid* for a strange landscape bereft of any
creature "yformed be Nature" (l. 490). His nervousness finds
expression in a prayer:

> "O Crist," thoughte I, "that art in blysse,
> Fro fantome and illusion
> Me save!"   (*HF*, 492–94)

The dreamer's association of "fantome" with "illusion" inti-
mates his fear that the images in the Temple are nothing but

delusions, imaginative impressions drawn from nothing outside the mind and bearing no relation to external reality.[30]

At this point Dante's eagle swoops down to pluck the
dreamer from the desert of his uncertainty. Dante, it seems,
will guide Chaucer as Virgil had guided Dante. The dreamer's
quest, forced upon him by the eagle, is for an alternative way
to account for the visible speech of Book I, a way to understand
it as something other than "fantome and illusion." To this end,
the eagle promises to show Geffrey "tydynges," which he thinks
of as new material to write about. The eagle is an appropriate
guide out of Book I; as the symbol of empire in the *Commedia*,
he follows Aeneas from Troy to Carthage and thence to Rome
(*Par.* VI, 1–3). His presence gives the first hint about the nature
of tidings, for he is also Dante's emblem of history.[31] The rest
of the poem is devoted to a "natural history" of tidings, and
traces the journey of received texts (in the order Geffrey discovers it) through the mind of the reader. For the sake of clarity, I will summarize this journey in sequential order: backward.[32]

Best defined as "the reports of events,"[33] tidings originate in
speech. As sound, or "eyr ybroken" (l. 765), they first rise to
Fame's realm in the sphere of air. Here they enter the House of
Rumor, a whirling, noisy labyrinth made of twigs.[34] Spreading
and growing, as rumors do, they finally escape through the gaps
in the porous structure. But they don't always leave as they
came:

> And somtyme saugh I thoo at ones
> A lesyng and a sad soth sawe,
> That gonne of aventure drawe
> Out at a wyndowe for to pace;
> And, when they metten in that place,
> They were achekked bothe two,
> And neyther of hem moste out goo
> For other, so they gonne crowde,
> Til ech of hem gan crien lowde,
> "Lat me go first!" "Nay, but let me!"
> And here I wol ensure the

Wyth the nones that thou wolt do so,
That I shal never fro the go,
But be thyn owne sworen brother!
We wil medle us ech with other,
That no man, be they never so wrothe,
Shal han on [of us] two, but bothe
At ones, al besyde his leve,
Come we a-morwe or on eve,
Be we cried or stille yrouned."
Thus saugh I fals and soth compounded
Togeder fle for oo tydynge.   (HF, 2088–2109)

This is the combinative function of the imagination, with its
creative ability to conjure up absent things and join them in
ways never before seen.[35] The compound tidings of the House
of Rumor give an imaginative explanation of the juxtaposed
versions of the Dido story in Book I.

Having escaped from the House of Rumor, the composite
tidings are blown to Fame's palace. Here the capricious goddess, with little regard for merit, awards them name and du-
ration. The House of Fame is a memorial structure;[36] the store-
house of images, it not only determines which tidings will live
on, but also is built of tidings. The pillars supporting its
vaulted roof are the premier poets (mainly historical) of the
Western literary tradition.

In sum, *The House of Fame* records the imaginative process by
which tidings are received and created, combined with other
tidings, and remembered or forgotten. The natural history of
tidings explains how the images of Book I came into being, but
does little to resolve the issues of truth and authorship they
raised. For tidings are the children of chance ("Aventure, / That
is the moder of tydynges," ll. 1982–83), and Fame's judgments
as well are governed by whim and caprice. The Middle Ages
saw the imagination as a potentially dangerous faculty, unreliable at best. Instead of trying to minimize its waywardness, as
Dante had done by attributing the products of his imagination
to God's artistry, Chaucer embraces it as the foundation of his

poetic practice. A "feble fundament" it is; and many of the
poem's readers have been unsettled by its insistence on the prerational, apparently anarchic roots of poetry. The journey of
tidings through imagination and memory, far from resolving
the impasse at the end of Book I, seems rather to magnify its
troubling suggestion that reading and writing result in nothing
but "fantome and illusion." True, false, or "fals and soth com-
pouned" (l. 2108), tidings seem to abandon any pretense of veracity. There can be many tidings for one event, as we have seen
in Book I; there can be tidings for nonevents. And there is no
way of distinguishing among their possible relations to truth;[37]
you either believe them or you don't. With them, Chaucer
seems to accede to the scholastic accusation that poets lie: for in
the world of tidings, truth and falsehood are indeterminate;
and poems, when they are read, seem to elude the control of
both author and reader. Thus the fictions of humankind seem
doomed to inauthenticity.

But I have left for last the most astonishing aspect of tidings:
their form. When the eagle sets Geffrey down in Fame's aery
realm, he explains how there could be so much noise in a place
populated by no living thing:

> "Whan any speche ycomen ys
> Up to the paleys, anon-ryght
> Hyt wexeth lyk the same wight
> Which that the word in erthe spak,
> Be hyt clothed red or blak;
> And hath so verray hys lyknesse
> That spak the word, that thou wilt gesse
> That it the same body be,
> Man or woman, he or she.
> And ys not this a wonder thyng?"   (HF, 1074–83)

This is Chaucer's most striking use of the Dantean idea of visible speech.[38] Clothed in the form of those who spoke them, tidings embody a radically different means to truth: not the imaged truth of historical events, which had eluded the dreamer
in the Temple of Venus, but the truth of the teller. Remarkable

in this age of the impersonal poetic "I,"[39] they shift emphasis away from the kind of authenticity that warrants reports of real events, and toward the rather different authority of the reporter. Tidings are thus at the heart of Chaucer's "impersonated" poetic practice, with its full-bodied (and often comically substantial) narrative personae.[40] They make visible the idea behind Chaucer's limited, well-defined narrators, that human beings speak in particular voices even when they claim to utter universal truths.

The House of Fame shifts in Book II from a visual world to an auditory one. The shift does not mean that Chaucer has turned his attention away from stale old books and looks now to the fresh world about him for his poetic material. Howard has suggested that it is instead a matter of digging deeper, finding the roots of poetry in the ephemeral world of speech.[41] But tidings are not exclusively oral. Though the outside of Fame's hall includes figures from popular and largely oral culture—minstrels, jugglers, and magicians—the interior is literary. And despite the acoustic origin of tidings in "eyr ybroken," the red or black in which they may be clothed suggests black-letter manuscripts with red capitals and rubrics. To distinguish sharply in this case between the written and the oral would be misleading; reading was not usually the silent affair it is today. John of Salisbury, following Isidore, defines writing as "shapes indicating voice"; letters "speak voicelessly the utterances of the absent."[42] His language betrays the primacy he attaches to the aural; writing for him was literally visible speech. One might recall Augustine's amazement that Ambrose could read without moving his lips;[43] and M. T. Clanchy shows that, until the advent of print, reading remained primarily something heard rather than seen.[44] The sound taken up into Fame's realm as tidings, then, can be spoken by readers and writers as well as by oral reporters.

And indeed Chaucer attributes voice to the great literary masters he reads. When Geffrey sees the poets who perpetuate the fame of Troy, he also hears the babble of their conflicting voices:

But yet I gan ful wel espie,
Betwex hem was a litil envye.
Oon seyde that Omer made lyes,
Feynynge in hys poetries,
And was to Grekes favorable;
Therfor held he hyt but fable.   (*HF*, 1475–80)

This passage, which suggests that Chaucer was already thinking seriously about the matter that was to occupy him in *Troilus
and Criseyde*, explicitly frames the issues of poetic authority and
truth so important to both poems. Shrouded in antiquity, the
real history of Troy is lost; what remains are various tidings.
Homer lied, say the Trojan partisans, because he took up for the
Greeks. "Envye" (a kind of poetic competition)[45] results as they
all vie for the title of greatest authority. It is tempting to specu-
late (and impossible to prove) that Chaucer may have come to this
"voiceness" through Dante's treatment of Virgil in the *Commedia*. Faint through long silence when he first appears ("per
lungo silenzio parea fioco"; *Inf.* 1, 63), Virgil acquires compelling reality through the voice Dante gives him. This voice can
come only from being read; and Virgil's voice in the *Commedia*
owes as much to Dante as to the Latin master himself.[46] Authors
need the help of readers to make their voices heard.

   Like Dante, Chaucer hears the voices of the poets when he
reads. But more important, voice is also central to *The House of
Fame*'s analysis of poetic borrowing. Book II's shift to the auditory signals a new approach to the problem of authorial responsibility raised by the visible speech of Book I, and it is
through the eagle Chaucer borrowed from Dante that we can
best see what answer tidings offer. The eagle is a tiding born of
reading, the most extensively developed in the poem. He promises to bring Geffrey to hear tidings, but when his argument
about sound sprouts beak and tail, it becomes clear that the
bird is what he promised to show:

   "A ha," quod he, "lo, so I can
   Lewedly to a lewed man
   Speke, and shewe hym swyche skiles

> That he may shake hem be the biles,
> So palpable they shulden be.
>   . . .
>
> And with thyne eres heren wel
> Top and tayl and everydel . . ."   (*HF*, 865–69, 879–80)

This is no mere metaphor fit for an eagle; the words actually create the likeness of their speaker.[47] Chaucer's eagle, like Dante's in *Paradiso*, is visible speech. The words he embodies are initially Dante's, as shown by the introductory description. As long as he remains something seen, he is a very Dantean bird. But as soon as he begins to speak—with an "Awak!" very like the scream of a real eagle—he becomes the product of a different imagination. The more we hear from him, the harder it is to envision him as the majestic eagle of the initial description. His voice creates a different being: loquacious, perhaps a bit pedantic, certainly bossy. He is no longer the exalted symbol of empire and justice which carries Dante aloft in his dream and which, appearing later in another form, expounds the theology of divine justice. But he embodies equally the magic of fiction, with its ability to build, from black and red marks on a page and from the baseless fabric of the imagination, worlds animated by beings we can see and hear.

The eagle is a deliciously witty demonstration of the nature of Chaucer's debt to Dante. Dante may be the impetus behind Chaucer's new exploration of theoretical literary issues, but Chaucer uses the eagle, his chief Dantean borrowing, to steer clear of poetry in the Dantean vein. In addition to its immediate source in the dream of *Purgatorio* IX, the flight of Book II has a long lineage of distinguished forebears; Geffrey duly notes them, for what he sees reminds him (not surprisingly) of Boethius, Alain de Lille, and Martianus Capella. Such flights generally signify a philosophical or religious journey to truth. But whenever Geffrey edges too close to Dante's flight to the Empyrean, the eagle forestalls him. "Thow demest of thyself amys" (l. 596), he cries when Geffrey imagines, in a Dantean echo (of *Inf.* II, 32), that he is about to be "stellyfyed." And

when Geffrey quotes Dante and St. Paul to wonder whether he
journeys in body or in spirit (compare *Par.* 1, 73–74, and 2 Corinthians 12:2–4), the eagle breaks into his thoughts with a dis-
missive "Lat be . . . thy fantasye!" (l. 992).

Geffrey's journey, like Dante's, is an inward one, but the
truths he finds are not those of the *Commedia*. Dante had used
the eagle to fuse the subjective experience of conversion with
the objective nature of the universe; Chaucer uses the eagle as a
guide to the inward hall of fame "that in myn hed ymarked ys"
(l. 1103)—surely as exotic a setting as any in the *Commedia*.
Here truth is personal, influenced by the subjective concerns of
writers and readers, and therefore indeterminate. The eagle's
preemptory dismissal of Geffrey's "fantasye" helps to create our
image of the poet as a bumbling hack—an image that would
not be funny if it were true. But combined with Geffrey's calm
self-assurance when he refuses to subject himself to Fame's
judgments, the dismissal also reflects a critical distance from
the *Commedia*. The eagle measures both Chaucer's dependence
on Dante and his independence from him.

The eagle also demonstrates a realism new to Chaucer. In
some respects it is difficult to speak of originality in Chaucer's
works. Like most medieval poets, he reworks material already
to hand; seldom does he invent something entirely new. The
imitation of Virgil, Ovid, and Dante in *The House of Fame* is
typical of his practice. Chaucer generally borrows what we
"see" as we read: visual images and plot. To this, Chaucer adds
what we "hear." I know of no other poet so concerned with what
we hear, not in the sense of the music of language—for many
poets are equally attuned to this—but in the sense of John of
Salisbury's definition of writing: shapes that speak voicelessly
the utterances of the absent. We hear the voices, whether of a
character like the eagle or of the narrator, so vividly that we
imagine the speakers as fully present. Chaucer's new realism is
that of the teller. A narrator like the Wife of Bath is so real to
us that we easily forget how much she is based on previous literature; part of the reason for this is the degree to which her

voice requires our imaginative participation. We think of her as a real, and fully realized, character partly because we have helped to create her.

For Chaucer as for Dante, visible speech is a resonant image for the craft of poetry. Dante's *visibile parlare* is art written by God and imitated by the human vessel of his inspiration; it thus lies at the heart of the *Commedia*'s claim to truth. Chaucer's visible speech suggests a poetry profoundly different from Dante's. *The House of Fame* acknowledges frankly the "made-up" quality of poetry: it is fiction, it depends on the imagination, and its relation to truth is not easy to discern. Appealing to the eye and ear and building a world in the imagination, it seems to exist at a fundamentally prerational level. Although the poem is unfinished, the ending we have seems appropriate.[48] Geffrey hears the tidings he came to find, but does not report them; and the "man of gret auctorite" with which the poem breaks off must, like so many others encountered along the way, remain nameless. In a poem in which the highest attainable truth is only what people say,[49] he could say nothing to restore verifiable truth to his authority. Because he says nothing, the focus remains where it belongs: not on any substantive result of Geffrey's quest for tidings, but on the marvelous process by which they are created.

The oddity of *The House of Fame* derives in no small measure from Chaucer's refusal to authenticate the poem. He repeatedly builds up the standard devices for assuring the truth of a medieval narrative, only to draw back from them, leaving the issue of truth for his readers to judge. In the proem, he breathlessly lists all the arguments for the truth of dreams, but distances his own vision with the framing prayer "God turne us every drem to good!" (ll. 1 and 58). He asks only that his dream be useful, and calls it wonderful without claiming it to be true. It takes place in the evening, whereas only morning dreams were thought to be true.[50] And in the mock curse of the first invocation, he warns his readers not to "mysdeme" (l. 97) the dream, but gives no guidance as to what might constitute a proper interpretation. By these means Chaucer arouses our desire to know in what way we should believe the narrative—and then frustrates the desire. *The House of Fame* is in part a consideration of why narrative authentication seems necessary, an unwritten contract between author and reader. But the poem invokes authenticity without guaranteeing it. And the pointed absence of authentication—the devices are present only to stress their artificiality—is *The House of Fame*'s broadest response to Dante.

Chaucer's skepticism about Dante's endeavor in the *Commedia* is apparent in several aspects of *The House of Fame*. Two I have already discussed: first, the transformation of the eagle from a resplendent image of heavenly justice (the only kind of fame that finally counts in the *Commedia*) into a bossy didact, authoritarian rather than authoritative; second, the metamorphosis of Dante's journey through otherworldly realms into a subjective exploration of Chaucer's own mind. But the third feature in which his skepticism finds voice will reappear in *Troilus and Criseyde*, for it is not bound to the specific images or plot of this poem: the view of history as tidings and literature as fame. To equate literature with fame—notoriously slippery in its relation to real achievement—and history with what people say is to raise the issue of authenticity. In doing so, Chaucer implicitly counters the view of history that animates the *Commedia*.

There is no better illustration of Dante's bold historiography than his treatment of Henry VII of Luxemburg. The Holy Roman Emperor whom Dante saluted as the second coming of Christ[51] invaded Italy in 1310, but died near Siena without having firmly established his imperial authority. Dante reserves an empty throne in the Empyrean for "l'alto Arrigo, ch'a drizzare Italia / verrà in prima ch'ella sia disposta" (the lofty Henry, who will come to set Italy straight before she is ready; *Par.* xxx, 137–38—can "Italia . . . in prima" possibly echo the *Aeneid*'s first lines?). Blind mortal history records the failure of Henry's Italian expedition, but for Dante Henry remained the ideal em-

peror and savior of Italy. That phenomenal events did not
match providential truth only measures the distance between
exiled mankind and God; Henry will be enthroned in paradise
and in the poem that records paradise. Wherever the *Commedia*
departs from the actual course of events, Dante grounds his
poem in the authority of God's book of history. The *Commedia's*
history is providential, typological in structure, and infused
with the meaning of the Incarnation. It is God's history, written across the pages of human time with events that incremen-
tally reveal the fullness of divine intention.

In contrast, *The House of Fame* offers an incipiently antitypological vision of history as mere stories, recorded in literature, which, like fame, has no secure relation to truth. History
here is purely human, the product of memory and imagination
rather than the record of God's providence unfolding in time.
Like the names of famous people written in the melting ice of
Fame's mountain, whatever providential meaning history
might hold is liable to be effaced in the telling and retelling.
History in this poem is not incremental; it does not tend toward
ever fuller revelation. Instead, it merely repeats itself, shrink-
ing or growing or getting mixed up as it does. Once transposed
into human language, it is too frail a vessel to preserve the providential meaning Dante sought to reveal in the *Commedia*.
Hence the deliberate inauthenticity of Chaucer's imitation of
Dante.

The shortcoming of *The House of Fame* as a challenge to
Dante's view of history, and to the *Commedia* itself as authentic
history, is that it does not represent an alternative that appeals
as strongly to the reader's willingness to assent to invented
worlds. About the nature of literature itself, and the difficulties
of transposing events into verbal images, *The House of Fame* indeed invites skepticism toward authentication. But the real
test—and consequently Chaucer's fullest response to Dante—
comes only when he creates a world in need of authentication
to vie with the world of the *Commedia*. This he does in *Troilus*

and Criseyde. Like *The House of Fame*, Chaucer's great Troy poem casts a skeptical eye at claims of truth in literature; yet simultaneously, like any realistic historical poem, it also needs authenticating.

Authentication is central to realistic narrative art. By telling us what sort of truth a narrative claims and by substantiating this truth-claim within an invented world, the authenticating level places the narrative with respect to the world in which we live. It gives us leave to assent to something we know to be made up, so that we might then take seriously whatever designs the narrative might have—by analogy and interpretation—on our own world. The air of truth we seem to require of our narratives can be established in a variety of ways. Morton Bloomfield, in his seminal essay on Chaucer's authenticating realism, discusses four: framing devices that explain how the author came to know about the inner narrative; an "I" who either participates in the action or observes it; an authorial voice whose tone guarantees authenticity (or sometimes deliberately subverts it); and realistic background details—localities, names, dates—that place the narrative in the known world.[52] Authentication can be seen as the level of a narrative in which the author addresses his readers, directly or implicitly. At its broadest, it partially subsumes even the referential aspect of the narrative, for the manner in which the author represents reality can be a powerful argument for the truth of his fiction. This is, of course, a tautology, of which Bloomfield comments that "the authenticating level also in a way makes us more aware of the fact that the inner story is a creation which needs authenticating."[53]

The charge that poets were mere liars seems to have been a particularly grave problem during the later Middle Ages; one need only recall Thomas Aquinas's hostility toward fictions, or Boccaccio's rather defensive apology for poetry in the *De genealogie*.[54] Such attacks may account for the elaborateness of both Dante's and Chaucer's authenticating levels, but truth-claims and their substantiation were fundamental to medieval fiction even without the spur of the schoolmen. Medieval writers used two main claims to establish an air of truth for their fictions. One appeals to the authority of an old written tradition. Popular romances often tell old stories already familiar to the audience; those which do not make this claim anyway. The author does not necessarily expect his audience to believe his tale as literally true; rather, his claim gestures toward an older oral culture. In oral culture the entire situation—the presence of a speaker and listeners as well as their shared knowledge of the story—guaranteed authenticity by forging anew the link to a supposedly historical past.[55] The implied minstrel and audience of many popular romances remain as traces of this cultural milieu. When an author places his story within a tradition, he invokes the seriousness of storytelling in a culture defined by its stories. Such appeals to tradition were not limited to popular romances; writings of the high intellectual culture, Latin or vernacular, were just as likely to assert their truth by claiming continuity with the authenticating classical tradition that defined knowledge for the Middle Ages.[56]

A second truth-claim rests on the authority of personal experience. The armchair pilgrim who wrote *Mandeville's Travels* claimed to have seen, or heard and believed himself, everything he actually culled from other books. Mandeville's report seems worthy of belief for two reasons. First, he distinguishes judiciously between the credible and the incredible; since he does not believe every anecdote he hears on his pilgrimage, we are invited to trust his critical judgment. Second, he carefully limits his eyewitness claim. Of the Earthly Paradise, for instance, he says: "Of Paradise ne can I not speak properly, for I was not there. It is far beyond, and that forethinketh me, and also I was not worthy."[57] Dream visions also base their authenticity on personal experience. No matter how fantastic or unrealistic the dream may be, the narrator nonetheless dreamt it.[58] Beyond this minimal truth, the literary dreamer can also turn to the long scriptural and philosophical tradition of dream interpretation to specify how his dream holds true in the waking world as well.

These examples illustrate the main axes along which medieval truth-claims range themselves. Narratives are true insofar as they remain faithful to the old experience preserved in authoritative tradition, or to the new personal experience of a trustworthy narrator. In the *Commedia*, Dante incorporates both of these traditional elements into a sweeping truth-claim of audacious magnitude. He derives his authority from God, and his poem (divided into hell, purgatory, and heaven) mirrors the book of God's creation.[59] The *Commedia* also imitates God's book of history by invoking Exodus to present the pilgrim's conversion as a repetition of this basic pattern of Christian sacred history.[60] Christ's Incarnation, the moment that gives meaning to all prior and subsequent events in sacral time, also infuses Dante's poem with its meaning and provides a model for the poetic representation of the pilgrim's experience. The authenticity of the *Commedia* rests on a typological theory of history, leading Dante to his characteristic poetic modes, allegory and the vast system of analogies by which poet and poem are raised, by recapitulation and fulfillment, to the Empyrean.

And the poet is the scribe of God, a finite version of the *Deus artifex* who made the bas-reliefs of the terrace of pride. In a passage often taken as a programmatic description of the *dolce stil nuovo*, Dante describes himself as a poet inspired by love:

> "I' mi son un che, quando
> Amor mi spira, noto, e a quel modo
> ch'e' ditta dentro vo significando."　　(*Purg.* XXIV, 52–54)

("I am one who, when Love inspires me, takes note, and goes setting it forth after the fashion which he dictates within me.")

But Love in this poem is not only the fiction of courtly poets, or even the feeling itself, to which the poets of the movement claimed to return. It is also "l'amor che move il sole e l'altre stelle" (the Love which moves the sun and the other stars; *Par.*

XXXIII, 145): God himself. Moreover, the religious shading of "spira" here suggests a parallel between Dante's poetry (born of his mother tongue and his poetic forefathers, and then inspired by Amor) and the "embryology" of the following canto.[61] There too a human being is created out of the conjunction of mother and father, grows through the stages governed by nature, and at last receives an immortal soul breathed into it by God.

The similarity between God's creation of the human soul and Dante's creation of poetry can be no accident.* In these cantos the language is also infused with suggestions of the Incarnation. The landscape and all it holds are animated by the presence of the sacred:

> E quale, annunziatrice de li albori,
>   l'aura di maggio movesi e olezza,
>   tutta impregnata da l'erba e da' fiori . . .

> (*Purg.* XXIV, 145–47)

> (And as, heralding the dawn, the breeze of May stirs and smells sweet, all impregnate with grass and with flowers . . .)

The breeze hints at the spirit of poetry (with the pun on *lauro*), and suggests again the breath of divine inspiration. This is almost an annunciation scene, with the breeze ("annunziatrice" and "impregnata") both bearing and receiving the blessing. Natural generation, inspiration, and poetry are all bound together in one image of the Incarnation. These cantos, along with Dante's imitation of divine artistry in *Purgatorio* X–XII and *Paradiso* XVIII,[62] constitute Dante's claim to write divine, incarnational poetry. The authority he follows is God; the authenticity of the *Commedia* rests partly on Dante's claim, as the human vessel of divine inspiration, to mirror in his poetry God's own creativity.

---

*In *Purg.* XXVI, Guido Guinizelli says of Arnaut Daniel that he "fu miglior fabbro del parlar materno" ("was a better craftsman of the mother tongue"; l. 117). This refers to the vernacular, the language a child learns from his mother. Dante characterizes Guido as "il padre mio" (my father; ll. 97–98). In *Purg.* XXIV, the verb used by Bonagiunta da Lucca to ask Dante if he is the poet of the *dolce stil nuovo* is "fore trasse" (drew forth; ll. 49–50), also used of midwifery.

Dante's claim to imitate God's books of nature and history, as well as the manner in which they were written, corresponds to other poets' more modest reliance on the authority of previous written sources to guarantee the authenticity of their narratives. The *Commedia* also depends on the authentication of personal experience. As a record of the pilgrim's conversion to God, it copies yet another book, that of memory, in which Dante preserves "quant' io del regno santo / ne la mia mente potei far tesoro" (so much of the holy kingdom as I could treasure up in my mind; *Par.* I, 10–11). Although this treasury occasionally falls short at the heights of his vision, it is "la mente che non erra" (unerring memory; *Inf.* II, 7) in what it does record. Along with the muses and Dante's own "alto ingegno" (high genius; *Inf.* II, 7), the "mente che scrivesti ciò ch'io vidi" (memory that wrote down what I saw; *Inf.* II, 8) is one of the powers to which Dante appeals in his first invocation. The metaphor of writing suggests that his remembered experience is an authoritative text in its own right.

Thus the *Commedia* carries traditional truth-claims to a unique extreme. The veracity of the poem depends on the unerring book of memory, recorded by a pilgrim whose conversion, justifying him in the sight of God, has empowered him to imitate, in process and substance, God's books of nature and history. *Troilus and Criseyde* also combines the traditional authority of previous texts and personal experience to produce a similar collocation of truth-claims. In pointed contrast to Dante, however, Chaucer validates his narrative by claiming to transmit the books of man. As he does throughout his works, he relies on "olde bokes" as the repositories of a continuous tradition of human knowledge, accepted as true now because they have been so accepted in the past. In the *Troilus*, he bases himself primarily on "myn auctour," Lollius. The main truth-claim of the *Troilus* thus resides in Chaucer's pose as a historian. Admitting that he does not know how old Criseyde was or whether she had any children, he invites our belief in the *Troilus* as an objective report transmitted by a responsible historian. The "inner story" is a third-person narrative about people and events for which Chaucer claims factual existence, despite the impossibility of his having witnessed a history that unfolded so long ago.

Thus the historical authentication differs from Dante's, which depends on the author's participation in events molded by the patterns of sacred history. Chaucer says he has no direct experience of either this love story or any love whatever. Nonetheless, he claims for his poem the truth of personal experience, for, like the *Commedia*, the *Troilus* copies the book of memory. The narrator preserves his encounter with Lollius's old Trojan history, alternating (as Bloomfield has taught us) between distanced historical style and intimate close-ups of events and conversations as they take place.[63] In addition, he constantly intrudes on a straightforward account of past events to tell us how he reacts to them. Both characteristics stem from Chaucer's presentation of the poem not as a transmission of a historical source, but rather as the story of his experience of reading that source. In this respect, the *Troilus* parallels the first book of *The House of Fame*. Although Chaucer never calls the poem a book of memory, his initial summary of the entire history indicates how much the narrative depends on memory. The only personal experiences Chaucer offers are those of reading and remembering; the only participation, that of an imaginative encounter with his sources.

Chaucer's authenticating claims are knives that cut both ways. The narrator's imaginative participation in his story is an important element in making us believe in the realistic inner love story.[64] Yet it also compromises Chaucer's pose in the frame as a historian, reporting events from a distanced, objective point of view. The conflict between frame and inner story undercuts Chaucer's authentication, and in large measure dictates his characteristic poetic mode, irony.

The irony runs deeper than the conflict between history and personal reading experience, for the text Chaucer claims to have read and remembered never existed. It is not uncommon to prefer "olde bokes," with their power to preserve within an authoritative tradition, to a more modern actual source. Guido delle Colonne also suppressed his modern source, the *Roman de Troie* of Benoît de Ste.-Maure, in favor of the "eyewitness" accounts of Dares and Dictys. And Guido's pretense was apparently successful; the *Historia destructionis Troiae* was immediately accepted for the authentic history it claimed to be. Yet Guido's case is not entirely parallel to Chaucer's; he probably did believe that Benoît's account was basically true, if too romantic and poetic. In correcting these excesses, he attempted to restore his Troy book to the historical tradition of the fraudulent Dares and Dictys.[65]

Chaucer, however, asserts as his primary source a history written by Lollius, whom Robert A. Pratt has shown to be nothing but a misreading.*[66] In the proem to Book II, one of the poem's central passages on authentication, Chaucer discusses the difficulties he faces in preserving ancient written tradition from time's oblivion. His own ignorance, and changes in language and culture generally, interfere with his effort to mediate between Lollius's old Latin text and his own fourteenth-century English audience:

> Ye knowe ek that in forme of speche is chaunge
> Withinne a thousand yeer, and wordes tho
> That hadden pris, now wonder nyce and straunge
> Us thinketh hem, and yet thei spake hem so,
> And spedde as wel in love as men now do . . .   (*TC*, II.22–26)

Primarily, these lines beg indulgence for the exotic strangeness of his source. If it were not for Lollius, we could consider them

---

*As Pratt has shown, in "Chaucer's Lollius" (p. 184), the only known Lollius is the actor to whom Horace addressed his second epistle (*Epistolae*, I, ii, 1–2): "Troiani belli scriptorem, maxime Lolli, / Dum tu declamas Romae . . ." (While you recite at Rome the writer of the Trojan War, O greatest Lollius; trans. mine). John of Salisbury quotes the first line of the epistle in the *Polycraticus*, VII.9. Pratt (p. 185) discovers the misreading "scriptor*um*" (a genitive plural) for "scriptor*em*" (an accusative singular) in a twelfth-century manuscript of the *Polycraticus*; the sense is thus rendered "O Lollius, of the writers of the Trojan War the greatest" (trans. mine). The merely an extension of the proem's modesty topos, the apology an inverted assertion of authenticity. Chaucer here appeals to Clio, the muse of history, and after all, even problems in transmission imply that transmission indeed occurs.

However, all the while insisting on the need for the authenticity provided by old sources, Chaucer quite deliberately pulls the rug out from under his feet by basing his authentication on a fiction. Since Lollius never wrote a history of Troy, none could have survived for Chaucer to translate. He may well have believed that such a history had once existed, and that it had been lost. But he knew that he had not read it. Consequently, his pose of merely transmitting a historical account ultimately collapses; with this collapse, his claim to have experienced the history by reading and remembering it is subverted as well. To claim Lollius as a source is to build ignorance, forgetting, and oblivion—the failure of individual and collective knowledge and memory—into a text that is a history and a remembered experience. Chaucer does not acknowledge *Il Filostrato* as the basis for the *Troilus* because the fiction of Lollius embodies, far more resonantly than the admission of any newer, surviving source could, the problematic authenticating endeavor of *Troilus and Criseyde*.

By undermining his truth-claims in such a fashion, Chaucer makes the task of narrative authentication a major issue in the *Troilus*. His ambivalence about the truth of his fiction results in a position about the relation of his text to the world vastly different from that of the *Commedia*. Chaucer's authenticating devices had been complex before he read Dante.[67] But as *The House of Fame* shows, his ambivalence toward authentication crops up simultaneously with clear evidence of Dante's influence. In the

misreading is easily explained as a confusion of the similar abbreviations for the inflectional endings. Pratt (p. 186) supports his finding with Foullechat's 1372 translation of the *Polycraticus*, which says, citing Horace, "que Lolli fu principal ecrevain de la bataille de Troie" (that Lollius was the chief writer of the Trojan War; trans. mine). In this manner, Lollius may have attained his legendary status as a chief authority on the Trojan War. Chaucer, though he made use of the legend, would still have known that he had read no such source for his tale.

Troilus Chaucer again alerts us to the Dantean connection through a major borrowing. He alters his main source, *Il Filostrato*, so that it partially resembles the story of Paolo and Francesca from *Inferno* v. In the following chapter, I will establish the influence of Francesca's doomed love in the *Troilus*. Chaucer's use of her story, which is concerned with both love and the morality of romantic fiction, clearly indicates that he did not assent to Dante's treatment of either; in other words, he did not assent to the role prescribed for him as a reader by the authenticating devices of the *Commedia*. He responded by authenticating the *Troilus* in such a way that it matches and counters the *Commedia* point for point, and in such a way too that he calls authentication itself into question.

2. A Text and Its Afterlife: 'Inferno' V and 'Troilus and Criseyde'

The busy presence of Pandarus transforms the consummation scene of *Troilus and Criseyde* into something both comic and profound. Criseyde's uncle and Troilus's older friend, Pandarus traces his literary ancestry to the mediating "friend" of courtly romance and, of course, to Criseida's young cousin Pandaro in *Il Filostrato*.[1] But Pandarus goes further than any other courtly friend: he throws the unconscious Troilus into Criseyde's bed, helps her to revive him, and dims the lights to create an atmosphere more conducive to love. Only when Troilus finally gathers Criseyde into his arms does Pandarus, with a parting admonishment to Troilus not to faint again, betake himself to bed.[2]

The extent to which Pandarus manages the action is confirmed in a thread of fire images running through the scene. To Troilus, huddled in the "stuwe," Pandarus says, "So thryve I, this nyght shal I make it weel, / Or casten al the gruwel in the fire" (III.710–11). To Criseyde, he emphasizes the need for swift action to reassure Troilus:

> "Nece, alle thyng hath tyme, I dar avowe;
> For whan a chaumbre afire is or an halle,
> Wel more nede is, it sodeynly rescowe
> Than to dispute and axe amonges alle
> How this candel in the strawe is falle." (III.855–59)

As the Wife of Bath knows, "peril is bothe fyr and tow t'assemble" (*CT*, III.89). Although Pandarus intends his description of domestic conflagration in the first place to impart a sense of urgency to the reluctant Criseyde, his proverbial language also reveals the cause he says is useless to seek: the fires of passionate ardor with which Troilus has burned since he first saw Criseyde.* Having united the diffident lovers in Criseyde's chamber (thinking, perhaps, that they no longer need his aid but not willing to risk failure now), Pandarus withdraws to a discreet distance:

> And with that word he drow hym to the feere,
> And took a light, and fond his contenaunce,
> As for to looke upon an old romaunce.   (III.978–80)

The candle Pandarus lights from the fire captures in little the vicarious satisfaction he seeks from the love affair.

But, as Howard has shown us, these lines are odd for another reason: their apparent clarity blurs in any attempt to define what Pandarus does here. He "assumes a certain appearance 'As for to looke upon an old romaunce.'" Does "looke upon" mean "read" or "watch"? And what is the "old romaunce"?[3] We are left to wonder which romance Pandarus "looks upon"—a book in his hand, or the one he "wrote" himself, now about to unfold across the room from him. Pandarus's comic but disquieting intimacy here is balanced by the poet's distance.[4] Retreating into the old books that both join and separate narrator and characters, Chaucer intermittently views the love scene from afar. Together, Pandarus's closeness and the poet's distance mark balanced poles that also govern the telling of the entire story, and that in this case make it difficult to respond to the consummation as a simple scene of romantic fulfillment.

This scene reflects the most important change Chaucer made in Boccaccio's Pandaro, the striking correspondence between Pandarus and the poet himself.[5] In the frame, the poet mediates

---

*Chaucer uses a similar proverb in the Merchant's Tale, where the fire's suggestion of passionate ardor is equally evident: "O perilous fyr, that in the bedstraw bredeth!" (CT, IV.1783). Domestic treachery is the main point of this apostrophe, but its power to suggest the precise nature of Damyan's betrayal lies in fire's association with sexuality. See also below, pp. 132–33.

between his audience and his source; as "the sorwful instrument, / That helpeth loveres, as I kan, to pleyne" (I. 10–11), he
embraces the role of go-between. To avail the cause of lovers in
his audience, he retells the ancient Trojan love story he read in
Lollius's Latin, glossing it in passing with other sources as well.
Chaucer's mediating role thus has a double aspect: textually, he
translates a venerable written tradition for his fourteenth-
century audience; and socially, he offers his listeners a compen-
dium of the conventional words and behavior of love after
which they may pattern their own lives. Following the precepts
of rhetorical theory, this servant of the servants of Love (I.15)
constructs a poem in order to accomplish his textual and ama-
tory mediations. Similarly, Pandarus mediates between the lovers in the inner story. He fashions the romance of Troilus and
Criseyde according to the poetic theory outlined in Geoffrey of
Vinsauf's *Poetria nova*:[6]

> For everi wight that hath an hous to founde
> Ne renneth naught the werk for to bygynne
> With rakel hond, but he wol bide a stounde,
> And sende his hertes line out fro withinne
> Aldirfirst his purpose for to wynne.
> Al this Pandare in his herte thoughte,
> And caste his werk ful wisely or he wroughte.   (I.1065–71)

When Pandarus describes his role in furthering love, his
words often apply as aptly to the poet and his mediating roles.
Both are unsuccessful in love; nonetheless, Pandarus justifies
his efforts with a proverb that also validates the poet's efforts to
advise lovers: "I have myself ek seyn a blynd man goo / Ther as
he fel that couthe loken wide" (I.628–29). To rationalize his inadequacies as a redactor, Chaucer modifies this proverb—and
reverses its force—to include a pun on the colors of rhetoric ("A
blynde man kan nat juggen wel in hewis"; II.21). There is a vast
difference in tone, but none at all in premeditated rhetorical design, between Pandarus's advice to Troilus about how to write
a love letter ("Biblotte it with thi teris ek a lite"; II.1027) and

Chaucer's somber invocation to the fury Thesiphone ("Thise woful vers, that wepen as I write"; I.7). All of these parallels reinforce the analogies between Pandarus and poet, love affair and poem.

Pandarus also creates love fictions in order to further the romance between Troilus and Criseyde. His account to Criseyde of finding Troilus in the throes of desire differs markedly from the scene we saw in Book I; highly romanticized (though no more conventionally literary), Pandarus's story minimizes his own part and lacks the humor of the original. But it serves beautifully to answer Criseyde's first glimmering of interest, her question "Kan he wel speke of love?" (II.503). Pandarus's final story is the fiction of Horaste in Book III. For this tale of jealousy and betrayal, he has no prior authority—although it foreshadows Criseyde's eventual infidelity in Book V. Pandarus fabricates it out of whole cloth, guided not by truth but by his rhetorical design to move Criseyde to pity. His fiction making plays a crucial role in bringing the lovers together.[7]

Thus the author of the *Troilus*, both as the creator of a romance and as a go-between, resembles Pandarus, the author of the inner love affair. But the go-between, Pandarus, himself resembles a book. He is a walking encyclopedia of *sententiae*, never without an appropriate saying to suit any occasion. He shares his bookishness chiefly with the poet. The proverbs and maxims of the *Troilus* serve the same function as the "olde bokes" Chaucer mentions in the *Parlement of Foules*:

> For out of olde feldes, as men seyth,
> Cometh al this newe corn from yer to yere,
> And out of olde bokes, in good feyth,
> Cometh al this newe science that man lere.   (*PF*, 22–25)

As the parallel between proverb and maxim in this passage suggests, both books and oral wisdom are the repositories of a continuous tradition of human knowledge; any new work that relies on them, including the *Troilus*, validates its own authority. The lore associated with the poet and his double in the inner story is thus intimately bound up in Chaucer's authenticating level.

This bookishness, along with the poem's more convention-ally romantic treatment of love, is one of the major ways in which Chaucer "medievalized" his adaptation of *Il Filostrato*.[8] C. S. Lewis, whose outline of Chaucer's changes has guided the direction of *Troilus* criticism ever since, referred only to the augmented use of "sentence," both learned and popular, and to the frequent citation of written sources in the *Troilus*. By "bookishness," however, I also mean to suggest a broader char-acteristic of the poem. Bookishness subsumes, among other things, the reliance on authority I discussed in the first chapter. It also reflects a general structural principle of the poem, for a central narrative device here is Chaucer's pose as a reader re-porting to his audience the contents of a prior text. Finally, it includes the doubling of Pandarus and poet, in which the poet acts as a bookish mediator between his old Trojan history and his audience of lovers, and in which the mediator of the inner story comes to resemble both an author of romance and an au-thoritative book.

Defined thus broadly, the bookishness of the *Troilus* not only medievalizes the poem, but in distancing it from its source in *Il Filostrato*, moves it closer to the story of Paolo and Francesca in *Inferno* v. Howard H. Schless has written that "the fact that Chaucer never made use of the Francesca story from *Inferno* v is one of the most striking problems of the Chaucer-Dante rela-tionship."[9] For him, the treatment of love in each poem is too conventionally romantic, in both word and deed, to argue for decisive influence; the resemblances between canto and poem are but slender, accidental, and structurally insignificant.[10] But the conventionality of Francesca's language as she tells how she and Paolo fell in love over a book is precisely the point, for *In-ferno* v unmasks romantic fiction itself. And it is in the con-junction of romance and reading that Chaucer follows Dante here. Like *Inferno* v, the *Troilus* combines both romantic and antiromantic threads in its treatment of love. And like *Inferno* v, it interweaves bookishness and love into an extraordinary analysis of literature's role in mediating between lovers.

Texts and their afterlife are central to the *Commedia*, both structurally and thematically; thus, to understand how the afterlife of *Inferno* v animates the *Troilus*, we must look at the canto in its original context. As with the *Commedia*'s other literary episodes, *Inferno* v derives its full significance from its analogy to the central textual encounter that generates the whole poem: Dante's reading of Virgil.[11]

Virgil is, so to speak, literally present in Dante's work. That is, he is as much the text of his works as he is an imagined historical character come miraculously to guide Dante in person, and Dante's relation to him is that of a reader and a poet to the author he most reveres. Some of the evidence for this comes from the manner in which Virgil appears and disappears in the *Commedia*. When, faint from long silence, he approaches Dante in the first canto, he identifies himself by describing the *Aeneid*:

> "Poeta fui, e cantai di quel giusto
>   figliuol d'Anchise che venne di Troia,
>   poi che 'l superbo Ilïón fu combusto."   (*Inf.* 1, 73–75)

("I was a poet, and I sang of that just son of Anchises who came from Troy after proud Ilium was burned.")

He also places himself historically; he lived under Augustus and "nel tempo de li dèi falsi e bugiardi" ("in the time of the false and lying gods"; *Inf.* 1, 72), and to these he must finally return. His truest afterlife is textual, and for this reason his gradual disappearance in *Purgatorio* xxx is particularly poignant. When Beatrice appears to supersede him as the pilgrim's guide, Virgil melts from the poem in a sequence moving from direct quotation through close translation to oblique allusion to his poems.[12] Barred from the Earthly Paradise, Virgil is defined at the moment of his disappearance wholly in terms of his works. Although his historical existence and context are also important to his role in the *Commedia*, he is present first and last as a book.

If reading the *Aeneid* is central to Dante's poem, the figure of Statius offers clear evidence of its moral effects.[13] Like many other characters, Statius serves as a surrogate for Dante himself. Both are poets; both learned their craft from Virgil. Statius says:

> "Al mio ardor fuor seme le faville,
> che mi scaldar, de la divina fiamma
> onde sono allumati più di mille;
> De l'Eneïda dico, la qual mamma
> fummi, e fummi nutrice, poetando:
> sanz' essa non fermai peso di dramma." *(Purg.* XXI, 94–99)

("The sparks which warmed me from the divine flame whereby more than a thousand have been kindled were the seeds of my poetic fire: I mean the *Aeneid*, which in poetry was both mother and nurse to me—without it I had achieved little of worth . . .")

And Dante:

> "O di li altri poeti onore e lume,
> vagliami 'l lungo studio e 'l grande amore
> che m'ha fatto cercar lo tuo volume.
> Tu se' lo mio maestro e 'l mio autore,
> tu se' solo colui da cu' io tolsi
> lo bello stilo che m'ha fatto onore." *(Inf.* I, 82–87)

("O glory and light of other poets, may the long study and the great love that have made me search your volume avail me! You are my master and my author. You alone are he from whom I took the fair style that has done me honor.")

Virgil authored both Statius and Dante in a spiritual sense as well. Following a widespread reinterpretation of the Fourth Eclogue, Statius attributes his conversion to Christianity to his reading of the Latin master:

> "Tu prima m'inviasti
> verso Parnaso a ber ne le sue grotte,
> e prima appresso Dio m'alluminasti.

Facesti come quei che va di notte,
   che porta il lume dietro e sé non giova,
   ma dopo sé fa le persone dotte,
quando dicesti: 'Secol si rinova;
   torna giustizia e primo tempo umano,
   e progenïe scende da ciel nova.'
Per te poeta fui, per te cristiano . . ."   (*Purg.* XXII, 64–73)

("You it was who first sent me toward Parnassus to drink in its
caves, and you who first did light me on to God. You were like
one who goes by night and carries the light behind him and
profits not himself, but makes those wise who follow him,
when you said, 'The ages are renewed; Justice returns and the
first age of man, and a new progeny descends from heaven.'
Through you I was a poet, through you a Christian . . .")[14]

In predicting the return of Astraea and the advent of a new
Golden Age, Virgil had intended to celebrate the new secular
Roman empire. But long after his ideals had turned to dust, his
work survived in a sort of afterlife as a prophecy of Christ's virgin birth. Virgil never envisioned the significance it would acquire when the Christian Middle Ages read these lines and, miraculously, found in them a veiled version of their own beliefs.
In the *Commedia*, this afterlife enables Statius to convert.

Dante invented the story of Statius's Virgilian conversion in
order to strengthen the parallel to his own relation to his poetic
master. Statius, having already cited the crucial role the Fourth
Eclogue played in engendering his newfound belief, then patterns his secret conversion after the same Exodus figure that
controls Dante's own turning to God. Alluding to an incident
in the *Thebaid*, Statius says, "E pria ch'io conducessi i Greci a'
fiumi / di Tebe poetando, ebb' io battesmo" ("And before I had
led the Greeks to the rivers of Thebes in my verse, I received
baptism"; *Purg.* XXII, 88–89).[15] In the parallel story from Exodus, the children of Israel are led to the banks of the Jordan;
this event prefigures baptism in the New Testament. It also prefigures Dante's journey through the desert to the River Jordan,
which appears in various guises throughout the *Commedia*. Vir-

gil, an unsaved soul, cannot cross the stream; for Dante as well as for Statius, he carries the lantern but does not see by the light himself. It requires no great leap of the imagination to extend the parallels between Statius and Dante one step further: Dante's reading of Virgil—like Dante a poet in search of a political Golden Age—also influenced the spiritual experience underlying the *Commedia*. Dante's conversion, like Statius's, results from his Christian reading of the *Aeneid*.[16]

Statius exemplifies literature's power to rewrite its readers; his conversion figures a positive paradigm to which Dante seeks to conform in his own work. But other episodes in the *Commedia* illustrate the traps literature can set for its readers, and chief among them is the canto of Paolo and Francesca. *Inferno* v has always exerted a powerful attraction on its readers,[17] but Dante's intimate moral and aesthetic involvement here springs not from his tolerance of Paolo and Francesca's behavior, but from his strong convictions about the proper use of his literary art. To a large extent, the canto concerns a kind of love literature that endangers its readers. And Dante, a love poet first and last, is implicated in the social effects of love literature, for good or for ill.

Character, language, and plot secure *Inferno* v's affinity with the tradition of chivalric romance. Virgil describes the lovers in his catalogue as romantic rather than heroic figures; although many of them come to us from classical epic, here they are doomed to the eternal winds of the second circle for their treatment in love literature. Even Achilles and Paris resemble their romance companion Tristan more than their Homeric originals.[18] And Dante speaks of them with the words of chivalric romance: "Le donne antiche e' cavalieri" (the ladies and the knights of old; *Inf.* v, 71). Francesca's name and courtly idiom place her as well in the French tradition. When she echoes Guido Guinizelli's canzone "Al cor gentil ripara sempre amore" (Love always shelters in the gentle heart), she attributes love's genesis to the physicality of Paolo's *piacer* (delight, a Provençalism); in general, her language is the aristocratic diction of romance.[19]

Critics have long recognized that Francesca's story follows the plot of the Old French prose Lancelot, in which the go-between Gallehault arranges the rendezvous at which Guinevere first kisses Lancelot.[20] Dante transforms this tale into one of two lovers brought together by a different sort of go-between, a book. The book creates the lovers in its image when Paolo and Francesca imitate what they read in its pages. Dante apparently fuses the proper noun "Galeotto" (Gallehault's name in the Italian version of the Lancelot romance) with the common noun *galeotto* (pilot or steersman), which is applied to two guide figures in the *Commedia*: Phlegyas, who ferries Dante and Virgil across the Styx (*Inf.* VIII, 17); and the angel who ferries souls across the sea to purgatory (*Purg.* II, 27). The pun makes Gallehault's mediating role in the romance that of a steersman in love, a guide who brings people to a new station in life.[21] Francesca attributes just such a role to the book she and Paolo read when she says, "Galeotto fu 'l libro e chi lo scrisse" ("A Gallehault was the book and he who wrote it"; *Inf.* V, 137). Francesca does not duplicate the Lancelot romance as such; rather, she tells what happens when people read it.

Francesca actually tells two versions of her fall. The first, a romance, adopts that genre's language and ideals, but makes no mention of the book behind the incident. Until she must admit how thoroughly her love has been conditioned by her reading, Francesca endorses the romantic conventions that enable her to evade responsibility for her actions. Like Tristan, who was excused by a love potion, she implies that love's irresistibility absolves her of blame:

> "Amor, ch'al cor gentil ratto s'apprende,
>   prese costui de la bella persona
>   che mi fu tolta; e 'l modo ancor m'offende.
> Amor, ch'a nullo amato amar perdona,
>   mi prese del costui piacer sì forte,

che, come vedi, ancor non m'abbandona.
Amor condusse noi ad una morte.
Caina attende chi a vita ci spense."   (*Inf.* v, 100–107)

("Love, which is quickly kindled in a gentle heart, seized this
one for the fair form that was taken from me—and the way of
it afflicts me still. Love, which absolves no loved one from loving, seized me so strongly with delight in him, that, as you see,
it does not leave me even now. Love brought us to one death.
Caina awaits him who quenched our life.")

But she is wrong. Her presence among the damned gives the lie
to her self-deception. When pressed, she offers a second version
of her fall. An antiromance, it concedes the crucial role of the
book, and reduces rarefied courtly periphrasis ("il disïato riso,"
the longed-for smile; *Inf.* v, 133) to raw physicality ("la bocca,"
my mouth; *Inf.* v, 136). Francesca errs by accepting the book's
romantic conventions and believing that she could act them out
in her own life with impunity. The result is her absolute ego-
tism, which reduces Paolo to a silent figment of her desire. Ultimately, she bears full moral responsibility for her choice and
the actions that follow upon it.

But in one sense she is also a victim. Renato Poggioli best
summarizes the canto's moral import when he states that "writing and reading romantic fiction is almost as bad as yielding to
romantic love."[22] Mutually shared moral responsibility, like
love itself, multiplies rather than divides; the book does not escape culpability merely because Paolo and Francesca must pay
the reckoning for having responded to it as they did. Dante includes fictions and their authors in the key line "Galeotto fu 'l
libro e chi lo scrisse." And by this inclusion, he hints at the possibility that he and his *Commedia* could also be implicated for
ill rather than for good.[23]

The mediation of the Lancelot romance in *Inferno* v inverts
the moral valence of literary mediation in the *Commedia* as a
whole. Dante writes the poem in order to recreate his experience of conversion in the lives of his readers, thus bridging the

gap between himself and those whom he seeks to lead along the path he traversed. To make it clear that the poem is an act of mediation, in which the reader is joined by a go-between (the book and he who wrote it) to the proper object of love (God), Dante exemplifies his experience as an act of reading. He, like Statius, read Virgil and converted to God. But Paolo and Francesca read the Lancelot romance, and the "solo un punto" (one moment alone; *Inf.* v, 132) that conquers them is worlds apart from the "un punto solo" (*Par.* XXXIII, 94) that defeats Dante's memory at the end of the poem. Anna Hatcher and Mark Musa ask why Dante plays the "cruel authorial trick"[24] that traps Francesca into lifting the veil from her self-deception, but I think the answer is clear. Had he not uncovered her error, he would have perpetuated it, endangering his own soul as well as pandering to more Paolo's and Francesca's. As the "pietade" (pity; *Inf.* v, 140) he feels for Francesca suggests, this danger is real, for in Francesca's first version of her fall, Dante has just written a perilous piece of romantic fiction. Thus it cannot be, as Poggioli suggests, that Dante attacks a kind of love literature that he did not himself write. The fame of Paolo and Francesca as romantic (rather than antiromantic) figures may be due to misreading, yet their inclusion alongside the great lovers of Western literature suggests a subterranean desire on Dante's part to enter the romantic competition. Only by laying bare the beautiful deceit of love literature—including his own—could Dante avoid misleading his readers.

Hence he makes the canto an antiromance, and an ironic antithesis to his own great love poem. The opposition between part and whole becomes clear through another underlying text, Augustine's *Confessions*. Francesca's reticent conclusion to her story of the book's role, "quel giorno più non vi leggemmo avante" ("that day we read no farther in it"; *Inf.* v, 138), echoes Augustine's "nec ultra legere volui" (No further would I read), from the scene in which he converts to God by means of another book, Scriptures.[25] This scene itself echoes and corrects an earlier stage in Augustine's life, characterized by his delight in the story of Dido and Aeneas.[26] It is on this earlier scene, in which Augustine remorsefully recalls the seductive appeal of vain, deceitful fictions, that Francesca's second story depends. She remains eternally in the spiritual condition from which Augustine later turns; she dooms herself by taking up a romantic fiction, reading, and molding her own life according to its ideology. Her second account thus inverts Augustine's conversion by the book.

But Dante imitates Augustine's conversion rather than Francesca's fall. Like the *Confessions*, the *Commedia* is an account of a soul journeying to God, traveling from the books of youth (both read and authored) to the Book—Scriptures or the bound volume to which Dante likens God at the end of the *Paradiso*. However, as Giuseppe Mazzotta demonstrates, Dante models Francesca's story "on Augustine's reading of the *Aeneid* in order to register his disagreement with it."[27] The canto is part of the rehabilitation of Virgil that enables the Latin poet to lead Dante two-thirds of the way toward the Book he sees at the end. Thus in *Inferno* V, Dante distinguishes two kinds of reading that nonetheless share the same process of mediation. Paolo and Francesca create an afterlife for the Lancelot romance by repeating it in their own lives, and so win damnation. Dante seeks a better afterlife for his poem (and for the *Aeneid*) by setting *Inferno* V in counterpoint to the *Commedia* as a whole.

In order to avoid the dangers exemplified by *Inferno* V, Dante does not simply leave the fate of his text to the vagaries of his readers. Instead, he limns in an ideal reader whom he controls by often monitory direct addresses:

> O voi che siete in piccioletta barca,
>   desiderosi d'ascoltar, seguiti
>   dietro al mio legno che cantando varca,
> tornate a riveder li vostri liti:
>   non vi mettete in pelago, ché forse,
>   perdendo me, rimarreste smarriti.   (*Par.* II, 1–6)

(O you that are in your little bark, eager to hear, following behind my ship that singing makes her way, turn back to see again your shores. Do not commit yourselves to the open sea, for perchance, if you lost me, you would remain astray.)

Dante seeks to prevent abuse of his text by making the reading conform to his intentions; his ideal relation to his reader parallels Virgil's relation to him. Just as Virgil's book rescued Dante from the perils of the prologue scene, so Dante's book should rescue the reader from the woeful spiritual passes of his own life. Dante thus embraces Francesca's summation: "Galeotto fu 'l libro e chi lo scrisse."

But despite the imperious directives Dante issues to guide the use to which his poem is put, reading remains the province of readers. In Chaucer, Dante found a reader who would not assent to the role prescribed for him. Far from following docilely in his mentor's wake, in the *Troilus* Chaucer uses the *Commedia* against itself. In the proem to Book II, he characterizes himself as a *galeotto* scarcely able to steer his course through the rough seas of his story:

> Owt of thise blake wawes for to saylle,
> O wynd, o wynd, the weder gynneth clere;
> For in this see the boot hath swych travaylle,
> Of my connyng, that unneth I it steere.
> This see clepe I the tempestous matere
> Of disespeir that Troilus was inne . . .   (II.1–6)

Imitated from the *Commedia* (*Purg.* I, 1–3), this passage is one of the most overt links Chaucer makes between love and poetry, and is thus central to the role *Inferno* V plays in the *Troilus*. Like *Inferno* V, Chaucer's poem tells the story of two lovers brought together by a bookish mediator, written by a poet who poses as a go-between.

The parallel extends to the book Paolo and Francesca read as well. The length to which Troilus carries his diffidence, especially in the consummation scene, is amusingly exaggerated.[28]

However, he has good literary precedent for his bashfulness, for he acts much as Lancelot does in the romance bearing his name.[29] Two passages from the Gallehault scene bear particular scrutiny; in the first, the Dame of Malehout's presence non-plusses Lancelot, for she was once his paramour:

> Et cil en fu si angoisseus par un pou que il ne pasma . mes la peor des dames qui lesgardoient le retint et la reine meesmes sen dota parce que ele le uit palir et color changier . si le prist par le braz quil ne chaist et apela Galehout et il salt sus si uient a li corant .

> (And he was in such sore anguish thereat that he well-nigh swooned, but the fear of the ladies who were looking at him kept him therefrom; and the Queen herself was in fear thereof, for she saw him turn pale and change color. And she took him by the arm lest he should fall, and called Gallehault. And he leaped up and came to her running.)[30]

Having sworn to his constancy in the Queen's service, Lancelot nearly faints when confronted with the evidence of his inconstancy. When Troilus is confronted with Pandarus's contrived fable about Criseyde's inconstancy, he does faint (III. 1086–92). In both cases, when the men lose their nerve, the women must take the initiative:

> Lors se traient tuit troi ensemble et font semblant de conseillier . et la reine uoit bien qui li cheualiers nen ose plus fere . si le prent par le menton et le bese uoiant Galehout assez longuement .

> (Then they all three drew together and made as if they took counsel. And the Queen saw well that the knight dared do no farther, and she took him by the chin and kissed him before Gallehault no short space . . .)[31]

The *Troilus* as a whole bears no great resemblance to the Lancelot romance. But Pandarus is like Gallehault, both as a go-between and as a faithful friend.[32] And Troilus resembles Lancelot in the Gallehault scene. Both are valiant in war and easily abashed in love. And both belong to the tradition of romantic fiction embodied in *Inferno* v's catalogue of lovers rather than to the kind of love literature Boccaccio wrote in *Il Filostrato*.

Criseyde too shares a common history with *Inferno* v's heroines, notably with Dido. Dante's periphrasis for the souls of the second circle, "la schiera ov' è Dido" (the troop where Dido is; *Inf.* v, 85), identifies their sin as Didonian. Virgil mentions Dido without directly naming her: "L'altra è colei che s'ancise amorosa, / e ruppe fede al cener di Sicheo" ("The next is she who slew herself for love and broke faith to the ashes of Sichaeus"; *Inf.* v, 61–62). Dido's defining presence suggests that the sin punished here is not simply adultery or incest (both of which can be applied to Paolo and Francesca). Dante includes Dido either because she (like Troilus) died for earthly love, or because she (like Criseyde) broke faith in love.

Chaucer's own Dido teasingly resembles his Criseyde. In *The House of Fame*,[33] Aeneas's deserted queen speaks eloquently about the power of rumor, canonized in literature, to traduce. Criseyde's speech lamenting her future literary treatment parallels Dido's:

> "Allas, for now is clene ago
> My name of trouthe in love, for everemo!
> For I have falsed oon the gentileste
> That evere was, and oon the worthieste!
>
> "Allas, of me, unto the worldes ende,
> Shal neyther ben ywriten nor ysonge
> No good word, for thise bokes wol me shende.
> O, rolled shal I ben on many a tonge!
> Thorughout the world my belle shal be ronge!
> And wommen moost wol haten me of alle.
> Allas, that swich a cas me sholde falle!" (v. 1054–64)

And when Criseyde looks down at Troilus's triumphal progress through the streets of Troy, she asks herself, "Who yaf me drynke?" (ii.651). Both Root and Robinson gloss "drynke" as "love-potion," the drink that removes love from the sphere of volition.[34] While Criseyde's question is not as sharply defined as this gloss implies—it could refer merely to a heady sensation of the kind caused by strong wine[35]—it nonetheless delicately suggests that Criseyde should be placed in the romance tradition of Tristan and Isolde. This is certainly the interpretation offered by the *Disce mori*, a fifteenth-century treatise for women religious, which quotes the *Troilus* to exemplify carnal love. The treatise consistently interprets the poem in terms of the drink of sweet poison Criseyde's question seems to suggest.[36] The medieval Dido too belongs in the love potion tradition; the *Roman d'Eneas* describes the sudden passion she conceives for Aeneas as a draught of mortal poison.[37]

Thus the "spontaneous combustion" excused by love potions appears not only in *Inferno* V, but also in the *Troilus*. Troilus as well falls in love instantaneously. The poet assures us that this is a matter of necessity, like the "Amor, ch'al cor gentil ratto s'apprende" (Love, which is quickly kindled in a gentle heart; *Inf.* V, 100). The second element of Francesca's romantic anaphora has its turn later on, when Pandarus uses "Amor, ch'a nullo amato amar perdona" (Love, which absolves no loved one from loving; *Inf.* V, 103) as an argument to persuade Criseyde:

> "That is wel seyd," quod he. "Certein, best is
> That ye hym love ayeyn for his lovynge,
> As love for love is skilful guerdonynge."   (II.390–92)

This argument apparently moves Criseyde, for she later says to herself, "Ek sith I woot for me is his destresse, / I ne aughte nat for that thing hym despise" (II.719–20).

But Criseyde's words here show a tentative quality that Francesca's had lacked, and a few lines later, Chaucer's heroine rejects the notion that she is obliged to reciprocate Troilus's love (II.734–35). With Criseyde's hesitations, the plots of *Inferno* V and the *Troilus* begin to diverge. Chaucer develops the similarities only up to a point, beyond which he vitiates the possibility of absolute identification. Verbal and plot correspondences between *Inferno* V and the *Troilus* serve as a forum of shared concept, enabling Chaucer to highlight the doubts and qualifications so fundamental to his poem and its love affair, and so foreign to the *Commedia*. Chaucer has first assured us that they are indeed the same story; now he asks us to see that story in a different light.

The perspective from which Chaucer asks us to consider this story precludes both damnation and transcendence. The location of the *Troilus* within the world of time and flux counters the *Commedia*'s eternal realm seen under the aspect of death and final judgment. Dante claimed insight into the state of souls after death, and thus absolute knowledge of the moral state of people in this world. But such knowledge is absent from the *Troilus*. Chaucer's poem is fraught with uncertainty, as his treatment of Criseyde best shows. In Benoît, Guido, and Boccaccio, Criseyde's infidelity defined her with a fixity corresponding to Dante's flat judgment of souls.[38] Yet here she has become an enigma. In her first portrait, the only certain fact is her name:

> Criseyde was this lady name al right.
> As to my doom, in al Troies cite
> Nas non so fair, forpassynge every wight,
> So aungelik was hir natif beaute,
> That lik a thing inmortal semed she,
> As doth an hevenyssh perfit creature,
> That down were sent in scornynge of nature.   (1.99–105)

For the rest, we depend on the poet's judgment of what she resembles.[39] He knows neither her age (v.896) nor whether she had children (1.132–33), although Boccaccio said she had none. Even the nature of her final infidelity is uncertain, for the poet reports hearsay he is unwilling to warrant: "Men seyn—I not—that she yaf hym hire herte" (v.1050). The poet (as in *The House of Fame*) knows only what is said of her, and such definition in the *Troilus* is grounded at least as much in what people wish to believe as in what actually is. Chaucer does not change Criseyde's history, but by dwelling on the limitations of knowledge and the contingency of our interpretative acts, he makes it very difficult to condemn her.[40] And without such absolute judgment, there can be no *Inferno*.

Consequently, actions eternal and changeless in Dante remain here temporal and mutable. Time's mutability causes things to fall apart, but also occasionally allows amelioration. This is the case at the moment of Troilus's despair immediately after the Trojan parliament has decided to exchange Criseyde for Antenor. Chaucer borrows from the *Inferno* to describe Troilus's bleak state:

> And as in wynter leves ben biraft,
> Ech after other, til the tree be bare,
> So that ther nys but bark and braunche ilaft,
> Lith Troilus, byraft of ech welfare,
> Ibounden in the blake bark of care,
> Disposed wood out of his wit to breyde,
> So sore hym sat the chaungynge of Criseyde.   (IV.225–31)

Chaucer draws this description from two passages themselves borrowed from Virgil, the simile in *Inferno* III comparing the souls of the damned to falling leaves and the *contrapasso* of *Inferno* XIII. Dante altered the "generations like leaves" simile to reflect the difference between paganism and Christianity; his version stresses the individuality of each soul's fate, seen from the God-like perspective of the tree.[41] Chaucer absorbs Dante's changes in the first four lines of this stanza, but makes a Dantean reading impossible by adding Dante's version of Polydorus, Pier della Vigne.[42] In *Inferno* XIII, Pier's soul was imprisoned within a tree, which after the Last Judgment will serve as a gallows for his body. His punishment ironically inverts his suicide, by which he had violently rent soul and body asunder. Until this apocalyptic reunification, his inhumanity to himself is manifested in the distortion of his speech,[43] produced with great difficulty from the wound Dante makes when he breaks off a twig. His loss of human speech epitomizes his damnation:

> Come d'un stizzo verde ch'arso sia
>   da l'un de' capi, che da l'altro geme
>   e cigola per vento che va via,

sì de la scheggia rota usciva insieme
   parole e sangue . . .   (*Inf.* XIII, 40–44)

(As from a green brand that is burning at one end, and drips
from the other, hissing with the escaping air, so from that broken twig came out words and blood together . . .)

In Chaucer's poem, Troilus is figuratively metamorphosed
into a tree; he too loses the power of speech (IV.249). This
would seem to consign Troilus to Pier's infernal thicket,[44] but
Troilus does not sustain the first intensity of his despair. He
soon regains his speech (IV.250), and time assuages his initial
pain somewhat (IV.253–55). Chaucer's treatment of Troilus in
this passage springs from the same root as his insistence on Criseyde's ultimate mysteriousness: the idea that knowledge becomes final and change ceases only at the point of death.
Dante's removal of his poem to the otherworld is based on this
precondition; but Chaucer borrows from the *Commedia* to show
that it does not hold in the *Troilus*, and that the status of his
characters hence differs from the status of the characters in
Dante's poem.

If there can be no inferno in the *Troilus*, neither can there be
transcendence. The failing that dooms infernal souls is a misdirected desire for transcendence; Francesca, for example, fixes
her love on an object (Paolo, or rather Paolo loving her) inferior
to the supreme good. Troilus shares their error. He tries to
transform brief, mutable earthly love into something divine,
stable, and eternal. And he expresses his transcendent desire
with words drawn from the *Paradiso*; the hymn "O Love, O
Charite!" (III.1254–74) echoes Bernard's prayer for the Beatific
Vision (*Par.* XXXIII).

Indeed, the whole of Book III uses Dante to exalt Boccaccean
love. With the proem and Troilus's final song, the book is
framed by celebrations of love as the binding force of the universe. Although the proem derives from the first six stanzas of
Troiolo's similar song (*Filostrato*, III.74–89), Chaucer ceases to
follow Boccaccio before Troiolo directs his praise of Venus to-

ward her role in aiding his physical love for Criseida. Lacking the specificity and the erotic charge of Troiolo's song, Chaucer's invocation instead characterizes love chiefly as the bonds of cosmic and natural harmony. Hence it closely resembles the natural love "sempre sanza errore" (always without error; *Purg.* XVII, 94) to which Beatrice refers as the motive force that "la terra in sé stringe e aduna" ("binds together and unites the earth"; *Par.* I, 117).

Here too—as with Troilus's hymn at the moment of consummation—Chaucer seems to have had his eye on *Paradiso* XXXIII, for he ends the proem's invocation of love with an echo of Bernard's prayer to the Virgin Mary:

> Now, lady bryght, for thi benignite,
> At reverence of hem that serven the,
> Whos clerc I am, so techeth me devyse
> Som joye of that is felt in thi servyse.   (III.39–42)

Chaucer's appeal to love's "benignite"—a detail absent from Boccaccio—is drawn instead from "La tua benignità" (Thy loving-kindness; *Par.* XXXIII, 16), to which Bernard appeals in Mary. And where Troiolo had asked Venus to govern his and Criseida's ardor (*Filostrato*, III.89), Chaucer instead asks her to help him write about the joy of his lovers. The new structure of mediation recalls Chaucer's role as "I, that God of Loves servantz serve" (I.15), itself an echo of the papal title *servus servorum Dei* (the servant of the servants of God).

All of these changes transform love into something considerably more exalted than in *Il Filostrato*. Troilus's song at the end of the book (III.1744–71) confirms these changes. Here— the original place of Troiolo's song in Boccaccio—Chaucer substitutes an imitation of the Boethian passage also underlying Beatrice's discourse on the cosmic bonds of love in *Paradiso* I.[45] Even without direct Dantean echoes, then, Troilus's final song recalls the Dantean framework of natural love established by the proem. The concept of love framing Book III is clearly "paradisal" in nature.

Yet both framing passages—the proem and Troilus's final song—contain disturbing reminders of Francesca's story, a tale in which misdirected elective love turns the soul from natural love's unerring path. These echoes undercut Troilus's idealistic attempt to gain "hevene blisse" (III.704) through his love of Criseyde. The proem refers to the gentle heart of Francesca's romantic first version: "Plesance of love, O goodly debonaire, / In gentil hertes ay redy to repaire!" (III.4–5). Boccaccio also mentions the gentle heart in the passage Chaucer adapts here.[46] However, the Chaucerian version translates the first line of Guinizelli's canzone "Al cor gentil ripara sempre amore," and so resembles more closely, both verbally and conceptually, the gentle heart Francesca invokes to absolve herself of blame. And Troilus's song at the end of Book III includes a formal echo of the anaphora (*Inf.* V, 100–106) initiated by the gentle heart:

> "Love, that of erthe and se hath governaunce,
> Love, that his hestes hath in hevene hye,
> Love, that with an holsom alliaunce
> Halt peples joyned, as hym lest hem gye . . ."   (III.1744–47)

Francesca's voice is only a whisper; the attributes of love here resemble those of the *Paradiso* far more closely than those of *Inferno* V. Troilus also mitigates the similarity to Francesca's anaphora by adding a fourth repetition after the one-line hiatus:

> "Love, that knetteth lawe of compaignie,
> And couples doth in vertu for to dwelle,
> Bynde this acord, that I have told and telle."   (III.1748–50)

Faint though these echoes are, they join with the plot similarities to reinforce the irony: *Inferno* V, with its misdirected love, lurks behind the divine love Troilus seeks to attain in Book III.

Thus far, it would seem that Chaucer follows Dante in exposing false transcendence mistaken for its true counterpart. In this sense, the *Troilus* shares the antiromantic quality of *Inferno* V. The idealistic love of Book III is no more than Troilus's futile desire for transcendence. No matter how much he wishes to fix his love at the moment of "hevene blisse," its demise approaches as inexorably as the fall of the city whose name he bears. But I do not believe that Chaucer aims his critique at Troilus alone. He could easily have told the story of Troilus as a pagan sinner enthralled in the bonds of fleshly love without the fusion of infernal and paradisal language that characterizes the love of Book III. The Dantean language in a story set in ancient Troy embodies a commentary on the *Commedia*, and it is in this respect that the utterly different surfaces of the two works, Christian and pagan, become important.

The pagan quality of the *Troilus* is double-edged.[47] Although Chaucer develops the Troy setting far more extensively than Boccaccio had done, the *Troilus* does not share *Il Filostrato*'s starkly pagan tone. In effect, Chaucer rehabilitates human love by softening the pagan attitudes of his primary source.[48] Criseyde decides to love Troilus not merely because he is fair and she lusty, as is true in *Il Filostrato*, but at least partly because Troilus's moral virtue allays her fears. Her statement to that effect ("But moral vertu, grounded upon trouthe— / That was the cause I first hadde on yow routhe"; IV. 1672–73) should be taken as a serious reason, not simply as a rationalization of more elemental, purely sexual urges.[49] Troilus's moral virtue plays an important role in her considerations after she first looks down at him from her window, and the narrative supports her evaluation of his character.

Moreover, Troilus's virtue derives from love's ennobling power. Initially he is a rather callow young man, convinced of his own wit when he jeers at the plight of lovers, but the feeling he conceives for Criseyde reforms him:

> For he bicom the frendlieste wight,
> The gentilest, and ek the mooste fre,
> The thriftiest and oon the beste knyght
> That in his tyme was or myghte be.
> Dede were his japes and his cruelte,
> His heighe port and his manere estraunge,
> And ecch of tho gan for a vertu chaunge.   (I. 1079–85)

When the love affair reaches its peak, so too does his virtue:

> And though that he be come of blood roial,
> Hym liste of pride at no wight for to chace;
> Benigne he was to ech in general,
> For which he gat hym thank in every place.
> Thus wolde Love—yheried be his grace!—
> That Pride, Envye, Ire, and Avarice
> He gan to fle, and everich other vice. (III.1800–1806)

Francis Lee Utley even argues that Troilus exhibits, in addition to the classical virtues one might expect of a pagan hero, a close approximation of the Pauline theological virtues as well.[50] Throughout the poem, Chaucer links love and virtue in a causal chain. Love leads to Troilus's virtue, which then helps to inspire Criseyde's love for him; her love in turn increases Troilus's virtue.

Although the decreased paganness of the *Troilus* ameliorates human love vis-à-vis *Il Filostrato*, paradoxically the poem's increased paganness rehabilitates human love vis-à-vis *Inferno* V. As Christians (and relatives by marriage), Paolo and Francesca have no excuse for electing each other over God, and so diverting the tendency of natural love to return to its source. But as pagans, Chaucer's Trojan lovers do. Living under the law of nature, they have no access to the order of grace that would grant them knowledge of the object of desire (God) commensurate with the transcendent longings Troilus instead invests in Criseyde. Moreover, Chaucer's emphasis on Troilus's virtue transforms his love from Francesca's grammatically reflexive "Amor, ch'al cor gentil ratto s'apprende" into the grammatically transitive love Dante associates with Statius and Virgil: "Amore, / acceso di virtù; sempre altro accese" (Love, kindled by virtue, has ever kindled other love; *Purg.* XXII, 10–11). Chaucer perhaps equivocates by embedding his reactions to the *Commedia* in a tale set in pagan time, but this choice allows him to avoid the thorny issue of ultimates and instead to examine love as a process of positive, if limited, moral discovery. Dante had chosen the most extreme case, that of Christians who betray both husband and brother, to illustrate the perils of earthly romantic love. Chaucer's choice of pagans allows him to present human love as a positive, though secondary, good.

When Troilus is translated to the spheres at the end of the poem, he is taken out of time. The difference between his death and that of Paolo and Francesca is significant. Francesca concludes her first story with "Amor noi condusse ad una morte" ("Love brought us to one death"; *Inf.* v, 106); she and Paolo suffer a spiritually destructive *Liebestod* that dooms them to be whirled forever in the winds of the second circle. Troilus, after suffering the double sorrow of love and loss, dies in battle apart from Criseyde; then "His lighte goost ful blisfully is went / Up to the holughnesse of the eighthe spere" (v.1808–9). In contrast with Francesca, who learns nothing about the nature of her love, Troilus gains a perspective that separates him more thoroughly than even death could from his former self. His posthumous translation counters the destructive unity of Paolo and Francesca's death, and so shifts Chaucer's focus away from the final judgments found in the *Commedia*.

Earlier I compared Criseyde to the Dido of *The House of Fame*. In fact, this is part of a larger pattern, for both lovers bear striking resemblance to Dido and Aeneas, and in such a way as to suggest that Chaucer's use of Virgil comes to him through Dante. Troilus, who immolates himself when he is deserted, appropriates this part of Dido's history—though with a difference. He is ennobled by love, not destroyed; and whatever his ultimate fate, it is difficult to read it as the kind of punishment with which Dante afflicts Dido in naming the sin of the second circle after her. And Criseyde's departure from Troy echoes Aeneas's history, both in his desertion of Dido and in his treachery in the last act of the Trojan tragedy.[51]

The effect of this pattern is difficult to judge. By opening the perspective onto epic vistas, it complicates our response to Troilus and Criseyde and deepens the poem's capacity for seriousness. More specifically, Dido's shadowy presence focuses some of the same questions about literature and history that surround her in *The House of Fame*. Dante, by patterning himself after Aeneas, had rescued Virgil and his providential view of history from Augustine's condemnation in the *Confessions*. If Mazzotta is correct that "reading emerges as the fundamental metaphor upon which Dante's view of history depends,"[52] then Chaucer's altered configuration of Virgilian character types registers his reluctance to accept Dante's use of the story of Dido and Aeneas. As in *The House of Fame*, the story signifies for Chaucer not the askesis of revisionist history progressing toward providential truth, but rather the intractability and uniqueness of the past. The problem of recovering historical truth is a central one in the *Troilus*, and here too it is exemplified as an act of reading. But the view of history Chaucer arrives at does not subsume the pagan past into the scheme of Christian typology; it preserves a certain distance from a past he cannot wholly know.

Thus the paganness of the *Troilus* rehabilitates earthly love in comparison to both *Il Filostrato* and *Inferno* v. Yet Chaucer's greater emphasis on the Troy setting does not function consistently to distance the narrative.[53] Book II's proem, with its meditation on changing customs in language and love, tells us in part that the more people change the more they stay the same. Troilus's lack of access to Christian salvation does not vitiate the significance his story holds for readers of a later, Christian age, or Chaucer would not have retold it to help "loveres, as I kan, to pleyne" (I.11). The Trojan scene serves also to insist on historicity per se—the story's setting in time, as opposed to the *Commedia*'s setting in eternity. In our temporality, we are all like Troilus before he dies, perhaps seeking transcendence, but with no guarantee that we have found it.

The present relevance the *Troilus* holds for Chaucer's audience lies largely in the antiromantic quality it shares with *Inferno* v. As antiromance, the *Troilus* illustrates the dangers of ignoring the limitations to which human love is subject in this world. Yet Troilus, while living the plot of *Inferno* v, uses the

language of the *Paradiso* to celebrate the illusory romantic transcendence the *Troilus* ultimately warns against. By fusing *Inferno* and *Paradiso*, Troilus effaces the distinctions between true
and false transcendence that Dante had labored to build. And
this is no egregious error on his part; despite Dante's effort to
free his poem from all the failings literary flesh is heir to, the
same words of human love are used for Francesca and for Beatrice. In fact, since part of his purpose is to show how easily the
counterfeit passes for the true coin, Dante must differentiate
the two only very subtly. But the consequences for any reader
who does not follow him in conversion, as Dante warns, can be
to lose oneself utterly. Such a reader cannot perceive the subtle
but crucial distinctions between the love that leads to perdition
and the love that leads to salvation.

In Troilus, Chaucer offers a model of just such an unconverted reader. For him, the *Commedia* is only the most exalted
in a series of love poems that lend him the words and deeds by
which he patterns his own behavior. He believes he can mold
his love affair according to the conventions of literary love language, and so attain the transcendence into which Dante trans-
mutes his devotion to Beatrice. In a sense, the *Commedia* is Troilus's bookish *galeotto*, a steersman guiding him to the fulfillment of his desires. Dante indeed intends his poem as just such
a *galeotto*, guiding his readers to the Empyrean, yet Troilus's
Dantean words subvert Dante's purpose. Troilus's idealism is
admirable, but it fails. And in this failure, Chaucer illustrates
the dangers Dante's poem might hold for readers who, like
Troilus, do not share Dante's conversion. The bookishness of
the *Troilus*, like that of the *Commedia*, embodies a concern for
the moral effects of literature on its readers. Chaucer, however,
aims this concern at Dante's poem, to show how the *Commedia*
might be as false a guide as the Lancelot romance. The Dantean
borrowings of the *Troilus* turn the story not only into an antiromance, but also into an anti-*Commedia*.

If the *Troilus* is to succeed as a commentary against the *Commedia*, Chaucer must furnish a way for us to assent to his poem

as more true to the world than Dante's poem. This endeavor is fundamentally concerned with narrative authority. Hence my task now is to explore what I have called "primary authentication," the manner in which the "I" of each poem establishes itself as a trustworthy voice capable of illuminating the nature of reality. Chaucer's problem in representing a version of the world opposed to Dante's is formidable, for Dante's authority in the *Commedia* is daunting. Chaucer's solution to this problem includes questioning the validity of narrative authenticity itself.

3. The Narrators and Their Readers

At crucial junctures in *Troilus and Criseyde*, Chaucer positively invites misreading. There is good reason for the extraordinary range of interpretations that scenes such as this, relating the events of the morning following the consummation, have called forth:

> Pandare, o-morwe, which that comen was
> Unto his nece and gan hire faire grete,
> Seyde, "Al this nyght so reyned it, allas,
> That al my drede is that ye, nece swete,
> Han litel laiser had to slepe and mete.
> Al nyght," quod he, "hath reyn so do me wake,
> That som of us, I trowe, hire hedes ake."
>
> And ner he com, and seyde, "How stant it now
> This mury morwe? Nece, how kan ye fare?"
> Criseyde answerde, "Nevere the bet for yow,
> Fox that ye ben! God yeve youre herte kare!
> God help me so, ye caused al this fare,
> Trowe I," quod she, "for al youre wordes white.
> O, whoso seeth yow knoweth yow ful lite."
>
> With that she gan hire face for to wrye
> With the shete, and wax for shame al reed;
> And Pandarus gan under for to prie,
> And seyde, "Nece, if that I shal be ded,
> Have here a swerd and smyteth of myn hed!"
> With that his arm al sodeynly he thriste
> Under hire nekke, and at the laste hire kyste.
>
> I passe al that which chargeth nought to seye.
> What! God foryaf his deth, and she al so

Foryaf, and with here uncle gan to pleye,
For other cause was ther noon than so.
But of this thing right to the effect to go:
Whan tyme was, hom til here hous she wente,
And Pandarus hath fully his entente.   (III.1555–82)

Here Criseyde, who all along has chosen to maintain a certain blindness toward Pandarus's arrangements, finally shows that she understands them perfectly. Paired with its symmetrically placed counterpart near the beginning of Book III, in which Pandarus speaks openly to Troilus about his role as a "meene / As maken wommen unto men to comen" (III. 254–55), this scene contrasts Criseyde's worldly experience to Troilus's idealistic innocence. With Troilus, Pandarus has to spell out the ethical problems his mediation poses; even then some question remains of whether Troilus understands the potential difficulties.[1] With Criseyde, no such openness is necessary.

The peculiarity of this scene lies in the willful blindness it encourages in its critics. By blindness I mean the tendency to interpret Criseyde's and Pandarus's behavior in an extreme manner, either as wholly innocent or as shockingly debased; and then, by under- or overreading, to gloss over any evidence that might uphold the validity of the opposite extreme. In a "debased" reading, Pandarus "rummages under the bedclothes" to get at his niece; the sword he mentions acquires powerful sexual suggestiveness; and in the end he has his way with Criseyde.[2] Coming so soon after the consummation, such behavior seriously damages Pandarus's character; it destroys Criseyde's. It proves how fickle she can and will be, and how immoral she is in love. The narrator's effort to wriggle out of the obvious and disturbing significance of the scene, with "I passe al that which chargeth nought to seye," only confirms its enormity. Pandarus and Criseyde demonstrate conclusively the moral degradation that ensues when lovers elevate appetite over reason.

An "innocent" reading results in a very different scene. Pandarus is avuncular; Criseyde becomingly modest; and their intercourse purely verbal, a delightfully witty exchange between two people who are fond of one another.[3] Pandarus pulls the bedsheet down only far enough to uncover Criseyde's face, which she has hidden in her embarrassment. Pandarus's sword exists only in a manner of speaking, with no physical referent and certainly no sexual suggestion. Their physical contact is strictly limited; no part of Criseyde's body below the neck appears, and Pandarus's kiss is one of happy triumph over the success of his plan. Their play, as in Book II, is the verbal interchange in which both clearly take such pleasure. Pandarus's "entente," which is mentioned only after Criseyde has gone home, is nothing more than his effort to bring Troilus and Criseyde together. And the narrator's interjection suggests no more than an artistic choice to summarize the rest of a conversation of which only the first part bears upon the story. The worst face one can put on the scene is that it shows Pandarus and Criseyde to be comfortable in one another's presence in a way that Criseyde and Troilus are not, and Criseyde to reveal a practical recognition of the deceptions and logistics of love that Troilus lacks.

What happens here rests first on what one makes of Pandarus's "entente." We don't know what that intent is. Wetherbee recognizes this, and adds that "we do not need to know."[4] But I think we do need to know, for much depends on what it would reveal about Pandarus and Criseyde. That Chaucer frustrates our desire for knowledge creates in us a drive toward certainty that will not admit doubt. Hence the polarized examples of interpretative blindness I have described above: the first distorted by overreading, the second by a near refusal to read at all.

The second interpretative key is Chaucer's interjection: "I passe al that which chargeth nought to seye." Its evasiveness resembles that of his refusal, in a moment equally fraught with significance, to discuss the Wife of Bath's relationships with men:

> Housbondes at chirche dore she hadde fyve,
> Withouten oother compaignye in youthe—
> But therof nedeth nat to speke as nowthe.   (*CT*, 1.460–62)

"Withouten" means both "lacking" and "in addition to," and how we understand the Wife depends on which meaning applies here. But we cannot, or should not, decide. On the one hand, as we later discover, the Wife's first marriage at the age of twelve might preclude very much "wandrynge by the weye" (*CT*, 1.467); on the other, she may have been unfaithful to the husband(s) of her youth. Chaucer's refusal to discuss the matter here may simply mean that we'll find out later, from the Wife herself; but it could also be a coy invitation to conclude that the Wife indeed had "oother compaignye in youthe." The passage is irreducibly ambiguous, and the Wife of Bath's autobiographical prologue does not clarify the double focus of "withouten." Nothing she says on the subject lends itself to interpretative certainty.[5] Torn like the shepherd between wolf and lamb, we are uncertain which way to run. Chaucer leaves the puzzle for us to figure out. And ultimately, what we decide about the Wife will depend on what we want to think: that is, on our own desires.

Desire is the crucial factor in the morning-after scene of the *Troilus*, too, and in the interpretative blindness it encourages in its readers. By desire I do not mean only that of Criseyde or Pandarus; I should confess that my own reading tends rather more toward the innocent than not. But the scene requires more explanation than the innocent reading can provide. It raises the specter of betrayal, though the violation it points to is, I think, considerably more elusive than the literal one suggested in the debased reading. Criseyde has not been allowed to remain the subject she so clearly was in her long interior monologue in Book II; instead she has become the vessel into which both men pour their very different desires—Troilus's for "hevene blisse," Pandarus's for his own problematic and vicarious "entente," which, as this scene shows, he has substituted for hers. By manipulating, pressing, forcing the issue with his fiction of Horaste, and finally throwing Troilus into Criseyde's bed, Pandarus permits her only one side of her desires. Throughout the courtship, he "Felte iren hoot, and he bygan to smyte"

(II.1276); he is the maker, she his creation. In this it must be said that Criseyde acquiesces; herein lies the obscurity of the violation. Yet the delicate equipoise—will she? will she not?—that characterizes her when she is most herself is not allowed to exist for long.

By fulfilling Troilus's desires, Pandarus also obscurely violates the lyric idealism of his young friend's love. Here too he has substituted his own "entente" to the extent that he has narrowed Troilus's desires to those that may be incarnated in the world of action. And—most unsettling of all—since Pandarus is the poet of the inner love story, both violations reflect on the poet's parallel role as the "meene" who brings together not women and men (III.254–55), but his ancient Trojan history and his present readers. Like *Inferno* V, then, the morning-after scene clearly points to the ethical problems posed by reading and writing love literature. But the *Troilus* is also a history; and the scene points more broadly to the ethical difficulties Chaucer saw in turning the inviolate private lives of his Trojans to the more public—and vicarious—uses of literature. Whether we read the *Troilus* for pleasure or instruction (and whether the instruction is exemplary or monitory), we, like Pandarus, light our candles from the fire as we "looke upon an old romaunce" (III.979–80). If there is a violation in the morning-after scene, it belongs to poets and readers as well.

The innocent reading cannot see that Pandarus's "entente" is problematic at all; the debased reading cannot see that it is problematic not because it is direct, but because it is vicarious. Each fails to recognize the full extent of kinship, now made profoundly unsettling, between Pandarus's intent as the *galeotto* of the inner love story and Chaucer's own as the *galeotto* of the poem. The blindness of both innocent and debased readings, then, can be partly remedied by focusing on the outer story of Chaucer's narrative presentation. If, having recognized the kinship of "ententes," we attend to Chaucer's interjection—the second interpretative key—we see how precisely it doubles the *limits* of Pandarus's vicarious fulfillment of desire. Choosing not to complete his story, Chaucer instead, at a particularly awkward spot, withdraws. The pressures of frustration nearly force us either to flee or to complete the story for him—and thus entrap us thoroughly in our desire to preserve or to overleap the bounds of decorum. To understand (if not escape) the traps this scene sets, perhaps we need a little simplemindedness. The questions we should pose are: what does the narrator mean by his stated desire to suppress "al that which chargeth nought to seye"? what desires do scene and interjection engender in the reader? and what desires of the poet are embodied in the interplay of scene, narrator, and reader?

The narrator's desires are perhaps the easiest to understand. He wants to identify the "pleye" between Pandarus and Criseyde as insignificant and fundamentally irrelevant to the main lines of his story. But his sudden eagerness to drop the scene, after the way in which he has related it thus far, raises the very questions that "innocent" readers wish to gloss over, and answers those questions for others. It suggests the possibility that he wishes to exonerate Pandarus and Criseyde; if so, then the interjection simultaneously arouses and confirms the suspicion of wrongdoing. As so often, the narrator creates an effect quite opposed to the one he seems to want.

The desire of the reader is embodied in his interpretation, and may indeed be its chief determinant. Those who, like the narrator, wish to forestall any criticism of Criseyde, will adopt the innocent reading. Those who see the poem as an exemplum about the spiritual corruption of earthly love will incline to the debased reading. In between, the subtler interpreters of the *Troilus* are also moved by desire. Wetherbee's contention that Troilus resembles Dante's pilgrim, for instance, entails contrasting Troilus's sexual purity with Pandarus's "debased 'entente,'" as well as with Criseyde's compromised experience and practicality.[6] The reader's desire in this case—to preserve Troilus as a spiritually pure pilgrim—requires the "baldly suggestive" interpretation Wetherbee offers.[7]

The poet's desires in this scene are the most elusive, for we infer them only from the structure of the scene, the intentions of the narrator, and our own responses. He clearly wishes to frustrate the reader's desire for certainty; he also wishes to distinguish (as in *The House of Fame*) between the irrecoverable events of his Trojan history and the form in which they are recorded—whether in Lollius's book, in his own memory of reading, or in this retelling—and thus to stress the made, fictional qualities of the scene. The distinction suggests that any representation is a misrepresentation to the extent that it is shaped—as a history must be—by authorial intent. And so from this distinction also arises the most general effect: Chaucer foregrounds the role of desire itself both in the telling and in the reading of the poem.[8] We have already seen how the scene conforms itself to the desires of various readers; my purpose in the present chapter is to explore how the poem as a whole embodies the poet's intentions and desires.

The poet's desires in the telling determine the doubled narrative pose which we see in this scene's distinction between narrative and commentary, and which Chaucer adopts throughout the *Troilus*. The authenticating qualities of this pose are also doubled. One side of the narrator is the sympathy and imaginative participation with which he records most of the conversation between Pandarus and Criseyde; this enables him to tell the story in intimate, close-up detail, as if it had happened before his eyes. The distance reflected in his withdrawal from the scene supplies the other half of the narrator's authentication, his fidelity to history and the books of man. The two sides argue respectively for subjective and objective truth: the "I have seen it" of personal witness, and the authority of impersonal history. Chaucer's narrative stance, then, expresses not only his desire for authenticity (perhaps the chief desideratum of the rhetorical poet) but also the subversion of his authenticating effort. For to the instability of the human historical record (a concern here as well as in *The House of Fame*), Chaucer adds the finally irreconcilable tension between his twin truth-claims of personal witness and history.

Chaucer invented the narrator of the *Troilus* as a guide (unreliable though he may be) in the reader's search for meaning, and as a device in his own exploration of how his story means. Looking at Chaucer's narrator in this manner results in an account of him somewhat different from the two commonly proposed—that he learns and grows during the poem so that, by the end, he is united with the poet;[9] or that he remains an ignorant foil throughout, as much a character as Troilus, Criseyde, or Pandarus.[10] The narrator in my view maintains no steady relationship to the poet; he is Chaucer, putting on poses of varying kind and intensity, and he does not consistently differ from the poet either in time (unlike the temporally divided "I" of the dream vision) or in the degree to which he understands his story. Rather, the narrator, always pointing beyond himself to the poet, is a deictic device. Just as Chaucer altered the love story of the *Troilus* to point toward and comment on *Inferno* V, so too his deictic narrative voice points toward the *Commedia*. Both authors combine the truth-claims of personal witness and objective history to authenticate their fictions; Chaucer adopts Dante's doubled pose in order to comment on it. Indeed, the way in which Chaucer's narrative pose both supports and undermines the authenticity of the *Troilus* counters Dante almost point for point. To see more clearly how this works, and how it affects the story itself—and since the differences between the *Commedia*'s first-person narration and the *Troilus*'s alternating third-person narration and first-person commentary are far more readily apparent than the similarities—I must describe Dante's primary authentication of the narrator in some detail.

The *Commedia* is a spiritual autobiography in the form of a conversion story.[11] In order to gain our assent to his narrative as true rather than feigned, Dante must convince us of the competence and good intentions of the "I" who tells it in the present, after the conversion. The process by which the narrator justifies himself, then, is crucial to primary authentication. This most personal of narratives depends on Dante's ability to persuade the reader that he has left behind his old life and, converting to God, written a new variety of reformed poetry. To achieve these ends, the "I" of the *Commedia* bridges the gap between objective and subjective modes of language and thus blurs the opposition between fact and fiction.

In general, first-person narrative contains no identifiable linguistic anomalies that would allow us certainly to distinguish fiction from fact. True or feigned, a first-person point of view shows the same combination of discours and histoire—a linguistic structure Dante exploits. For Dante's blurring of truth and fiction depends on his precise, consistent use of deixis, the pointing function of language.[12] Like other autobiographies, the *Commedia* uses the temporal, spatial, and personal systems of both discours and histoire to create two "I"'s and two temporal moments in the text.[13]

The poem begins with the remembered journey, expressed in the *passato remoto* and the *imperfetto*, respectively the narrative and stative tenses of histoire:

> Nel mezzo del cammin di nostra vita
> mi ritrovai per una selva oscura,
> che la diritta via era smarrita.   (*Inf.* I, 1–3)

(Midway in the journey of our life I found myself in a dark wood, for the straight way was lost.)

Yet the word "nostra" (the inclusive "our") establishes the *I–you* relationship typical of discours but not of histoire. Indeed the next *terzine* shift to the remembering poet's *qui* and *or*, the here-and-now moment of composition:

> Ahi quanto a dir qual era è cosa dura
> esta selva selvaggia e aspra e forte
> che nel pensier rinova la paura!
> Tant' è amara che poco è più morte;
> ma per trattar del ben ch'i' vi trovai,
> dirò de l'altre cose ch'i' v'ho scorte.
> Io non so ben ridir com' i' v'intrai. . . .   (*Inf.* I, 4–10)

(Ah, how hard it is to tell what that wood was, wild, rugged, harsh; the very thought of it renews the fear! It is so bitter that death is hardly more so. But, to treat of the good that I found in it, I will tell of the other things I saw there.

I cannot rightly say how I entered it. . . .)

The present and future tenses of discours predominate. And when Dante shifts again from present emotion (l. 8) to past experience, his speaker-anchored spatial adverb ("vi," l. 9) locates him in the present with us, far from the scene of his journey. The present tense of these lines reappears in the first simile of the poem:

> E come quei che con lena affannata,
>   uscito fuor del pelago a la riva,
>   si volge a l'acqua perigliosa e guata,
> così l'animo mio, ch'ancor fuggiva,
>   si volse a retro a rimirar lo passo
>   che non lasciò già mai persona viva.   (*Inf.* I, 22–27)

(And as he who with laboring breath has escaped from the deep to the shore turns to look back on the dangerous waters, so my mind which was still fleeing turned back to gaze upon the pass that never left anyone alive.)

The act of comparison belongs to the realm of discours. It results from the speaker's interpretation rather than from the event or object elucidated by the comparison. Hence the simile contains an element of subjectivity that strict histoire would preclude.

The pattern established in the opening lines continues throughout the *Commedia*. Even the narrative sections, told in histoire's *passato remoto* and described in the *imperfetto*, are oriented to the narrator. The tenses of histoire tell his past time, his *then*; but he stored up this experience from the past so that he can communicate it to us now:

> Lo giorno se n'andava, e l'aere bruno
>   toglieva li animai che sono in terra

> da le fatiche loro; e io sol uno
> m'apparecchiava a sostener la guerra
> sì del cammino e sì de la pietate,
> che ritrarrà la mente che non erra.   (*Inf.* II, 1–6)

(Day was departing, and the dark air was taking the creatures on earth from their labors; and I alone was making ready to sustain the strife, both of the journey and of the pity, which unerring memory shall retrace.)

Every verse can be located with respect to the narrator, for Dante uses the deictic forms of discours with great precision, carefully distinguishing the *qui* (here) and *or* (now) of his writing desk, in this world at the moment of composition, from the *là* (there) and *allor* or *poi* (then) of his remembered journey: "Allor mi dolsi, e ora mi ridoglio / quando drizzo la mente a ciò ch'io vidi" (I sorrowed then, and sorrow now again, when I turn my mind to what I saw; *Inf.* XXVI, 19–20). Here the tenses of histoire and discours—respectively "dolsi" (sorrowed) and "ridoglio" (sorrow again)—sort themselves out precisely in accord with the adverbs of temporal distance ("allor") and proximity ("ora"). The more discursive time references of the *Commedia* serve a similarly double function:

> Quanto tra l'ultimar de l'ora terza
> e 'l principio del dì par de la spera
> che sempre a guisa di fanciullo scherza,
> tanto pareva già inver' la sera
> essere al sol del suo corso rimaso;
> vespero là, e qui mezza notte era.   (*Purg.* XV, 1–6)

(As much as between the end of the third hour and the beginning of the day appears of the sphere that is always playing like a child, so much now appeared to be left of the sun's course toward nightfall: it was evening there and here it was midnight.)

Such a passage tells the time *then*, oriented to the speaker; Dante also puts time as only he saw it into a more universal temporal frame of reference, which he shares with all the inhabitants of this world. Because the tense ("era") and adverbs ("là," "qui") remain speaker-oriented, they show Dante to be a mediator between the two worlds, bringing the unfamiliar into the sphere of the familiar. Even in the absence of personal pronouns, the temporal and spatial deixis alone adumbrates an *I–you* relationship between speaker and audience.

This *I–you* relationship controls the poem. The first-person narrator directs himself throughout—always implicitly, often openly—to his reader. The addresses to the reader, appearing at regular intervals throughout the *Commedia*, subordinate the story to the communicative relationship between the narrator's *io* (I) and the reader's *tu/voi* (you).[14] The Letter to Can Grande illuminates their importance:

> Genus philosophiae sub quo hic in toto et parte proceditur est morale negotium, sive ethica; quia non ad speculandum, sed ad opus inventum est totum et pars. Nam si et in aliquo loco vel passu pertractatur ad modum speculativi negotii, hoc non est gratia speculativi negotii, sed gratia operis; quia ut ait Philosophus in secundo *Metaphysicorum*: "ad aliquid et nunc speculantur practici aliquando."

> (The branch of philosophy to which the work is subject, in the whole as in the part, is that of morals or ethics; inasmuch as the whole as well as the part was conceived, not for speculation, but with a practical object. For if in certain parts or passages the treatment is after the manner of speculative philosophy, that is not for the sake of speculation, but for a practical purpose; since, as the Philosopher says in the second book of the Metaphysics: "practical men occasionally speculate on things in their particular and temporal relations.")[15]

By identifying the *Commedia*'s purpose as ethical and practical, Dante reveals his intent to change his reader. The addresses are the most obvious means by which Dante pursues his modifying design. Through them, he creates an ideal reader, whom he molds by warning, exhorting, and encouraging into conformity with his own will. The addresses shape the ideal reader's responses, and outline for him a guide to the journey so that he will not founder in the trackless seas and deserts of the otherworld.

Dante also reports the inner action of other characters with great discretion; he never transgresses the limits set on the insight of a real conversational participant. Generally he reports direct discourse, allowing others to speak for themselves and, in the course of their speeches, to reveal their own states of mind. When Dante does describe inner action, he couches his report in speculative terms, as in "El mi parea da sé stesso rimorso" (He seemed to me smitten with self-reproach; *Purg.* III, 7), where Dante divines Virgil's unspoken feelings. Elsewhere he uses the "novelist's alibi," the grand "seems" of simile.[16]

Many of the *Commedia*'s similes go beyond the simple "as if" report of inner action, and support the *I–you* relationship between narrator and reader in other ways as well. One of the most touching compares Dante to a victorious gambler:

> Quando si parte il gioco de la zara,
>   colui che perde si riman dolente,
>   repetendo le volte, a tristo impara;
> con l'altro se ne va tutta la gente;
>   qual va dinanzi, e qual di dietro il prende,
>   e qual dallato li si reca a mente;
> el non s'arresta, e questo e quello intende;
>   a cui porge la man, più non fa pressa;
>   e così da la calca si difende.
> Tal era io in quella turba spessa,
>   volgendo a loro, e qua e là, la faccia,
>   e promettendo mi sciogliea da essa.   (*Purg.* VI, 1–12)

(When the game of hazard breaks up, the loser is left disconsolate, repeating the throws and sadly learns. With the other all the people go along: one goes in front, one plucks him from behind, and at his side one brings himself to mind. He does not stop, but listens to this one and that one; each to whom he reaches forth his hand presses on him no longer, and thus from the throng he defends himself. Such was I in that dense crowd, turning my face to them this way and that and, by promising, I got free from them.)

Dante, surrounded by the souls marveling at his shadow, clearly resembles "l'altro," the winner of the simile's vehicle. But the loser in the game of chance has no apparent counterpart in the tenor. We must imagine the scene in order to understand that he is Virgil, for Dante is walking with his master. The loser's sorrow transfers to the Latin poet no less completely for the absence of overt application. In fact, by suppressing the second identification, Dante achieves a greater poignancy, for Virgil, born too soon, has lost in a far greater game of chance; he cannot follow his follower beyond the bourne of the Earthly Paradise. In *Purgatorio* VI, however, there is no immediately obvious reason to compare Virgil to a loser at dice; we must involve ourselves in the text in order to discover the meaning of the simile. By making us seek, Dante recreates in us the emotional desolation of Virgil's damnation. And by making us draw the conclusions he only hints at, he further joins us to himself.

Thus one major function of similes in the *Commedia* is to overcome the strictures imposed on the knowledge of the first-person narrator. Part of discours, they impart the narrator's commentary about what he has seen rather than the things themselves. In addition, they strengthen the *I—you* relationship by establishing parallels between the unfamiliar landscape the pilgrim traverses and the familiar world the reader shares with the poet. Finally, and in despite of the distancing we are accustomed to expect from similes, they create an emotional and intellectual community between the narrator and his reader. Throughout the *Commedia* the subjectivity inherent in the pragmatic communication between a speaker and the *you* he addresses prevails; only the mixed tense system prevents us from assenting at once to Benveniste's characterization of autobiography as discours.[17] Thus the questions become: what causes the poet to use the undeniably past *passato remoto* rather than the retrospective tense of discours, the *passato prossimo*? And what aspect of the *passato remoto* does Dante mean to suggest?

For the *Commedia*, the answers lie in the pilgrim's conversion. Paul describes conversion as a form of death; the old man withers away, allowing the new man to be born.[18] In the otherworld Dante traverses, death marks a radical break with the past. The souls he meets there stress this discontinuity by the manner in which they introduce themselves: "Io fui di Montefeltro, io son Bonconte" ("I was of Montefeltro, I am Buonconte"; *Purg.* v, 88) or "Cesare fui e son Iustinïano" ("I was Caesar, and am Justinian"; *Par.* vi, 10). The shift from the *passato remoto* of their former earthly existence, embroiled in political intrigue and personal iniquity, to the present tense of the afterlife shows the magnitude of the intervening gulf. The "io fui" / "io sono" formula of introduction recurs so frequently that the rare exceptions stand out. The siren of Dante's second dream begins: " 'Io son,' cantava, 'io son dolce serena . . .' " ("I am," she sang, "I am the sweet Siren . . ."; *Purg.* xix, 19). When Beatrice introduces herself, she repeats the siren's obdurate negation of pastness with "Guardaci ben! Ben son, ben son Beatrice" ("Look at me well: indeed I am, indeed I am Beatrice!"; *Purg.* xxx, 73).[19] Beatrice speaks in a kind of eternal present; Dante matches it in *Paradiso* by the present tense with which he refers to her even yet as "quella che 'mparadisa la mia mente" (she who imparadises my mind; *Par.* xxviii, 3). The siren's present tense is a case of the false transcendence Dante repudiates so often in the *Commedia*. Beatrice's eternality, on the other hand, does transcend mundane distinctions between past and present, and she in fact helps Dante to recover his own past and reform it into "la sua vita nova" (his new life; *Purg.* xxx, 115).

The link between the *passato remoto* and death is most explicit in *Inferno* x. The tense expresses a range of aspects in both modern and fourteenth-century Italian, among them a single, noniterative action in the past; an action far (*remoto*) in the past; and an action with no connection to the present.[20] The last aspect, the past absolute, can imply the most extreme discontinuity between past and present: death.[21] This is how Cavalcante de' Cavalcanti interprets the answer to the question he directs at Dante: why does his son Guido not accompany the two poets? Dante's response sets Guido in the *passato remoto*:[22]

E io a lui: "Da me stesso non vegno:
colui ch'attende là per qui mi mena,
forse cui Guido vostro *ebbe* a disdegno."

(*Inf.* x, 61–63; my italics)

(And I to him, "I come not of myself. He who waits yonder, whom perhaps your Guido had in disdain, is leading me through here.")

But what aspect of the tense does Dante intend? Dante further complicates the question of aspect with Cavalcante's next agonized query:

"Come?
dicesti 'elli ebbe'? non viv' elli ancora?
non fiere li occhi suoi lo dolce lume?" (*Inf.* x, 67–69; my italics)

("How? Did you say 'he had'? Does he not still live? Does the sweet light not strike his eyes?")

Cavalcante has clearly interpreted "ebbe" as a past absolute, meaning that Guido is dead. But with "dicesti," he uses the same *passato remoto* to designate a verbal action performed just seconds previously, and moreover, very closely linked to his present. Singleton suggests that we should interpret both instances of the tense in a rather more *prossimo* sense: because "dicesti" is used for a single action in a precisely defined but very recent past, "ebbe" should be interpreted in the same way. He then suggests a hypothetical recent moment, nine hours before, when Guido made the one-time choice to disdain Virgil, that is, not to accompany Dante on his journey.[23] This reading has the advantage of making Dante's answer a cooperative response to Cavalcante's first question, but I believe it misses the point. To clarify the problem, I must set the exchange in its context.

First, "ebbe" is not the problem. Its ambiguous aspect—past absolute, remote past, or precise one-time past—is necessary to illustrate the peculiar oracular vision of the souls here. *Inferno* x is filled with misinterpretations caused by this vision. The souls can see far into the past and future, but less clearly as events approach more closely, and not at all when they melt into the present. Such vision inverts the structure of human memory, which sees the past more clearly the more recent it is. Blindness to the present is ironically appropriate to the Epicureans of the sixth circle, who, in denying the immortality of the soul, live only for the present. Cavalcante, cut off from knowledge of the present, misinterprets the pilgrim's *passato remoto* in the most pessimistic manner possible, leaping to the conclusion that his son must be dead. But at Easter, 1300—the fictional date of the *Commedia*—Guido still had four months to live.[24] His case in *Inferno* X, though it concerns only death by misinterpretation, clearly illustrates the scission between past and present that physical death, expressed in the *passato remoto*, can bring about.

The real problem is the unambiguous "dicesti," the *passato remoto* that designates an action in the very proximate literal and psychological past—for Cavalcante. As Singleton notes, the *Commedia* is filled with such *remoto* verbs apparently used in a more or less *prossimo* sense.[25] However, the tense, as exemplified by "dicesti" here, indicates not the proximity and present relevance of "ebbe," but the absolute remoteness from the poet Dante of everything connected to the pilgrim Dante. The use of the *passato remoto* in the *Commedia* is the cornerstone of the distanced objectivity with which the "I" now views his former self. But since Dante suffers no physical death, not even in the distraught imagination of a Cavalcante, the absolute pastness of even the recent past can adumbrate only a metaphorical death.

This spiritual death, which disjoins past and present as much as does the physical death suffered by those Dante meets, is conversion. Its distancing power engenders a common paradox of autobiography, that the "I" in the story is not quite the same person as the "I" telling the story. Conversion causes such a radical transformation in Dante that he may speak of himself and the past experiences of his exemplary journey as if he were dead, a figure relegated to the historical past and the *passato re-*

moto. The distance of this tense implies Dante's objectivity about a former self with whom he is no longer personally involved. The events he reports changed him; therefore he has no need to change them out of nostalgic or apologetic impulses. Conversion, then, allows Dante to combine the subjective authentication of *discours* with the objective authentication of *histoire*. The personal forms I have outlined provide the authenticity of personal witness and participation—the characteristic supports to the truth-claim "I saw it." The distanced *passato remoto* of *histoire* provides the authenticity of an objective history that the speaker does not distort in order to vindicate his past self—a support to the truth-claim "*I* did not see it."

Because the private nature of the *Commedia*'s autobiography precludes extratextual substantiation, Dante must convince us that the essential self-justification of the narrator is directed toward the present rather than toward the past. Here again, his conversion is crucial. The *Commedia* itself furnishes the best and only evidence of its narrator's conversion, the change of state that protects him from the accusation of lying. In order to confirm the authenticity suggested by his distanced *passato remoto*, Dante includes in his poem not only the fiction of his journey, but also the text of his confession.[26] In this he imitates his predecessor in both conversion and autobiography, Augustine, who characterized conversion as "a certain death of the soul in the abandonment of former life and habits which is made through penance."[27] This also describes the symbolic death of conversion in the *Commedia*, and moreover suggests the process by which Dante accomplishes it in the penitential text of his poem. Since Dante is a poet, the former life and habits he must abandon are the literary habits of his past.

The authenticating effect of the palinodic literary episodes of the *Commedia* lies in this self-justifying abandonment. Because Dante's poetry makes public the private and usually inaccessible life of the mind, to retract it offers verifiable evidence that the poet's intentions have changed. *Inferno* v takes back Dante's

early love poetry; *Inferno* IX his *rime petrose*.[28] Even such a philosophical lyric as "Amor che ne la mente mi ragiona" (Love that
discourses in my mind; *Purg*. II, 112) is recanted as an interruption in the journey to salvation.[29] The palinodes suggest that
out of this reformation of the will, a new, reformed poetry
arises. This reformed poetry, the *Commedia* itself, is both the result and the proof of its author's conversion. Dante's vast poem
in praise of God, as a "good work," is quite literally his satisfaction for past literary and spiritual sins; it actually accomplishes the conversion it also narrates. Dante's literary retractions furnish the confessional acts upon which his narrator's justification, and hence his credibility, depend.

The authorial domain was traditionally one of persuasive eloquence; the poet's text is his instrument for persuading his
readers to take the action he urges upon them.[30] Eloquence can
mislead if it praises or blames the wrong activities; hence it is
of paramount concern to Dante that he whip the recalcitrantly
equivocal, earthbound tools of his craft—his persuasive
words—into conformity with a reformed, heavenbound will, so
that they move the reader for good rather than for ill. The Letter
to Can Grande, in assigning the *Commedia* to the sphere of practical ethics, also adopts this fundamentally rhetorical conception of poetry. Dante's goal of transforming his readers demands unblemished virtue on his part. He acquires such virtue
in all the literary palinodes, but chiefly in retracting the *Convivio*, the massive, incomplete philosophical banquet on which
he labored between the *Vita nuova* and the *Commedia*.[31] Because
its exclusively earthbound philosophy and poetry subordinated
eloquence to the wrong ends, it interrupted Dante's journey
to Beatrice. Dante rejects the *Convivio*—an act of literary retraction, theological contrition, and self-revision—primarily
through his damnation of Ulysses and of what we might call
"Ulyssean" poetry.

Ulysses' place in the *Commedia*, and the parallels between
Ulysses and Dante himself, are well known.[32] But Dante's re-
jection of Ulyssean poetry extends well beyond Ulysses' appearance in *Inferno* XXVI, and beyond even the subsequent

echoes and references to him that flesh out his role as a surrogate
for the Dante of the *Convivio*.[33] Dante's vulnerability to one aspect of Ulyssean poetry—the passion for philosophical knowledge and the consequent reliance on the powers of unaided human natural reason—continues to haunt him until the formal
confession scene of the Earthly Paradise. He is nearly seduced
by his dream of the Ulyssean siren in *Purgatorio* XIX,[34] who
reappears in the confession when Beatrice, administering the
strong medicine of reproof, phrases his error in terms of the sirens of natural knowledge:

> "Tuttavia, perché mo vergogna porte
>   del tuo errore, e perché altra volta,
>   udendo le serene, sie più forte,
> pon giù il seme del piangere e ascolta:
>   sí udirai come in contraria parte
>   mover dovieti mia carne sepolta."   (*Purg.* XXXI, 43–48)

("Still, that you may now bear shame for your error, and another
time, hearing the Sirens, may be stronger, lay aside the seed of
tears and listen: so shall you hear how in opposite direction my
buried flesh ought to have moved you.")

Dante must transcend the knowledge of this world (the *sapientia mundi* Ulysses always stood for in the medieval mythographic tradition)[35] in favor of supernatural knowledge. In a
poem in which virtue depends on conversion, he can no longer
equate, as he did in the *Convivio* and as Ulysses does here, natural knowledge with virtue. Hence when Dante returns to Beatrice in his confession, his retraction of this aspect of Ulyssean
poetry is complete.

But Ulysses compounds his passion for worldly wisdom
through the second of his traditional characteristics: persuasive
eloquence. The *contrapasso* of *Inferno* XXVI punishes Ulysses'
abuse of persuasive language; he speaks through a tongue of
flame ("come fosse la lingua che parlasse," as if it were a tongue
that spoke; *Inf.* XXVI, 89), the eternal version of the tongue
with which he urged his companions to share his final voyage
to perdition. Ulysses subordinates means to ends when, to con-

vince his sailors, he promises that the voyage will fulfill their
highest human nature: "fatti non foste a viver come bruti, /
ma per seguir virtute e canoscenza" ("you were not made to live
as brutes, but to pursue virtue and knowledge"; *Inf.* XXVI,
119–20).

The simile of the Sicilian bull, which begins the following
canto, illuminates the dangers of Ulysses' eloquence. This most
compelling image of the poet's implication in his potentially
duplicitous language compares the tongue of flame enveloping
Guido da Montefeltro to a product of human artifice, a brass
bull whose maker became its first victim:

> Come 'l bue cicilian che mugghiò prima
>   col pianto di colui, e ciò fu dritto,
>   che l'avea temperato con sua lima,
> mugghiava con la voce de l'afflitto,
>   sì che, con tutto che fosse di rame,
>   pur el pareva dal dolor trafitto;
> così, per non aver via né forame
>   dal principio nel foco, in suo linguaggio
>   si convertïan le parole grame.   (*Inf.* XXVII, 7–15)

(As the Sicilian bull [which bellowed first with the cry of
him—and that was right—who had shaped it with his file] was
wont to bellow with the voice of the victim, so that, though it
was of brass, yet it seemed transfixed with pain: thus, having
at first no course or outlet in the fire, the doleful words were
changed into its language.)

Imprisoned within his creature and set afire, the artisan cries
out; his pain is transmuted into the inarticulate bellowing of a
bull. The full horror of the torment, in which the artisan was
made creature by his creation, arises from its inversion of the
Incarnation, in which the Word of God was made flesh in
Mary's womb. One of Bernard's traditional praises of Mary in
his prayer for the beatific vision recalls the Sicilian bull:

> "tu se' colei che l'umana natura
>   nobilitasti sì, che 'l suo fattore
>   non disdegnò di farsi sua fattura."   (*Par.* XXXIII, 4–6)

("... thou art she who didst so ennoble human nature that its Maker did not disdain to become its creature.")

Just as the bull makes human language bestial, so the human soul descends to the level of the beasts when language, the most human characteristic, is used without reforming virtue. The *lingua ignis* suggests that Ulysses' gravest error was not his search for natural knowledge, but his use of verbal artistry to lead others as well on his final voyage to perdition. Through language unguided by supernatural virtue, Ulysses sacrifices his humanity and instead imitates the beasts.

Ulysses' tongue of flame punishes fraudulent counsel; we might specify this more closely as a kind of pragmatic political discourse in which the speaker's real intentions are disguised. Ulysses achieves his desired rhetorical effect by moving his audience's emotions so that, without ever giving informed rational consent, they nonetheless assent to his unstated purpose. In the context in which Dante places it, this discourse, appearing to bind men together as "frati" (brothers; *Inf.* XXVI, 112), actually subverts the social ties of human community, which were, as Aristotle proposed, formed by the proper use of language.[36] That it is Virgil who speaks to Ulysses in the idiom of classical heroic poetry also suggests that part of the Ulyssean problem is a disordered relation between authorial intent and social effect.[37] Virgil is the *Commedia*'s chief example of a poet whose intentions in writing did not match the effects he achieved in the reading. He wrote to glorify the secular providential empire, but when both Statius and Dante read him, his writings become the means of Christian conversion.[38] His works can thus participate in Dante's synthetic Christian and classical typology; yet because his intent did not correspond to the salvific way in which he is read, Virgil himself dwells in Limbo.

As the parallel to Guido da Montefeltro's pragmatic use of the language of the confessional suggests, Ulysses would have suffered no diminishment of his humanity had his speech, and his voyage, been guided by penance and conversion. Dante, in his own voyage to rectitude, distinguishes himself from Ulysses on precisely this point; unlike Ulysses, he puts on the reed girdle of humility upon reaching the shores before which Ulysses was a shipwreck (*Purg.* I, 130–32). But in rejecting the intellectual pride of Ulysses' reliance on natural reason, Dante at first goes too far in the other direction, and falls prey to another sort of human self-magnification. In the VOM acrostic of *Purgatorio* XII, he imitates not the beasts, but God. By matching the *visibile parlare* of God's artistry in *Purgatorio* X with his own literal visible speech, writing, Dante demonstrates a specifically poetic pride that requires a second act of self-revision and literary retraction.[39] That he accomplishes this within the *Commedia* itself—rather than in the relation of this poem to previous works outside the text—argues for the authenticity of his conversion; rather than having to take Dante's word for it, we can see for ourselves the process of theological justification achieved through literary revision. Moreover, Dante extends the confessional dialogue between his past Ulyssean self and the new self created in and by the *Commedia* to the *Paradiso* as well, for the poetic pride of the VOM acrostic is not fully recognized or retracted until the LVE acrostic of *Paradiso* XIX.

Paradiso XIX is concerned specifically with the intellectual pride of lesser creatures who aspire beyond themselves to divine understanding. Lucifer fell, says the heavenly eagle, "per non aspettar lume" ("through not awaiting light"; *Par.* XIX, 48). The eagle (the heavenly apotheosis of *visibile parlare*)[40] identifies this light with the Logos (l. 44): it is the "raggi de la mente" ("the rays of the Mind"; l. 53). If Lucifer was "corto recettacolo" ("too scant a vessel"; l. 50), how much the shorter will human vision fall before the mysteries of divine judgment:

> "Però ne la giustizia sempiterna
>   la vista che riceve il vostro mondo,
>   com' occhio per lo mare, entro s'interna;
> che, ben che da la proda veggia il fondo,
>   in pelago nol vede; e nondimeno
>   èli, ma cela lui l'esser profondo."   (*Par.* XIX, 58–63)

("Therefore the sight that is granted to your world penetrates within the Eternal Justice as the eye into the sea; which, though from the shore it can see the bottom, in the open sea it sees it not, and none the less it is there, but the depth conceals it.")

Still, at the day of judgment even the most darkened human intellect will read the fates, written in God's Book, of the unjust Christian princes against whom the eagle inveighs in the threefold anaphora of the LVE acrostic (*Par.* XIX, 115–41).

As it stands, the acrostic is illegible.[41] It thus obliquely mimes the Ulyssean disorder of disguised authorial intent and uncertain social effect. But in the text that contains it, Dante suggests not only how this fragment of God's Book but also how this acrostic should be read; for both, "la sua scrittura fian lettere mozze, / che noteranno molto in parvo loco" (the writing for him shall be in contractions that will note much in little space; *Par.* XIX, 134–35).[42] To complete the meaning of the fragmentary LVE, we must look to the central *terzina* of the passage:

> Vedrassi al Ciotto di Ierusalemme
>   segnata con un i la sua bontate,
>   quando 'l contrario segnerà un emme.   (*Par.* XIX, 127–29)

(It will show the Cripple of Jerusalem, his goodness marked with an I, while an M will mark the opposite.)

The I and the M are clearly numerals; for Charles II of Naples and Jerusalem, God's Book will record a lone virtue against a thousand vices. But they are also letters, and if we add them to the "lettere mozze" (literally, "broken letters") of the acrostic proper, they yield LVEIM.[43] Though still illegible in this form, the letters are nonetheless an anagram for *umile* (humble), a word that not only illuminates the local context of intellectual pride, but also answers the pride recorded in the VOM acrostic of *Purgatorio* XII.

The VOM acrostic, with its examples from classical and biblical history, defines pride as *uomo*, mankind itself. In its imitation of God's *visibile parlare*, it also exemplifies Dante's personal pride in the excellence of his art. Its legibility argues the truth of Dante's claim to be the perfect *scriba Dei*. The scribal role he asserts here might seem a sign rather of humility than of pride—an abandonment of Ulyssean self-reliance—since it demands sacrificing his personal creativity to the higher claims of a message emanating from God. Yet to read and record God's Word perfectly would result in the highest authority, inspiration, and truth to which a religious poet can aspire. With the VOM acrostic, then, Dante edges dangerously close to Lucifer's presumption; he expresses the pride of exceeding his human capacity. In describing the pilgrim's lesson on the greater value of humility, the poet has written yet another chapter in the book of pride.

But the LVE acrostic redefines mankind, and the man Dante, as "umile." This is no large etymological leap: both "uomo" and "umile" derive from the Latin root *hum-* or *hom-*, meaning earth or ground.[44] Thus "uomo" is literally "creature of earth," a meaning that undermines Dante's vaulting artistic ambitions in the VOM acrostic but that, in the sixth heaven, restores him to his true nature and middle place in the scheme of creation. The "trasumanar significar *per verba* / non si poria" (passing beyond humanity may not be set forth in words; *Par.* I, 70–71); and Dante, in his "trasumanar," discovers and declares his own humanity. This moral self-revision is accomplished in the very illegibility of the acrostic. In keeping with the human incapacity to penetrate God's Book of Judgments, the mutilated state of these "lettere mozze" stresses not the perfection of imitation, nor the identity between God's way of writing and Dante's, but rather the shortcomings, which the poet now humbly admits. Dante's text, like all created things ("ciò che per l'universo si squaderna," that which is dispersed in leaves throughout the universe; *Par.* XXXIII, 87), is but a contracted version of God's Book, partially erased and partially illegible. Thus Dante retracts the VOM acrostic, with its proud suggestion of scribal perfection, and so embraces the humility that finally exalts his poem.

Thus literary penance and confession join with the more traditional process of theological penance of the *Purgatorio* whereby Dante rids himself of the seven P's (for *peccatum*) inscribed on his forehead. Much as the P's are erased from his face, so too are Dante's previous literary efforts erased from the face of his book. The sins to which he confesses, although expressed in terms of moral error, are as much literary as theological in nature. This is true even in the explicit confession of the Earthly Paradise, where Dante stands accused before Beatrice. Dante's fault lies in lapsing from his devotion to Beatrice after her death, and turning instead to a series of literary ladies including the *donna petra* of the *rime petrose* and the *donna gentile* of the *Convivio*:[45]

> "Mai non t'appresentò natura o arte
>   piacer, quanto le belle menbra in ch'io
>   rinchiusa fui, e che so' 'n terra sparte;
> e se 'l sommo piacer sì ti fallio
>   per la mia morte, qual cosa mortale
>   dovea poi trarre te nel suo disio?
> Ben ti dovevi, per lo primo strale
>   de le cose fallaci, levar suso
>   di retro a me che non era più tale.
> Non ti dovea gravar le penne in giuso,
>   ad aspettar più colpo, o pargoletta
>   o altra novità con sì breve uso.
> Novo augelletto due or tre aspetta;
>   ma dinanzi da li occhi d'i pennuti
>   rete si spiega indarno a si saetta."   (*Purg.* XXXI, 49–63)

("Never did nature or art present to you beauty so great as the fair members in which I was enclosed and now are scattered to dust. And if the highest beauty thus failed you by my death, what mortal thing should then have drawn you into desire for it? Truly, at the first arrow of deceitful things you ought to have risen up, following me who was no longer such. Young damsel or other novelty of such brief enjoyment should not have weighed down your wings to await more shots. The young bird waits two or three, but before the eyes of the full-fledged in vain is net spread or arrow shot.")

The pun on "penne" manifests the degree to which literary and theological error and confession reflect one another. The word appears frequently in the *Commedia*, and unites the two meanings of "wings" (or "feathers") and "writing quills." The pilgrim's flight to God, then, is made not only with the metaphorical wings of the soul, but also with the literal writing tools of a poet.

The relation between spiritual and literary conversion in the *Commedia* can be summarized as follows: a spiritual conversion, or self-revision, is accomplished through a traditional theological process of contrition, confession, and penance. Literary conversion is a sign of spiritual conversion, and indeed the only possible evidence for it here. At the same time, however, the *Commedia* does not merely record Dante's literary conversion; the text actually performs the poet's painful turn from previous modes of writing. Thus the writing of the poem is an essential part of his spiritual self-revision, and if the poet changes as he writes, or by writing, we should revise Singleton's famous aphorism that "the fiction of the *Divine Comedy* is that it is not a fiction."[46] To the extent that the poem is performative, it is no pretense; it is true. The explicit confession scene of the *Purgatorio* suggests a punning reciprocity between spiritual and literary justification, and the LVE acrostic of the *Paradiso* confirms the inextricability of moral and poetic self-revision. Conversion in the *Commedia* thus circles in on itself, each aspect signifying and confirming the others.

Because the *Commedia*'s literary retractions both signify the narrator's conversion and demonstrate his poetic reformation, they form a fundamental part of Dante's authenticating self-justification. They assure us that he is in a significant sense no longer the person he once was; his report is thus untinged by nostalgia or apology. But we require one further justification: we want to know that Dante's intentions toward us are reformed, and that he uses his new eloquence, as Ulysses did not, to lead us aright. To provide this assurance, Dante creates an implied ideal reader whom he persuades to follow him in conversion. The addresses to the reader—the foundation of the *I–you* relationship to which the narrative proper is subordinated—give rise to this ideal imitator. Because he shows the salutary effects of Dante's reformed eloquence, the *Commedia*'s addresses contribute the final assurance of the narrator's justification.

To read rightly means to follow the converting pilgrim. Many of the addresses facilitate this imitation. Offering himself as a model, Dante asks the reader to imagine his reactions and, by imagining, to duplicate them:

> Pensa, lettor, se quel che qui s'inizia
> non prodecesse, come tu avresti
> di più savere angosciosa carizia;
> e per te vederai come da questi
> m'era in disio d'udir lor condizioni,
> sì come a li occhi mi fur manifesti.   (*Par.* V, 109–14)

(Think, reader, if this beginning went no further, how you would feel an anguished craving to know more, and by yourself you will see what my desire was, to hear of their conditions from them, as soon as they became manifest to my eyes.)

Leo Spitzer writes of such addresses:

The device . . . of *Pensa per te stesso, lettor,* is, of course, a clever diversion on the part of Dante, who influences the reader without giving the appearance of doing so: also in everyday conversations, in the moment in which the partner follows the suggestion "imagine how I felt!," he has already accepted the truthfulness of "what" was narrated and concentrates only on "how" it acted on his partner. To give the reader "something to do" about a matter difficult to imagine is a psychological inducement to make him accept this subject matter.[47]

Dante often isolates one particular reaction, that of disbelief:

> Se tu se' or, lettore, a creder lento
>   ciò ch'io dirò, non sarà maraviglia,
>   ché io che 'l vidi, a pena il mi consento.   (*Inf.* xxv, 46–48)

(If, reader, you are now slow to credit that which I shall tell, it will be no wonder, for I who saw it do scarcely admit it to myself.)[48]

By anticipating the reader's likely incredulity, Dante authenticates his narrative. Thus the reader's disbelief at what he reads once again imitates the pilgrim's reactions. Accepting the unbelievable himself, Dante encourages the reader as well to suspend disbelief, follow the pilgrim, and continue on the journey to justification.

Defining his ideal reader closely, Dante proves an exacting taskmaster who demands a great deal: interpreting properly, studying the poem hard, and, in sum, reading according to authorial intention. He admonishes the reader to interpret the truth from the veil of fiction:

> Aguzza qui, lettor, ben li occhi al vero,
>   ché 'l velo è ora ben tanto sottile,
>   certo che 'l trapassar dentro e leggero.   (*Purg.* VIII, 19–21)

(Reader, here sharpen well your eyes to the truth, for the veil is now indeed so thin that certainly to pass within is easy.)

The warning note he strikes here implies that misreading is the reader's responsibility, not the author's. Hence, if any reader of the *Commedia* ends up a Ulyssean shipwreck, Dante has absolved himself of responsibility. His intentions are reformed, his vision sharpened by the sight of God; and the reader must acquire equal acuity in order to follow the pilgrim.

Writing such an ideal reader into his text constitutes the most open authentication of Dante's narrator, and yet also the most tenuous, for it depends on a tautology. Dante does allow for the possibility of wrong readings, but denies their validity in determining the crucial positive effects of his poem on its readers. He taunts wrong readers as unsound of mind (*Inf.* IX,

61–63), as blear-eyed (*Purg.* VIII, 19–21), and as shipwrecks (*Par.* II, 1–6); these taunts weed out all potential readers who do not correspond to the implied reader. We may still read the poem, of course, but if we do not follow Dante in conversion, we are not qualified to judge the authenticity of Dante's self-presentation. Any ill effects we suffer from reading the poem—including skepticism—are our fault; if we do not allow Dante to rewrite us, we are the inauthentic ones. By defining wrong readers out of the text in this manner, Dante seeks to avoid the Ulyssean danger of eloquence put to dangerous ends. The only readers left are those who imitate Dante, and so substantiate the main elements of the narrator's self-justification: spiritual conversion, reformed poetry, and the *Commedia*'s positive social effect. Their implicit belief in the narrator, rewarded by the promise of salvation he holds forth, assures the authenticity of the poem. The *Commedia* seems a self-authenticating text, yet it achieves this status only by definition. The implied reader confirms the validity of the narrator's conversion, but, as Dante's creation, he may not correspond to any reader outside the text. Thus we see that the absolute control Dante claims to exert over his readers is actually considerably narrower than it seems; authorial control remains limited to the text itself.

The circular nature of the *Commedia*'s authentication does not escape Dante. When Geryon swims up from the depths in *Inferno* XVI, the poet stresses the fabulous appearance of his poem, "quel ver c'ha faccia di menzogna" (that truth which has the face of a lie; *Inf.* XVI, 124).[49] To such deceptive truths, he says, a man should seal his lips in order not to squander his credibility. But here he cannot remain silent: "e per le note / di questa comedìa, lettor, ti giuro" (and, reader, I swear to you by the notes of this Comedy; *Inf.* XVI, 127–28) that he truly saw the Ovidian fiction of Geryon. In what Hollander calls "a wink" to sophisticated readers,[50] Dante here acknowledges that the poem itself is the only warrant of its own truth, a truth whose surface (*faccia*, face or page) is a literary fiction. And yet this passage also asserts the narrator's reliability; his honesty is so pure that the incredible sight of Geryon, which he would suppress if he were less honest, compels him to risk disbelief and speak anyway. Thus here, one of the most playful passages in the *Commedia*, even the poem's obvious fictionality paradoxically supports the primary authenticity of the narrator.

That the narrative presentation of the *Troilus* differs from that of the *Commedia* is at once apparent. Indeed I have gone into such great detail about Dante's self-presentation so that, amongst all the obvious differences, the relationship between the *Commedia* and the *Troilus* can also emerge. Nominally an omniscient narration into which the author intrudes,[51] Chaucer's poem nonetheless defies description as a straightforward third-person story told by a nonparticipating narrator. The first-person narrator intrudes on the inner story so extensively—overcoming his distance from the story by insinuating himself into the perspectives of his characters[52]—that to describe the *Troilus* as third-person fiction does not really account for the poem. Instead, Chaucer tells two stories about two worlds.[53] Superimposed on the inner story of Troy is a frame in which the narrator, who mediates between this history and his audience, tells his own story. Both aspects of the *Troilus* are held together by the "I," who also guides our responses to the inner story.[54] The third-person narrative is thus controlled by the first-person frame, and the "I" is Chaucer's primary authenticating device. The narrator's story is one of personal experience; he has read the inner story, and remembers its end even as he begins to tell it to us. His struggle to recount it so that we will respond just right becomes as much a drama at times as the Trojan love story itself.

Like the *Commedia*, then, the *Troilus* combines a distanced, more objective inner story mediated by a more personal frame. But though the *Troilus* partially shares the *Commedia*'s autobiographical form, the differences remain significant. Dante tells both frame and inner story in the first person; only time intervenes between his experience then and the telling now, and even

this time is the narrator's own. Both discourse and story originate in Dante. But Chaucer had no real autobiographical im-
pulse;[55] the "I" of his poems is too veiled by his poses to reveal
much personal history. The frame of the *Troilus* tells the "I"'s
personal experience, but already distanced from Chaucer by his
narrative pose. Nor is there any clear temporal separation between the "I" of the frame and the narrator of the inner story.
The inner story does not originate in Chaucer; it is autobiographical only to the extent that it recreates the experience of
reading the story in his sources. Chaucer's chief source is the
fictional Lollius, but he also mentions in passing most of the
other writers of the medieval Troy tradition: Homer, Dares,
Dictys, and Statius. Those who actually told the story of Troilus and Criseyde—Benoît, Guido, and Boccaccio—are conspicuously absent.[56] But though Chaucer did not invent his
story, he alters it radically when he retells it as a reading experience, an impersonal story mediated by a personal frame.

By adding this frame, Chaucer makes his primary authentication, with its combination of subjective and objective systems of language, formally parallel to Dante's. In the *Commedia*, the bridge between discours and histoire closed the gap between interpretation and fact and justified the narrator. Every
element of primary authentication worked in concert with the
others to encourage belief in the "I." In the *Troilus*, however,
every element that urges primary authenticity also undermines
it; subjective and objective authenticating devices work against
each other. When Chaucer distances his point of view, the resulting objectivity argues the truth of a history that does not
depend on its teller. But this objectivity also allows gaps to
creep into Chaucer's text of historical memory. When he moves
closer and becomes implicated in the experience of his characters, his subjectivity offers the guarantee of personal witness
and participation. But it also bends the history according to the
narrator's desires when he tries to suppress aspects he would
prefer we did not know.[57] I termed the *Commedia* a self-

authenticating narrative; the *Troilus* offers instead an ambivalent anti-authentication in which Chaucer uses the same devices
to subvert the validity of his telling.

The added layer of the frame transforms Chaucer's Trojan
story into a work that reflects on the reading of literature in
general. The frame critically affects the bookish narrator's credibility by stressing his disjunction from the characters who
"lived" the inner story, and hence focuses this reflection on literary authentication. Because Chaucer got the fundamental
bookishness that defines the frame from the *Commedia*, his questioning of narrative authentication points specifically to Dante.
The tenuous authenticating value of Chaucer's narrator, then,
suggests a critical response to the circular, self-confirming authority of Dante's "I."

In contrast to Dante's claim to have copied the divine books
of nature and history, the *Troilus* narrator's primary truth-claim
rests on the books of human history. If the story depends on
authoritative sources for its truth, it also depends on Chaucer's
"transparency" as a mediator. In his pose as a diligent historian,
he insists on faithful transmission as a precondition for the authenticity of his tale. He often asserts that he has nothing at all
to do with his story, that it passes through him from Lollius's
Latin to his English audience as light through water.[58] Since he
does not move to the old dance of love himself, he is admirably
suited to be a neutral medium for his story; he does not have
the ulterior motive of, for instance, Boccaccio, whose clear
identification with Troiolo serves the lovelorn purpose of *Il Filostrato*. Chaucer's purported lack of experience in love allows him
to narrate the history as it happened; he does not distort it to
further his own love affairs, or to match his own conceptions of
love. He has none, he tells us. He affects the narrative only by
putting it into English rhyme.

The most stringent expression of Chaucer's transparency
comes with his first mention of Lollius, as he introduces Troilus's Petrarchan lyric in Book I:

And of his song naught only the sentence,
As writ myn auctour called Lollius,
But pleinly, save oure tonges difference,
I dar wel seyn, in al, that Troilus
Seyde in his song, loo, every word right thus
As I shal seyn; and whoso list it here,
Loo, next this vers he may it fynden here.   (1.393–99)

The historian has only minimal effect on the words of his source—and none at all on its "sentence."[59] He does not refract the story through his own concerns, but reports it just as he read it. Such perfect consonance between a text and its reading and retelling asserts the objective authenticity of histoire, where minimal focus on the circumstances of telling strives to make the speaker and his point of view irrelevant, and so to close the gap between event and report. Here, where the immediate event is a prior report of the ancient love history, the narrator strives equally to match his retelling to Lollius's account, neither adding to nor subtracting from it.

Given the disjunction between event and report in *The House of Fame*, we should be forewarned; the premise behind such fidelity to authority warrants investigation. When the narrator describes his function to reproduce "naught only the sentence" but also "every word right thus," he implicitly assumes that his source merits transparent transmission because it records events as such, unaffected by the translation into written history. Behind this assumption are others: that all deviation perforce involves degeneration from truth; and that neither the context in which a story is told, nor the purpose for which it is told, matters. By transmitting his source so faithfully, Chaucer presumably perpetuates an unbroken chain of human memory leading back to historical events themselves, and so insures the accuracy of his own version.

These attitudes behind the bookish pose of the narrator strike us as ironic and unpoetic;[60] the Chaucer we know from other works is intensely aware of the effects of narrative presentation and context. Nonetheless, the claim that narrative truth rests on absolute fidelity to authority also crops up in *The Canterbury Tales*, where Chaucer apologizes for the self-imposed constraints that force him to report every word, no matter how offensive, just as he heard it. The claim both asserts the independent existence of the tales outside his memory, and establishes him as a naive, unliterary, unreliable reporter: who could remember so much so perfectly?[61] In the Prologue to Melibee, Chaucer extends the correspondence between original and subsequent tellings of a tale one step further. As with the gospels, he argues, all versions of the same story "acorden as in hire sentence, / Al be ther in hir tellyng difference" (*CT*, VII.947–48). This amounts to a blind, unqualified assertion that the teller can never affect his tale significantly;[62] even if the narrator were to alter the wording of the other pilgrims' tales, he would not interfere with their meaning.

Of course, the context subverts the idea of the teller's transparency. The Canterbury collection as a whole plays with the wide range of effects achieved by varying speaker and surrounding context. Of all the elements that make up fiction, Chaucer varies plot, the skeletal structure of events, least. The tales of Knight, Miller, Merchant, and Franklin, for instance, all share one basic plot, yet differ from one another enormously.[63] Chaucer precludes reducing "sentence" to story alone, and stresses instead the difference wrought by style, teller, and the circumstances of telling: the effect of the discourse on the story. The tales embody the narrative possibilities of voice suggested in *The House of Fame*, where the dreamer found that the aery raw materials of human discourse took on the forms of those who spoke them (*HF*, 1073–83).[64] Ascertaining the truth of a story is not only difficult, *The House of Fame* argues, but also less important than attending to the teller and the circumstances of telling. This is just what we would expect from a habitual teller of twice-told tales: Chaucer asks us to consider the way authorial shaping affects the meaning of a story. The claim in the Prologue to Melibee that authorial revision revises nothing only calls attention to the changes in "sentence" that issue from any retelling.

Thus we instantly suspect the assertion of authorial transparency in the *Troilus*. But why is it here at all? It does not call attention to a collection of tales that, set off against one another, expose the claim as wrongheaded. If we suspend our skepticism for a moment, we can explore what narrative transparency accomplishes for Chaucer's version of the Troy story. Primarily, it reasserts the historicity Boccaccio's version lacks.[65] In adapting *Il Filostrato*, Chaucer attenuated the intense identification felt by the Boccaccean narrator for his Troiolo. Boccaccio tells Troiolo's story, he says, in order to move his own lady to pity; his open personal involvement obviates the need for historical authentication. His subjective purpose makes the past truth of his Trojan story unimportant; it matters only that the story is rhetorically effective in evoking the response Boccaccio seeks from his present audience. Consequently he pays only lip-service to "olde bokes."[66]

By removing this subjective purpose, Chaucer restores the historicity of the tale, and thus creates the need for historical authentication. Since his only subjective purpose in telling this tale appears to be a banal devotion to "just the facts," we are invited to trust his intentions if not his competence. His claim to reproduce "naught only the sentence" but also the very wording of his authority seems to insure that he delivers to us a tale he has left uninterpreted. In contrast with *Il Filostrato*—and even more strikingly with Francesca's first-person story in *Inferno* v, where self-delusion turns history into a self-exculpating nostalgia that casts suspicion on everything she says—the objective third-person *histoire* of the *Troilus* gains credibility from Chaucer's pose as a diligent, faithful, transparent mediator with no clear personal stake in the story he perpetuates. His stance is unpoetic; with it, he suggests that his story is no poet's fiction.

So far, Chaucer's strategy appears to parallel Dante's effort to erase the distinction between objective fact and subjective interpretation, though where Dante had redefined the quality of his subjectivity through conversion, Chaucer simply eliminates any reason we might have to suspect subjective reinterpretation of historical truth. However, while espousing the ideal of transparent transmission of history, Chaucer simultaneously undercuts the authenticity it lends his narrative. In Book III, he defends the completeness of his account with these protestations:

> But now, paraunter, som man wayten wolde
> That every word, or soonde, or look, or cheere
> Of Troilus that I rehercen sholde,
> In al this while unto his lady deere—
> I trowe it were a long thyng for to here—
> Or of what wight that stant in swich disjoynte,
> His wordes alle, or every look, to poynte.
>
> For sothe, I have naught herd it don er this
> In story non, ne no man here, I wene;
> And though I wolde, I koude nought, ywys;
> For ther was som epistel hem bitwene,
> That wolde, as seyth myn autour, wel contene
> Neigh half this book, of which hym liste nought write.
> How sholde I thanne a lyne of it endite?   (III.491–504)

Here he renews his assertion of absolute fidelity to his source.* But the very stiffness of his interrupted syntax—suggesting a sniff of injured dignity?—muddies the clear waters of his transmission. More important, this passage introduces the difference between event and report that Chaucer had sought to circumvent by his fidelity. His ignorance about love prevents

---

*A claim not consistently asserted; at III.1324, for instance, the narrator apologizes for not telling as much as his "auctour" did; it is hard to tell if he means he left something out, or whether he is simply incapable of telling it with the proper emotional resonance. He then tells his audience to leave out anything he may have added inadvertently because of his ignorance of love. Thus this passage expresses the will to fidelity, if not the perfect execution. At IV.799–805, he deliberately passes over the lovers' laments, feeling that he would "childlisshly deface" them if he tried. The locution "ich it pace" suggests to pass over on a page. We see then that though

him from interpolating anything that possibly or probably happened, but that his source omits; what began as a traditional authenticating claim based on old written authority, then, suddenly raises the specter of gaps in the record of human memory. Lollius's selective reporting has already interpreted the story. By the very manner in which Chaucer asserts the authenticity of his narrative here, he undercuts the truth of his source. Moreover, such historical inauthenticity seems to be a general characteristic of narrative: "I have naught herd it don er this / In story non. . . ."

This vanity is also implicit in Chaucer's pleas for the future of his version of the story. At the end of the poem he begs that the *Troilus* might survive without textual corruption or lapses in understanding:

> And for ther is so gret diversite
> In Englissh and in writyng of oure tonge,
> So prey I God that non myswrite the,
> Ne the mysmetre for defaute of tonge;
> And red wherso thow be, or elles songe,
> That thow be understonde, God I biseche!   (v.1793–98)

Underlying his plea for textual immutability is the poet's awareness that such stasis is impossible. The source on which he pins the authenticity of the *Troilus* as history, Lollius, is fictional. But even the source Chaucer in fact adapts, *Il Filostrato*, has undergone extensive change. Indeed, virtually every corroborating reference to "Lollius" or "myn auctour" comes in the midst of a passage Chaucer substantially invented himself.[67] Unattainable stability is demonstrated not only in the literary

---

the narrator espouses the ideal of transparent transmission, he himself feels incapable of achieving it. In other passages, such as I.260–66 and III.1408–9, it is not clear to me that the narrator summarizes Lollius; in the first, I think the "thing collateral" refers to his own story in the frame, which he does not wish to dwell on, not to something irrelevant in Lollius. At III.1408–9, he spares us the details of how the lovers slept; again, this merely confirms his unpoetic pose. At v.946–51, he summarizes his source for a different reason, which I will discuss below: Diomede's love talk is simply something he would prefer not to remember.

background of the *Troilus*, but in its subsequent fate as well. Henryson's question "Quha wait gif all that Chauceir wrait was trew?" prefaces the *Testament of Cresseid*'s revision of the story Chaucer had revised from Boccaccio.[68] The changes in the Troilus story from Boccaccio to Henryson illustrate the manner in which history varies according to the concerns of each successive author.

Thus Chaucer constantly questions his source, or, by the manner in which he defends it, causes us to question it. Faithful to a suspect source in both its inclusions and omissions, Chaucer's version inevitably deviates from the original events themselves. At other times, however, Chaucer undermines his own credibility as well. In his effort to present himself as a judicious reader, distinguishing among reliable and unreliable sources, he instead diminishes our sense of him as a reliable speaker and a competent historian. When he tells us of Criseyde's infidelity to Troilus, he refuses to warrant the certitude with which his sources affirm that she fell in love with Diomede:

> I fynde ek in stories elleswhere,
> Whan thorugh the body hurt was Diomede
> Of Troilus, tho wep she many a teere
> Whan that she saugh his wyde wowndes blede,
> And that she took, to kepen hym, good hede;
> And for to helen hym of his sorwes smerte,
> Men seyn—I not—that she yaf hym hire herte.   (V. 1044–50)

But we have Criseyde's own testimony implying that, despite her regret on Troilus's account, she did give Diomede her heart: "To Diomede algate I wol be trewe" (V. 1071).

Furthermore, the real difference between the two occasions on which Criseyde falls in love lies less in the process itself—it is nearly identical in both cases—than in the manner in which Chaucer reports it. When Criseyde reciprocates Troilus's feelings for her, the narrator tells us her thoughts and feelings— her inner action—as well as the externally observable aspects of the courtship. When she switches her allegiance to Diomede, however, the narrator distances his narration. We know little of the feelings behind Criseyde's words and deeds, and the narrator refuses to tell us the details of Diomede's wooing.[69] Consequently, though the flavor of the second courtship is vastly different from that of the first, this is the effect of the report, of the discourse on the story. Chaucer not only impugns the reliability of his sources; more important, he also emends them silently by what we would call poetic or stylistic means. When the narrator presents the second courtship from such a great aesthetic and emotional distance, he forces us to look back at the other "objective" parts of his narrative—chiefly, the first courtship—and find that they too contain the narrator's personal perspective. Chaucer has carefully separated history from poetic technique, only to show, despite all claims of dependence on his "auctour," that his history is shot through with poetic fiction.

For this reason, we should be suspicious whenever Chaucer's comments on his story seem to conflict with the information—presumably exactly what he found in his source's "sentence"—communicated in narrative scenes. The best example of conflict between commentary and narrative is the passage in which the narrator disputes the interpretation that Criseyde, seeing Troilus from her window, falls in love instantaneously:

> Now myghte som envious jangle thus:
> "This was a sodeyn love; how myght it be
> That she so lightly loved Troilus
> Right for the first syghte, ye, parde?"
> Now whoso seith so, mote he nevere ythe!
> For every thyng a gynnyng hath it nede
> Er al be wrought, withowten any drede.
>
> For I sey nought that she so sodeynly
> Yaf hym hire love, but that she gan enclyne
> To like him first, and I have told yow whi;
> And after that, his manhod and his pyne
> Made love withinne hire for to myne,
> For which by proces and by good servyse
> He gat hire love, and in no sodeyn wyse.   (II.666–79)

In the scene preceding this comment, it is perfectly obvious to anyone familiar with medieval literary love conventions that they are being used to suggest that Criseyde has indeed fallen in love at first sight.[70] Her reaction upon seeing Troilus for the first time since she has learned of his feelings for her is: "Who yaf me drynke?" (II.651). These words summon up Tristan and Dido, whose instantaneous passion is attributed to or metaphorically expressed as a draught of powerful love potion.[71] Within the *Troilus*, "drynke" also describes the sudden love of Troilus: "For ay thurst I, the more that ich it drynke" (I.406). It is a commonplace of medieval love literature—one Chaucer also uses with Troilus—that love enters the heart through the eyes; the *locus classicus* is Guillaume's Fountain of Narcissus in the *Roman de la rose*. With such an extensive literary background, the image could serve no other purpose but to imply that Criseyde indeed conceives her love instantaneously. I would hesitate to assert this inference as fact; in the subsequent scene, Criseyde's doubts and ambivalences are too real to discount, and they qualify the narrative information given here. I suspect that, like Troilus, Criseyde would never have *acted* on her feelings without Pandarus's arrangements, but this suggests nothing about what her feelings were, or when and how quickly she conceived them. Nonetheless, the narrator's commentary calls attention to the sudden onslaught of love on Criseyde's eyes and heart precisely as convention.[72] By questioning whether her responses to seeing Troilus through her window constitute love at first sight, Chaucer labels them as the customary manner in which a medieval romance heroine falls in love, and by an ironic inversion, directs his reader's attention to the conventions that influence any interpretation of the scene.

The narrator's disputation imperils the authenticating level of the *Troilus*. In taking issue with the interpretation the narrative suggests, Chaucer apparently forces us to choose between narrative and commentary; both cannot simultaneously be true. I think the initial tendency of most readers is to trust the narrative, and to dismiss the argument against it as specious.[73] The narrator's intervention destroys any lingering sense we might have that he is a reliable speaker. Not only does he differ from his source, but he is also internally inconsistent: for reasons extraneous to what he represents as the events themselves, he chooses to attach to this crucial scene an interpretation at odds with the evidence of the narrative. If, in first-person narrative, the character and reliability of the narrator is fundamental to authentication, then Chaucer here not only shows, but indeed stresses, the possible inauthenticity of the *Troilus*. His narrator is demonstrably incompetent at the historian's task he has set for himself, or an unreliable interpreter—or both.

Yet if we choose the truth of the narrative over the conflicting commentary, we fall into Chaucer's trap. We lull ourselves into thinking that we have astutely distinguished between Lollius's authentic version and the later interpretative accretions that attempt, with suspicious lameness, to revise it. In fact, the choice Chaucer encourages us to make is itself specious. In reality he added not only his quibbling comments but also the scene they dispute. The origin of the scene is Boccaccio's bare assertion, offered parenthetically, that Criseida's passions had already been kindled by Pandaro's report; there is no trace of the romantic progress of love striking through the eyes to a heart whose resistance has been weakened by a draught of love potion.[74] Had Chaucer been concerned merely to authenticate his story, he could have continued to claim the authority of Lollius's old history for the scene, and emended his fictional source silently. This is the practice followed in most twice-told tales. Yet Chaucer invented the scene and added a conflicting commentary, for his purpose is to disrupt easy authentication. We should not only distrust the narrator, but also wonder at the very idea that interpretation can be separated so neatly from narrative, and at the remarkable impasse in which we find ourselves if we trust to the truth of a narrative told by a narrator we distrust.

I asserted earlier that the first function of Chaucer's disputation is to stress the conventional romanticism it tries to dispel, that Criseyde falls in love instantaneously. Yet we should not therefore decide that Chaucer endorses the truth of this interpretation. Rather, he emphasizes the pervasive presence of interpretation itself, operating through the insistently medieval conventions from which we form our impressions. Such modernity is not consistent with the manner in which Book II begins. After first invoking Clio, the muse of history, and apologizing for his personal incompetence, Chaucer begs indulgence for the exotic, strange quality of his story:

> Ye knowe ek that in forme of speche is chaunge
> Withinne a thousand yeer, and wordes tho
> That hadden pris, now wonder nyce and straunge
> Us thinketh hem, and yet thei spake hem so,
> And spedde as wel in love as men now do;
> Ek for to wynnen love in sondry ages,
> In sondry londes, sondry ben usages.   (II.22–28)

From the perspective provided by the proem, the medieval conventions of the window scene are, like the disputation itself, later accretions to the original events. The narrator is apparently so completely and unconsciously controlled by the terms in which he and his contemporaries find it natural to conceive literary love that the medievalism of the scene issues willynilly.

Ultimately, then, the specious conflict between narrative and commentary demonstrates the inauthenticity of Chaucer's claim to transmit his tale without altering it. The glass is opaque whichever way we look through it, for the manner in which Chaucer disposes the narrative interprets it for us. Neither commentary nor narrative will lead us in any sure fashion back to the historical truth of how Criseyde fell in love; instead, both point to the way in which the *I–you* relationship between narrator and audience papers over this crucial gap in knowledge.

When Chaucer takes issue with his narrative, then, he directs us to the pervasiveness of implicit as well as explicit interpretative choices. But our initial response, to trust the narrative over the commentary, has some validity as well. Chaucer bases his historical truth-claim on his lack of personal involvement in his story. Nonetheless, his anxiety to dispel the dangerous idea that Criseyde offered her affections too lightly—dangerous because it lays the foundations for an equally light withdrawal of affections[75]—argues that he has indeed become personally implicated in his supposedly objective account of ancient Troy. Though it subverts the authenticity Chaucer seeks to gain from objective history, it also brings the inner story alive with the immediate realism of personal witness and imaginative participation.[76] Paradoxically, the most effective realism gained by such imaginative involvement is the most unabashedly fictional.[77] At times, the narrator effaces himself, nearly disappearing from our consciousness. For long stretches in such dramatic scenes as the conversations between Pandarus and Criseyde in Book II (ll. 85–595) and between Pandarus and Troilus in Book III (ll. 239–420), the narrator's only apparent contribution is the insertion of "quod he" or "quod she" into the direct discourse of his characters. His self-effacement makes it easy to forget that we witness these scenes only through an intermediary; as long as we are not forced to think of his anomalous presence in scenes he could not have witnessed, the verisimilitude of conversations as they take place every day supports authenticity.

Yet the deeper the narrator's participation, the more naked the fictionality. Book II's conversation between Pandarus and Criseyde not only shows us the externally observable actions of speech and gesture, but also tells us the inner experience behind them:

> Tho gan she wondren moore than biforn
> A thousand fold, and down hire eyghen caste;
> For nevere, sith the tyme that she was born,
> To knowe thyng desired she so faste;
> And with a syk she seyde hym atte laste,

"Now, uncle myn, I nyl you nought displese,
Nor axen more that may do you disese."   (II.141–47)

Criseyde, which that wel neigh starf for feere,
So as she was the ferfulleste wight
That myghte be, and herde ek with hire ere
And saugh the sorwful ernest of the knyght,
And in his preier ek saugh noon unryght,
And for the harm that myghte ek fallen moore,
She gan to rewe and dredde hire wonder soore,

And thoughte thus: "Unhappes fallen thikke
Alday for love, and in swych manere case
As men ben cruel in hemself and wikke;
And if this man sle here hymself—allas!—
In my presence, it wol be no solas.
What men wolde of hit deme I kan nat seye;
It nedeth me ful sleighly for to pleie."   (II.449–62)

These passages report Criseyde's unspoken thoughts as direct discourse and interpret the conversation as experienced from within her consciousness.[78] Since Chaucer does not qualify his report of her inner action, as Dante had done with his characters by means of similes and other distancing devices, he clearly violates the strictures on a first-person narrator's knowledge of subjective experience not his own. Yet it is precisely the interpretation of inner consciousness behind the spoken record that makes such scenes credible facsimiles of real conversation, seen from within.[79]

The best example of the narrator's fictive report of inner action is the sequence that follows Pandarus's departure from this conversation: starting with the scene in which Troilus rides under Criseyde's window; resuming, after the narrator's interruption, with her long interior monologue about the advantages and disadvantages of love; and ending with her dream of the eagle (ll. 596–931). Earlier I discussed the window scene as if it were unanchored third-person narrative, not oriented by the frame of reference of either narrator or character. Yet this is not the case; although no deictic locative or authorial statement tells us that "Criseyde saw" Troilus down below, we see the scene through her eyes. Chaucer achieves this point of view through a more subtle aspect of discourse: narrative ordering. The scene is surrounded by passages recording Criseyde's inner action; it begins (at l. 601) with her unspoken thoughts and feelings about what Pandarus has just told her, and ends with her momentous reaction to seeing Troilus:

> Criseÿda gan al his chere aspien,
> And leet it so softe in hire herte synke,
> That to hireself she seyde, "Who yaf me drynke?"   (ii.649–51)

Thus we should read the entire scene of Troilus's triumphal progress beneath her window as a seamless continuation of the workings of her mind and perceptual faculties. Despite the absence of openly deictic signals to locate our vantage, the verb of perception when "Criseÿda gan al his chere aspien" retroactively anchors the scene in her perspective. We now have a finite subject for the numerous infinitive verbs of inner action throughout the passage.* The narrator records the scene not objectively,[80] but as seen through Criseyde's window. Chaucer's narrative style here is remarkably subtle; because the verbs of perception are all infinitives, we all share her perspective, and see Troilus as she sees him.

The window scene might be described as Chaucer "telling" us what Criseyde saw, heard, thought, and felt as if he were only "showing" us what there was "to see." In order to gain our assent to the proposition that he knows her inner action and point of view—which will be necessary for his more audacious forays into her mind in the meditation and dream to follow— he must establish his authority for doing so. His pose as a derivative historian who retells only "As to myn auctour listeth for t'endite" (ii.700) does not enable him to evade the suspicion

---

*See "to loke" (l. 630), "to seen" (l. 632), "to seen" (l. 635), "to see" (l. 637), "to byholde" (l. 647), and the noun "sighte" (l. 628). The infinitives do not presuppose a seeing subject; they only indicate the possibility of seeing if such a subject were to be present.

that he fictionalizes his source; even displacing the inherent fictionality of the narrative onto his source does not explain the
provenance of his point of view here. Rather, the narrator's real
authority comes from the ahistorical imaginative participation
that enables him to share his characters' state of mind. During
Criseyde's monologue, he describes her changing inclinations
with this simile:

> But right as when the sonne shyneth brighte
> In March, that chaungeth ofte tyme his face,
> And that a cloude is put with wynd to flighte,
> Which oversprat the sonne as for a space,
> A cloudy thought gan thorugh hire soule pace,
> That overspradde hire brighte thoughtes alle,
> So that for feere almoste she gan to falle.   (II.764–70)

This simile narrowly precedes Criseyde's use of the same image
to express the variable nature of love:

> "For love is yet the mooste stormy lyf,
> Right of hymself, that evere was bigonne;
> For evere som mystrust or nice strif
> There is in love, some cloude is over that sonne."   (II.778–81)

By anticipating her thoughts, Chaucer suggests the perfect
consonance between character and narrator that enables him to
impart her interior monologue.[81]

This is not the first time Chaucer uses a shared image to suggest the narrator's participation in the experience of his characters. The "Canticus Troili" of Book I contains a typical Petrarchan conceit expressing Troilus's despair in love:

> "Thus possed to and fro,
> Al sterelees withinne a boot am I
> Amydde the see, bitwixen wyndes two,
> That in contrarie stonden evere mo."   (I.415–18)

Troilus uses a nautical metaphor when he imagines the bleak
result of his hopeless love: "God wold I were aryved in the
port / Of deth, to which my sorwe wol me lede!" (I.526–27).

Though Pandarus overhears neither of these images, he forestalls Troilus's despair by substituting a less final destination for
the ship of love: "Stonde faste, for to good port hastow rowed"
(1.969), he says of Criseyde when Troilus divulges his secret.

The narrator appropriates the same nautical imagery for himself in the opening lines of Book II:

> Owt of thise blake wawes for to saylle,
> O wynd, o wynd, the weder gynneth clere;
> For in this see the boot hath swych travaylle,
> Of my connyng, that unneth I it steere.
> This see clepe I the tempestous matere
> Of disespeir that Troilus was inne;
> But now of hope the kalendes bygynne.   (II. 1–7)

Nautical metaphors as references to poetry also abound in the
narrative tradition behind the *Troilus*.[82] Chaucer imitated these
lines directly from the beginning of the *Purgatorio*:

> Per correr miglior acque alza le vele
>   omai la navicella del mio ingegno,
>   che lascia dietro a sé mar sì crudele . . .   (*Purg.* 1, 1–3)

(To course over better waters the little bark of my genius now
hoists her sail, leaving behind her a sea so cruel . . .)

By rearranging the syntax of his translation so that "of my con-
nyng" floats unanchored by the "boot" it modifies, Chaucer
makes it nearly impossible to distinguish between his difficulties in writing and Troilus's in loving. Both must navigate what
appears to be the same sea. The nautical metaphors for love and
poetry thus confirm the importance of the *galeotto* roles—both
as go-betweens and as steersmen—of Pandarus and poet. And
by linking Troilus's love and his own poetry with the same image, Chaucer suggests the same consonance of experience that
he later shares with Criseyde as well.

All of this is unremarkable; and none of it distinguishes the
Troilus from third-person omniscient fictions with intrusive
narrators that ask us to suspend our disbelief without making

it difficult to do so. The straightforward fictive traits merely argue that the poem is fiction—and we knew that already. The crucial step (and one that happens in Dante only at the end) occurs when the narrator's imaginative participation leaves the narrated world of the inner story and invades the commentative world of the frame as well.

When his imaginative identification with his characters becomes too explicit, as we have seen in his attempt to dispel the notion that Criseyde fell in love too quickly, the narrator not only undermines his authority as an objective historian, but also calls too much attention to the fictionality this identification yields in the inner story. In the disputation, we suspect that Chaucer has not fully expunged the personal motivations with which Boccaccio had told his version, but it remains unclear why he seems so anxious to forestall the interpretation he also built into his narrative. When he celebrates the lovers' attainment of "hevene blisse" in Book III, at the joyous point of stasis before the narrative begins its downward trajectory, we suddenly recognize the new personal desires struggling to control the poem:

> O blisful nyght, of hem so longe isought,
> How blithe unto hem bothe two thow weere!
> Why nad I swich oon with my soule ybought,
> Ye, or the leeste joie that was theere?
> Awey, thow foule daunger and thow feere,
> And lat hem in this hevene blisse dwelle,
> That is so heigh that al ne kan I telle!   (III.1317–23)

In this apostrophe, the narrator openly wants time to stand still; his vicarious identification with his characters leads him to wish he could memorialize them at the lyric moment of perfect happiness. His desire to circumvent the passage of time here parallels the desire implicit in his effort to transmit and preserve history faithfully.

Yet this apostrophe belies the authenticity of the personal involvement of which it is possibly the strongest expression in the poem. The negative in "Why nad I" reiterates the "unlikly-nesse" in love that casts a pall over the narrator's authority to know and share the inner experience of lovers. Like Pandarus, he is useful as a whetstone to sharpen knives, but, as he often repeats, he does not know and cannot express the most intimate and powerful feelings of the lovers themselves. Moreover, the very expression of his desire for stasis points to its own futility. The narrator *knows* time won't stand still because he knows the story's outcome. His prayer for "hevene blisse" recalls the earlier prayer for lovers, in the somber grandeur of Book I's invocation, "That Love hem brynge in hevene to solas" (1.31). That other heavenly solace would console those lovers who, like Troilus, have lost the "hevene blisse," who have instead gone "Fro wo to wele, and after out of joie" (1.4). The narrator's desire to stop time in this apostrophe only forces us to recognize how thoroughly the imaginative participation, which makes the poem so resemble real experience as it unfolds, depends on a suspension of memory: in a word, on nostalgia.

By interjecting the narrator's personal implication into the frame as well as the inner story, Chaucer elevates the authenticating process from a literary technique to a thematic concern. After Book III, the narrator must relinquish the stasis he prays for in the apostrophe so that he can continue to follow Lollius's history; but he needn't like it.[83] His emotional involvement in the last two books openly conflicts with his role as chronicler; more and more frequently, his interpretations differ from those of his source, and he tries to suppress some of the more damaging aspects of the events he so clearly abhors.[84] Objectivity and subjectivity collide, but the result is not, as it was in the *Commedia*, a vindication of the objective truth of a first-person narrative, authentic because the narrator's pristine reliability and unerring memory purge nostalgic lingering over a past to which he does not wish to return. Instead, the two poles intermingle in a way that devastates both Chaucer's subjective reliability and the objective truth of the history he relates.

When the narrator resumes his tale of woe, he writes with
obvious reluctance and quaking pen:

> For how Criseyde Troilus forsook—
> Or at the leeste, how that she was unkynde—
> Moot hennesforth ben matere of my book,
> As writen folk thorugh which it is in mynde.   (IV. 15–18)

These lines come in the midst of Book IV's proem, in which
Chaucer heightens the pathos of the tragedy about to unfold.
The contrast between the end of Book III and this proem is
shocking, and so is the contrast within these lines. They link
the poem's baldest statement of Criseyde's infidelity with the
narrator's most conspicuous effort to ameliorate the tragedy he
has just heightened.[85] If his desire is to exonerate Criseyde (here
as well as in Book V, where he tries to impugn the veracity of
his sources and then, as a last resort, to "excuse hire yet for
routhe"; V. 1099), then he fails utterly to match intention to effect. Like Criseyde, he seems to scramble for weak rationaliza-
tions; hence the anticlimax of line 16 only increases the gravity
of their transgressions. Rather than alleviating our suspicions,
Chaucer provokes them, for if the only defense he can provide
is so weak, then she must indeed be guilty of actions far worse
than "unkynde."

Chaucer's intermingling of "olde bokes" and personal witness points to the degree to which the narrator has lost control
of his work. At every turn, his intentions are confuted by the
effects they engender. At first, it seems that he could exert control by abdicating it to his source; acting on the desire Chaucer
expresses elsewhere as well,[86] he intends to transmit history
faithfully in order to preserve the record of human memory.
The narrative structure of the *Troilus*, however, militates
against this endeavor; the work is not simply a history of things
past, but also an account of the narrator's experience of reading
about them, and his struggle to communicate that experience
to his audience. The personal involvement of this layer works
against the credibility of distanced history. More and more, the

narrator (the mediator of the frame) falls into complicity with Pandarus (the mediator of the inner story) and his efforts to bring and keep the lovers together. When Pandarus tells Criseyde how he discovered Troilus's love for her, he fictionalizes his account to make it more persuasive.[87] The difference between "history" and "fiction" in this case arises out of Pandarus's personal stake in successful mediation. Pandarus's fiction here provides a paradigm for what happens to the narrator as well, whose stake in successful mediation is equally great. His vicarious engagement in the inner experience of his characters causes him intermittently to suppress his knowledge of the story's outcome so that both he and we might savor the joy of their love for as long as possible. His nostalgic desire to retrieve the past before Criseyde forsook Troilus, and before he read of her infidelity, threatens his desire to preserve the general human memory of history.

Indeed, for a work that depends so heavily on both historical and personal memory, the *Troilus* contains an extraordinary amount of forgetfulness. In the last two books, the historical sources to which the narrator had relinquished control in order to guarantee the authenticity of his work become a grave burden, and his nostalgic desire to linger becomes instead a desire to exonerate Criseyde. In this too he fails, and the attempt only seals his own unreliability.

Thus we see that the *Troilus* is fraught with the consistent disparity between intentions and effects. Whatever the narrator desires to do—transmit history neutrally, linger over his story nostalgically, or exonerate Criseyde—he conspicuously fails in. His failure to achieve his desires reveals a broader strategy on Chaucer's part. By undermining the credibility of his narrator, whose character and reliability are supposed to assure primary authenticity, Chaucer instead shows how thoroughly the narrator's desires falsify his utterance. The falsity arises from his strain toward truth; it is the intermingling of first-person witness and third-person history that confutes his desires. And in a work that so consistently severs intentions from effects, we must extend this disparity to the broadest intentions of a rhetorical narrative poet: that his fiction have the desired effect on its readers, and that it persuade us that it truly describes the world beyond the text. Thus authentication itself embodies authorial desire. Chaucer uses the subversive paradigm of his unreliable narrator, whose futile desires distort his text of memory, to expose the act of authentication as a phantom of desire, a persuasive fiction suspect precisely in the measure that the author desires his argument about the world to be true.

The manner in which this "anti-authentication" of the narrator in the *Troilus* responds to the *Commedia* rests upon Chaucer's elevation of authentication from narrative technique to thematic concern. Chaucer also undermines the authentication of the *Troilus* in those aspects of the poem he borrows from Dante rather than from Boccaccio. Both the *Commedia* and the *Troilus* are texts of memory that insist on their historicity; and both bridge the gap between subjective discours and objective histoire. Where the *Commedia* had objectified its first-person narrative, Chaucer's poem subjects even third-person narrative to the distortions of his narrator's desires. Finally, the *Commedia*, like the *Troilus*, is a love poem—a text of desire. The organizing principle of sins, virtues, and beatitude throughout Dante's poem is love, whether misdirected or well directed. The *Commedia* recounts the journey of the pilgrim-lover to the object of his desire in the Empyrean, and the entire pilgrimage is the flight of desire aided by grace, without which "sua disïanza vuol volar sanz' ali" (his desire seeks to fly without wings; *Par.* XXXIII, 15). The pilgrim's goal is to unite "l'ardor del desiderio" (the ardor of my longing; *Par.* XXXIII, 48) with "[i]l fine di tutt' i disii" (the end of all desires; *Par.* XXXIII, 46). Dante records the successful attainment of this goal in his final lines, where the desiring pilgrim unites with the object of his desire ("il mio disio"), the Supreme Good, which alone can still all longing (*Par.* XXXIII, 143–45). This union gives Dante the knowledge and the purified language to write the poem. The fulfillment of his religious desire justifies Dante's assertion of uniqueness; alone among literary fictions—Virgil's *Aeneid* is the poem's chief counterexample—the *Commedia* fulfills the greatest authorial desire, to match intention to effect.

Through the negative authentication of the narrator, *Troilus and Criseyde* questions the truth of such an experience recorded in a literary fiction. The *Troilus* warns us that when a narrator claims to attain anything he so strongly desires, we must suspect him precisely because of the strength of his desire. By borrowing extensively from Dante—Francesca's story, the concern for literary mediation, the scattered verbal echoes, and the combination of subjective and objective truth-claims—Chaucer turns his critique specifically to the *Commedia*. The motive force of the *Commedia* is desire, and desire *is* personal implication. Dante claims successfully to join a fictional text of desire with the purgation of all distorting personal implication, to erase the distance between fact and interpretation, fiction and history. Chaucer, however, questions the possibility of such an authentic relation between a literary fiction and the world beyond the text. His skepticism is in large measure responsible for the enormous differences between the authoritative Dantean narrator and the unreliable Chaucerian narrator, and between the ways in which each speaks of love.

4. Figuring the World

Thus far I have concentrated on the deictics of narrative voice: how Chaucer, in response to Dante, places himself with respect to his audience and his subject. My focus now shifts to the deictics of narrative reference by which Chaucer creates the pagan world of the *Troilus*. The settings of both poems are exotic and otherworldly, the *Commedia*'s more obviously so than the *Troilus*'s. Yet the strange settings confront Dante and Chaucer with the same task: each poet must bring his distanced otherworld into the ken of his readers so that we will recognize it in some sense as our own. Consequently, their strategies of analogical language are crucial to secondary authentication. In the *Commedia*, analogical language confirms Dante's truth-claim that he is the *scriba Dei*, his poem a copy of God's book. But in the *Troilus*, analogical language, like the character of the narrator, subverts authenticity and confirms that the words of the poem are optative and based on desire.

Proverbs are a characteristic mode of analogy in the *Troilus*, and this stanza illustrates their problematic function:

> For ay the ner the fir, the hotter is—
> This, trowe I, knoweth al this compaignye;
> But were he fer or ner, I dar sey this:
> By nyght or day, for wisdom or folye,
> His herte, which that is his brestez ÿe,
> Was ay on hire, that fairer was to sene
> Than evere were Eleyne or Polixene.   (1.449–55)

The narrator has just described the "hote fir" (1.445) of Troilus's new love for Criseyde, a flame whose intensity continually

increases: "And ay the ner he was, the more he brende" (1.448).
In order to link the exotic love of ancient Troy to the experience
of his fourteenth-century audience, Chaucer then shifts to the
generalized present tense of a proverb, whose similar wording
follows quite naturally the description of Troilus: "For ay the
ner the fir, the hotter is." The proverb appeals to common sense
and a common analogical habit of thought. Whenever we encounter something of which we have no previous knowledge,
we try to synthesize it into our construction of the world, which
is based on the sum of past experience. We naturalize the new
information by making an analogy: "This may seem strange at
first, but really it is just like . . ." The proverb here is comic
because the audience is supposed to know more than the "unlikely" narrator about the sensations of love, and consequently
needs the analogy less. However, as part of a general pattern in
the *Troilus*, it has a serious function as well; it represents Chaucer's effort to bring Troilus and Troy into our experience by
means of naturalizing analogy.

But Chaucer retracts the analogy almost as soon as he proposes it. By line 451, we have only the illusion of a link between Troilus's fire and the proverbial fire. We are no longer
sure what the "fir" is—Criseyde, who warms Troilus like a fire?
But the previous stanza also described the "hote fir" as Troilus's
own emotions. Nor do we know whether Troilus is "fer or ner";
he burns regardless. The proverb, which seemed to suggest the
closeness and comprehensibility of distant time, place, and
people, only shows the limits of analogical understanding.

The proverbs of the *Troilus*, as well as the anachronistic language of medieval *amour courtois*, at once suggest an analogy between the two worlds of the poem—the pagan world of Troy,
and the world Chaucer shares with his audience—and show the
deceptions of such analogical understanding. The *Troilus*'s construction of reality seems very different from the *Commedia*'s,
and Chaucer's proverbs are instrumental in creating this disparity. Furthermore, along with the other forms of conventional language, they suggest a critique of the intellectual

premises behind the finely articulated, coherent analogies of the *Commedia*. Before describing Chaucer's strategies of figuring the world, then, we must look again to the poem it reacts against.

Of the three kinds of analogical language in the *Commedia*—metaphor, simile, and allegory—the first provides Dante with his basic fiction, the traditional metaphorical journey he maps onto his spiritual experience. Since Dante did not travel through hell, purgatory, and heaven, the pilgrimage removes the *Commedia* from literal truth. The other two strategies of analogical language operate against the background of this metaphor, whose fictionality creates the need for authentication. Through similes and allegory, Dante returns the text, if not to literal truth, then at least to credibility, spiritual truth, and hence authenticity. The similes, which embody the narrator's associations, primarily create what natural realism the *Commedia* achieves in its descriptions, and authenticate the poem as *discours*. The allegory creates a figural realism[1] that arises not from the narrator's perspective but from the structure of reality itself. It thus authenticates the poem as *histoire*.

Similes both establish and depend on the central *I–you* relation of author and reader.[2] Through them, Dante renders his exotic landscape in terms he already shares with the reader, and persuades us of his authority as an observer. To establish the authority of the comparative form itself, Dante uses a peculiar subclass, the so-called pseudosimiles.[3] Strictly speaking, these are not comparisons at all, for tenor and vehicle are identical:

> Ben discernëa in lor la testa bionda;
>   ma ne la faccia l'occhio si smarria,
>   come vertù ch'a troppo si confonda.   (*Purg.* VIII, 34–36)

(I clearly discerned their blond heads, but in their faces my sight was dazzled, like a faculty confounded by excess.)

Here Dante states a causal relationship as if it were a comparison.[4] Sight *is* a faculty. Rather than comparing the experience to a disparate but similar process, the second term offers a general principle to explain why Dante's eye loses itself: an excess rather than a deficiency of light. The simile interprets Dante's failed sight, but in distanced form. Nor is this a true simile:

> A guisa d'uom che 'n dubbio si raccerta
>   e che muta in conforto sua paura,
>   poi che la verità li è discoperta,
> mi cambia' io . . .   (*Purg.* IX, 64–67)

(Like a perplexed man who is reassured, whose fear changes to confidence when the truth is revealed to him, so I was changed . . .)

These lines establish an identity between the generalized man in the tenor and the "I" in the vehicle, and again present a causal relationship in distanced form. Here too the pilgrim is not like a perplexed man; he *is* such a man. The pseudosimiles raise a question: why does Dante fragment integral relations of causality and identity by casting them into the much looser form of comparison?

Three answers suggest themselves. First, pseudosimiles such as the one in *Purgatorio* IX help establish Dante as an exemplary figure, an individual representing the whole class of people he tries to create by leading his readers to conversion.[5] This he accomplishes by stating his emotions first in the general case, and only then applying them to himself. A second function of the pseudosimiles resembles the use of real similes to bridge the cognitive gap between the first-person narrator and the inner life of others;[6] but here the focus remains on Dante. When he expresses his feelings and experiences in such distanced form, he presents his own inner action as if it were that of another character. These pseudosimiles cannot be distinguished formally from real similes describing the inner action of others, as here, where Dante expresses Sordello's surprise at meeting Virgil:

> Qual è colui che cosa innanzi sé
>   sùbita vede ond' e' si maraviglia,

che crede e non, dicendo "Ella è . . . non è . . . ,"
tal parve quelli . . .   (*Purg.* VII, 10–13)

(As one who of a sudden sees a thing before him that he marvels
at, who believes and believes not, saying, "It is, it is not,"—
such seemed the other . . .)

In the pseudosimiles, Dante treats himself as he does Sordello—in the third person, so to speak. He furthers the separation between the pilgrim, who no longer exists, and the poet,
who was reborn out of his former self. The distance from self
blurs the distinction between interpretation and fact, and establishes Dante's authority to report the inner life of others.

The third function pertains less to the deictics of narrative
voice than to the capacity of the poem's genuine similes to render reality truthfully. The perplexed man of *Purgatorio* IX is
joined both by another pseudosimile and by a genuine one:

Non altrimenti Achille si riscosse,
    li occhi svegliati rivolgendo in giro
    e non sappiendo là dove si fosse,
quando la madre da Chirón a Schiro
    trafuggò lui dormendo in le sue braccia,
    là onde poi li Greci il dipartiro;
che mi scoss' io, sì come da la faccia
    mi fuggì 'l sonno, e diventa' ismorto,
    come fa l'uom che, spaventato, agghiaccia.   (*Purg.* IX, 34–42)

(Even as Achilles started up, turning his awakened eyes about
him and not knowing where he was, when his mother carried
him off, sleeping in her arms, from Chiron to Skyros, whence
later the Greeks took him away; so did I start, as soon as sleep
fled from my face, and I grew pale, like one who is chilled with
terror.)

Again, it is Dante who is chilled with terror after his prophetic
dream of Ganymede rapt to the heavens by an eagle of gold; we
accept such comparisons as fully credible because of the identity of tenor and vehicle. The authenticity of the pseudosimile

easily carries over to the genuine comparison that precedes it. The main simile compares identical reactions to similar events, for as we discover shortly, Dante's terror and astonishment stem not so much from his dream as from his discovery that he has been moved as he slept. Hence the final focus is on the similarity between the two unwitting journeys of Dante and Achilles. But since this simile describes Dante's own feelings as well, it acts as a bridge between the pseudosimiles, in which the two terms are identical or nearly so, and the genuine similes, in which Dante describes the world he traverses rather than his reactions to it. Through pseudosimiles, Dante establishes the authority of the comparative form to communicate, without lapses in knowledge, things he knows of a certainty from his own past experience. He uses them to transfer authenticity to the comparisons that link the world familiar to his reader to the strange otherworld of the poem.

The authoritative pseudosimiles make it easier for us to accept and believe such genuine similes as this:

> Quale ne l'arzanà de' Viniziani
> bolle l'inverno la tenace pece
> a rimpalmare i legni lor non sani,
> ché navicar non ponno—in quella vece
> chi fa suo legno novo e chi ristoppa
> le coste a quel che più vïaggi fece;
> chi ribatte da proda e chi da poppa;
> altri fa remi e altri volge sarte;
> chi terzeruolo e artimon rintoppa—:
> tal, non per foco ma per divin' arte,
> bollia là giuso una pegola spessa,
> che 'nviscava la ripa d'ogne parte. (*Inf.* XXI, 7–18)

(As in the Arsenal of the Venetians, in winter, the sticky pitch for caulking their unsound vessels is boiling, because they cannot sail then, and instead, one builds his ship anew and another plugs the ribs of his that has made many a voyage, one hammers at the prow and another at the stern, this one makes oars, that one twists ropes, another patches jib and mainsail; so, not

by fire but by divine art, a thick pitch was boiling there below,
which overglued the bank on every side.)

Such similes do the real descriptive work of the poem; the
vivid, oppressive detail with which Dante evokes the shared
world of the Arsenal establishes him as an observer of great authority. Through extended comparisons, he imparts new information in terms of "old"; they link the shared world to the unfamiliar one the poet asks us to accept as equally real. This
"world creating" leads Erich Auerbach to call Dante the poet of
the secular world; in his view the otherworld is a grand eschatological simile for this one.[7] He is surely right to connect them;
however, in authentication, the comparisons work in precisely
the opposite (and in fact the more usual, literal) direction. Epic
similes serve other functions as well; the Venetian arsenal simile, almost surreptitiously amidst all the natural realism, links
nautical imagery to divine art and thus once again confirms
Dante as a *galeotto*. But it is important not to lose sight of the
most immediate function of Dante's extended similes: they
present this strange world as similar to the one we know, and
thus make it easier for us to accept the often astonishing sights
Dante claims to have seen.

To impart new information in terms that allow the reader to
imagine along with the author is not an unusual use of simile.
But Dante's task would daunt a lesser writer; he must find ways
to describe a realm no reader has seen or can ever see. His solution depicts his eschatological pilgrimage, on Beatrice's rec-
ommendation, as a painter would:

> "voglio anco, e se non scritto, almen dipinto,
>   ch'l te ne porti dentro a te per quello
>   che si reca il bordon di palma cinto."   (*Purg.* XXXIII, 76–78)

("I would also have you bear it [the light of my word] away
within you—and if not written, at least depicted—for the reason
that the pilgrim's staff is brought back wreathed with palm.")

Similes serve Dante as the palmer's staff serves earthly pilgrims;
they support his claim to have made the journey. Thus Dante

appeals often to landmarks familiar to his audience, such as Montereggione seen through a gradually dissipating mist (*Inf.* XXXI, 34–45). The vividness they add to the text may not directly describe the terrain, but in their detail they assert the capaciousness of his memory; and by making the reader participate imaginatively in creating them, they lend credibility to incredible descriptions.

Beyond their descriptive realism, the similes of the *Commedia* serve a deeper strategy. They embody stylistically the philosophical argument about the structure of reality on which the poem is grounded. This argument attempts to persuade the reader that the universe, not only within but also outside the poem, comprises a hierarchy of analogically related levels that may be ascended gradually, step by step, from lower to higher and highest. When the poet uses similes, he proves his harmony with an analogical world he does not invent, but only describes as it really is.[8] The argument justifies the narrative structure of the poem, for it outlines the steps by which Dante rises, through his devotion to Beatrice, from the "selva oscura" of materially directed love to properly directed spiritual love for God. Beatrice's eyes, reflecting alternately the human and divine images of Christ as she gazes at the Griffin, show the essential unity of a universe in which love is the motive force of all things:

> Mille disiri più che fiamma caldi
>> strinsermi li occhi a li occhi rilucenti,
>> che pur sopra 'l grifone stavan saldi.
> Come in lo specchio il sol, non altrimenti
>> la doppia fiera dentro vi raggiava,
>> or con altri, or con altri reggimenti. (*Purg.* XXXI, 118–23)

> (A thousand desires hotter than flame held my eyes on the shining eyes that remained ever fixed on the griffin. As the sun in a mirror, so was the twofold animal gleaming therewithin, now with the one, now with the other bearing.)

The mirroring syntax of this passage ("li occhi a li occhi," "or con altri, or con altri") suggests the intimacy with which the phenomenal world both mirrors and participates in the spiritual world, which gives it meaningful being.

The analogical relation between higher and lower levels of the hierarchical universe also underlies the narrative structure of *Paradiso*. The *cantica* is based on vision, but as Dante ascends through the spheres, he encounters souls that are not really there. His error is not revealed to him until he has attained the capacity to perceive more truly. When he arrives in the Empyrean, he sees the true home of the souls at first as a stream between two banks "dipinte di mirabil primavera" (painted with marvelous spring; *Par.* xxx, 63) of grass and flowers. Beatrice interprets the River of Light in words that apply to the sights of the lower spheres as well:

> "Il fiume e li topazi
> ch'entrano ed escono e'l rider de l'erbe
> son di lor vero umbriferi prefazi.
> Non che da sé sian queste cose acerbe;
> ma è difetto da la parte tua,
> che non hai viste ancor tanto superbe."   (*Par.* xxx, 76–81)

("The stream and the topazes which enter and issue, and the smiling of the grasses, are the shadowy prefaces of their truth; not that these things are defective [unripe] in themselves, but on your side is the defect, in that you do not yet have vision so exalted.")

The souls, though at home in the Empyrean amphitheater, have condescended to Dante's vision to help him ascend. The sudden revelation that their earlier presence was but prefatory dissolves the narrative basis of the *Paradiso*: it depends not on vision, but on defective vision. Yet dissolution occurs only after Dante has already mounted, by the erroneous rungs of the mystical ladder, to the point where he can see that his ascent has been based on the unripe—but useful—fictions written by the heavens themselves.

The descent of the souls into the hierarchically ordered spheres matches the chain of condescension by which Mary, Lucy, and Beatrice intervene for Dante. Such condescension also corresponds to the Incarnation itself, in which God descended into a man in order to raise humankind back up to God. Incarnational poetry impels the *Commedia* from the corporeal vision of the *Inferno* to the imaginative vision of the *Purgatorio* and finally to the immaterial intellective vision of the *Paradiso*.[9] The condescension of the divine into the pilgrim's life raises his language from the palpable bodily poetry of hell, where souls are so material that Dante can step on Bocca degli Alberti's face and pull out his hair (*Inf.* XXXII, 78, 103–5), to the progressively more ethereal poetry of heaven, which finally can describe only the play of light on light. The similes of the *Commedia* argue stylistically that the structure of reality may be understood and acted on as a vast system of analogies. This argument is a crucial underpinning for Dante's claim that his human poetry is analogically related to God's Word, to God's books of nature and history; and that Dante's conversion recapitulates the central narratives of Christian sacred history, Exodus and the resurrection of Christ. The similes of the *Commedia*, though they themselves are present primarily as means to communicate— the human author's condescension to our ways of knowing— arise from a conviction that analogies are not arbitrary forms imposed from without; rather, they can express the essential relations of an allegorical universe.

Typological allegory constitutes a special kind of analogical language. Its salient features are first, that it operates through history, with prefiguring events of the Old Testament fulfilled in the New; second, that its prefiguration writes with things and events (*res*) as well as with words (*verba*), and that it is consequently both literally and figuratively true; and third, that as God's way of writing it does not originate from the personal desire that motivates merely verbal human analogies. The analogical relationship between figure and fulfillment resides in an "Urbild des Geschehens" (a primal paradigm of the event) eternally present and complete in God.[10] We may approach understanding of the analogy through retrospection, looking back from the New Testament to restore the veiled and incomplete meaning of the Old; but since the basis of the analogy dwells with God in eternity, full knowledge will come only at the moment toward which time has always been pointing, the second coming of Christ at the end of history. With this event, history itself will be subsumed into eternity.[11]

Allegorical analogies are not part of the world of commentary, or discours; rather, in Christian theology, they are part of the objective structure of history. They are not invented, but discovered. They exist because God has condescended to leave his imprint on history. His condescension also infuses the natural world, which exists in order to draw human beings "per creaturam ad Creatorem," from created things to the Creator.[12] If human language is characterized by its gestural function of pointing beyond words to meanings, so too the universe and time point beyond themselves to pure being. Allegory, which as a style of representation fundamentally points beyond, is also the form of human language best able to represent the gestures of the created world. Unlike similes, then, the analogies of allegory are not solely epistemological and linguistic. Because the world and time are God's texts, written to communicate to his people, allegory as a style joins human linguistic epistemology to ontology. The objective and the subjective, being and knowing (and teaching) are all fused in much the same way Dante's autobiographical "I"'s are fused. In Dante's design upon the world, the figures of allegory belong to the objective realm of histoire.

Dante's typological allegory consists chiefly in his use of the Exodus narrative. The centrality of the Exodus figure in the *Commedia*'s narrative of sacred exile and return has been well known since Singleton pointed it out.[13] The story, explicitly invoked by the souls singing Psalm 113, "In exitu Israël de Aegypto," at *Purgatorio* II, 46, retrospectively resolves the shadowy prologue scene of *Inferno* I into clear focus. When this landscape reappears as the sea-ringed desert slopes of *Purgatorio* I, Exodus enables Dante and us to reinterpret the spiritual journey with Lucy's vision. Lucy, the patron saint of the visually afflicted, looks down from heaven at the prologue's landscape and sees "la morte che 'l combatte / su la fiumana ove 'l mar non ha vanto" ("the death that assails him on that flood over which the sea has no vaunt"; *Inf.* II, 107–8). From her celestial perspective, she sees Dante, not pushed down a mountain by a ravening wolf, but foundering in the flooding waters of the River Jordan.[14] These swollen waters had also proved an impassable barrier to the Israelites until God (as he had with the Red Sea) parted its waters (Joshua 3:15–16). In the *Purgatorio*, we see in much more recognizable form the three passages of Exodus: the Red Sea, the long labor in the desert, and finally, the insignificant stream at the boundary of the Earthly Paradise, which is nonetheless as impassable as the flooding Jordan to Dante until he is infused with sanctifying grace.[15] Beatrice retrospectively glosses the successful outcome of Dante's journey in the Heaven of Gemini, where Dante has returned to his astral home, saying:

> "però li è conceduto che d'Egitto
> vegna in Ierusalemme per vedere,
> anzi ch 'l militar li sia prescritto." (*Par.* XXV, 55–57)

("Therefore it is granted him to come from Egypt to Jerusalem, that he may see, before his term of warfare is completed.")

Thus Dante's journey recapitulates the historical salvation of God's chosen people when they made their way from Egypt to the Promised Land, and the fulfillment and renewal of the promise of Exodus in Christ's redemptive sacrifice.[16]

The passages of Exodus do not end at the Earthly Paradise. The stream at the top of purgatory isolates the promised land of God's first contract with prelapsarian man from all subsequent human history; Eden is forever lost. But the promise is once again fulfilled through grace, and though Matelda and natural justification are no longer attainable in this fallen world,[17] Dante does reach the River of Light in *Paradiso*. The pastoral idyll he describes here fulfills the meadow of the Earthly Paradise:

> e vidi lume in forma di rivera
> fulvido di fulgore, intra due rive

dipinte di mirabil primavera.
Di tal fiumana uscian faville vive,
    e d'ogne parte si mettien ne' fiori,
    quasi rubin che oro circunscrive;
poi, come inebrïate da li odori,
    riprofondavan sé nel miro gurge,
    e s'una intrava, un'altra n'uscia fori.   (*Par.* xxx, 61–69)

(And I saw a light in form of a river glowing tawny between two
banks painted with marvelous spring. From out this river is-
sued living sparks and dropped on every side into the blossoms,
like rubies set in gold. Then, as if inebriated by the odors, they
plunged again into the wondrous flood, and as one was entering
another was issuing forth.)

The ontological status of this idyll is as difficult to decipher
as that of the prologue scene, whose shadows had been illumi-
nated by the light cast backward from the clear Exodus pattern
of the *Purgatorio*. Dante sees another repetition of the waters he
has been crossing repeatedly throughout his return from Egyp-
tian exile, but no subsequent revision illuminates this scene.
The same "Urbild des Geschehens" infuses both this vision and
its prior incarnation, the edenic garden at the top of purgatory.
In retrospect, the idyll of light transforms the Earthly Paradise
into a figure whose production we now witness in the translation of light into a spring scene of water, flowers, and gemlike
bees propagating the nectar of grace. But this vision is clearly
recognizable from the outset as a figure pointing beyond itself.
Beatrice has already announced its substance as "l'una a l'altra
milizia / di paradiso" ("the one and the other soldiery of Paradise"; *Par.* xxx, 43–44), and she makes clear afterward that
the stream, flowers, and gems are prefigurements (*Par.* xxx,
78). As in the Earthly Paradise, Dante must drink the metaphorical river in order to advance. When he does, the linear
river resolves itself into the circular form of eternity, and his
vision proves to be of the City of God. The pastoral language
remains, but it is less shadowy because Dante can now provide
(still metaphorical) antecedents: the rose is the court of heaven

blooming in the warmth of God, the Sun that creates this eternal spring; the angels of the second host dip in and out like bees gathering nectar.

The River of Light provides a model of how Dante, in generating his figurative journey, imitates the figures of God's speech that constitute human sacred history. Dante first experiences the pastoral landscape as literal; its tangible quality stands out primarily in contrast with the similes he uses to describe it. Moreover, the river is literal enough for him to drink from it with his eyes. And indeed, only by his act of "drinking" does the scene reveal itself to be a shadow of its real significance. The River of Light, and the Rose and amphitheater that successively replace it, are not so much figures of speech as of vision and experience. Thus, although the initial reality of the pastoral scene is contingent and limited, it nonetheless remains real enough to provide the means by which Dante transcends it. Its transformations correspond to the double nature of figural events in Scriptures. Old Testament history was real enough to those who participated in its events, and no less literally true because these events are "figures of experience" foreshadowing what is more fully present in Christ. Yet from the temporal perspective of the New Testament, the reality of the Old is contingent in the same way as the River of Light here. Looking back, we see them as shadows cast by the solid body of God's providence incarnate.

However, the Incarnation that fulfills Old Testament history is but another layer of figuration in God's discourse of history; the advent of the Word itself is a figure of the promised end. Augustine, writing about Paul's discussion of Christ as the corporeal fulfillment of God's intention, sheds some light on the essentially figurative nature of the Incarnation:

> Satis est ergo scire corporale aliquid vel proprie dici, cum de corporibus agitur, vel etiam translato vocabulo, sicut dictum est, *Quia in ipse inhabitat omnis plenitudo divinitatis corporaliter.* Neque enim divinitas corpus est, sed quia sacramenta Veteris Testamenti appellat umbras futuri, propter umbrarum com-

parationem corporaliter dixit habitare in Christo plenitudinem
divinitatis, quod in illo impleantur omnia, quae in illis umbris
figurata sunt, ac sic quodammodo umbrarum illarum ipse sit
corpus [Colossians 2:9, 17], hoc est figurarum et significa-
tionum illarum ipse sit veritas. Sicut ergo ipsae figurae signi-
ficative, translato utique vocabulo, non proprie dictae sunt umbrae; ita et quod ait plenitudinem divinitatis corporaliter habitare, translato verbo usus est.[18]

(It is therefore enough to know that something is called "corporeal" either literally, when it refers to bodies, or figuratively,
as when it is said: "For in him dwells all the fulness of the divine
corporeally." For divinity is not a corporeal thing, but because
[Paul] calls the promises of the Old Testament the shadows of
things to come, he said that the fulness of divinity dwells in
Christ corporeally due to the counterparts of the shadows. For
all things which are figured in these shadows are made full in
Him, and thus He is in a certain sense the body of these shadows [Colossians 2:9, 17]; that is, He is the truth of these figures
and foreshadowings. Therefore, just as these figures and foreshadowings are not called shadows literally, but certainly by
means of a figure of speech, so also when he said that the fulness
of divinity dwells "corporeally," he made use of a figure of
speech.)

In making the once solidly literal landscape of the Earthly Paradise—the scene of Christ's advent into his own life—a contingent foreshadowing of the River of Light, Dante precisely captures the forward thrust of the Incarnation as a figure and a
promise of things to come. Just as the Old Testament Exodus
was real enough for its participants, so too is the landscape at
the top of purgatory a literal scene of action for the pilgrim, at
least until it draws him up to the heavenly exemplar that infuses
it with meaning.

The two pastoral scenes place the *Commedia* in history with
respect to two paradises outside the poem. The Earthly Paradise
looks back to Eden, the beginning of human history and also,
since the Fall, the beginning of human allegorical language as

a necessary, indirect way of knowing God. If the Earthly Paradise looks forward within the poem to the River of Light, now the River of Light looks forward to the eternal garden that is the real City of God, tended by "l'ortolano etterno" (the Eternal Gardener; *Par*. XXVI, 65). In its final form, this too lies outside the poem, for only at the end of time will it be full of souls. Then it will finally erase the history and the created gardens of our world, which are God's means of leading us back to paradise. Beatrice tells Dante that only a few seats remain empty (*Par*. XXX, 130–31); the fullness of time is near. But until then, this narrative is defined by time and memory, both personal and historical; and the incompleteness of the *Commedia* is the incompleteness of human history itself.

Condescension and the pattern of prefigurement and fulfillment also inform Dante's "poetic typology."[19] As in Scriptures, earlier events within the *Commedia* are the *umbrae futuri* of their own later fulfillments. The relationship between the Earthly Paradise and the River of Light exemplifies this poetic typology when the heavenly pastoral idyll transforms its earthly predecessor. The special irony of the *Inferno* works in much the same manner, with fulfillments from "higher" in the poem retrospectively infusing "lower" scenes and completing the meaning they had initially lacked. The ghoulish figure of Bertran de Born, the Provençal political poet who put art to the service of strife in his poems glorifying war, and who supposedly set the "young King" Henry against his father, Henry II of England, captures the essence of infernal irony. Bertran carries his head severed from his trunk, swinging it like a lantern; and Dante writes "Di sé facea a sé stesso lucerna" (Of itself it was making a lamp for itself; *Inf*. XXVIII, 124). The full enormity of Bertran's abuse of political poetry is completed only by Statius's later praise of Virgil:

> "Facesti come quei che va di notte,
>   che porta il lume dietro e sé non giova,
>   ma dopo sé fa le persone dotte . . ."   (*Purg*. XXII, 67–69)

("You were like one who goes by night and carries the light behind him and profits not himself, but makes those wise who follow him . . .")

Only when we encounter the recapitulated lantern motif here
do we realize the Virgilian framework into which Bertran's
schismatic political poetry should, but does not, fit.[20] Though
his punishment is at first only grimly literal, it also embodies
a figure of speech: if there is a body politic, then he is the poet
who dismembered it. Dante consequently dismembers Bertran.

Examples abound of infernal irony retrospectively infused
with meaning; I will limit myself here to Francesca and Ugolino. Francesca, buffeted by the furious winds of the second circle, becomes entirely comprehensible only when we meet Piccarda in *Paradiso* III, and read Beatrice's distinction in the next
canto between the right will, which endures, and the will that
consents to the force of external violence. Piccarda, a nun of St.
Clare, was forced into a marriage to which her heart never consented. The steadiness of her will gives the lie to Francesca's
tale of involuntary imitation of the book she and Paolo read.
Within this framework, we realize that the hurricane material-
izes another figure of speech. It does not represent external circumstances, to which Francesca still sees herself subjected;
rather, it incarnates the internal winds of passion to which she
has consented. The very exteriority of the winds signals the distortion in Francesca's way of thinking.

The "bestial segno" (bestial sign; *Inf.* XXXII, 133) of Ugolino is more complex. Gnawing at Archbishop Ruggieri's neck
like a dog, Ugolino is the frighteningly literal bestialization of
an eminent man. His punishment translates the betrayals in the
political community of Pisa, the "novella Tebe" (modern
Thebes; *Inf.* XXXIII, 89), into the much more intimate betrayal
of family ties. The story Ugolino tells is filled with potentially
redemptive meaning, which he does not hear. His sons offer
themselves to him in language that recalls Isaac's uncompre-
hending willingness to allow Abraham to make of him a ho-
locaust. This filial sacrifice established the covenant between

God and Israel, and moreover prefigured the sacrificial Lamb of God who carried the act through on the cross (see "tal croce," such torture or such a cross; *Inf.* XXXIII, 87).[21] The selflessness of his children offers Ugolino the redemptive possibility of a communion sadly lacking in the Pisa he has betrayed:

> "Padre, assai ci fia men doglia
> se tu mangi di noi: tu ne vestisti
> queste misere carni, e tu le spoglia."   (*Inf.* XXXIII, 61–63)

("Father, it will be far less painful to us if you eat of us; you did clothe us with this wretched flesh, and do you strip us of it!")

Ugolino understands only a physical meaning for the flesh he needs, never the eucharistic bread that is food for the soul. In the reticently implied ending of his story—in which he first says that hunger overcame sorrow, and then sinks his teeth once again into his "fiero pasto" (savage repast; *Inf.* XXXIII, 1)—the bodily flesh of his children becomes his food. The action poisons his soul by turning the potentially spiritual communion offered by his sons into cannibalism. Here redemptive language, pointedly divested of its usual spiritual significance and become only flesh, exemplifies the materialization involved in infernal irony.

Yet Ugolino did not eat his children; or at least there is nothing in the historical record to suggest that he cannibalized the two sons and two grandsons with whom he was imprisoned and died in Pisa's Torre della Fame in 1289.[22] Whatever the historical truth of Ugolino's last days, Dante has used cannibalism as a metaphor to convey the horrific quality of political betrayal. That Ugolino's savage repast is metaphorical becomes clear only later, in the invective against "serva Italia" (servile Italy; *Purg.* VI, 76). Here Dante supplies the figure of speech that lies behind Ugolino's fictional act:

> e ora in te non stanno sanza guerra
> li vivi tuoi, e l'un l'altro si rode
> di quei ch'un muro e una fossa serra.   (*Purg.* VI, 82–84)

(and now in you your living abide not without war, and of those whom one wall and one moat shut in, one gnaws at the other!)

As we see from Ugolino, infernal irony is grounded in spiritual significance; it is the "affirmative irony" Judson Boyce Allen and Theresa Anne Moritz describe as a characteristic medieval habit of thought.[23] The absence of the divine spirit is a pointed one, and the meanings suppressed by Bertran, Francesca, and Ugolino issue finally anyway. Like God's writing in scriptural history, the meanings unfold to completion through narrative time. Allegory and irony, both "other-speaking" figures, are grounded in spiritual meaning originating in God. Even infernal irony does not prevent full meaning from issuing forth precisely in this finely articulated analogical universe written by the divine finger. The earlier events of the *Commedia* contain the seeds of their own fulfillment; they too are *umbrae futuri*, the shadow-bearing prefaces of their truth.

Thus Dante's typological allegory posits an analogical universe in which the spirit of divine significance is made flesh in the body of human language. Since Dante reports what he saw and heard on his journey, the eschatological universe created by God, the prefigurations and fulfillments of his allegories and ironies are not simply stylistic characteristics of the text. They are built into the structure of a universe he merely describes. Dante's analogies, through which he condescends to his readers' limited knowledge in order to make higher truths known, form the stylistic strategy that best reflects God's condescension into human history and into the history of the individual Dante. Moreover, the conversion this allegorical style presents reenacts tropologically the figural history of Exodus; this too imitates God's writing of history, for in conversion as in Exodus, God infuses his spiritual intentions into time in order to raise mankind again. Historical and moral truth are at one with Dante's allegorical style.

The *Commedia* culminates in a vision of the universe united in a single point of space and time. Dante uses the traditional metaphor of the created universe as a book written by God's finger to describe this sight, and to strengthen its analogy to his own poem:[24]

Nel suo profondo vidi che s'interna,
    legato con amore in un volume,
    ciò che per l'universo si squaderna:
sustanze e accidenti e lor costume
    quasi conflati insieme, per tal modo
    che ciò ch'i' dico è un semplice lume.   (*Par.* XXXIII, 85–90)

(In its depth I saw ingathered, bound by love in one single volume, that which is dispersed in leaves [disquartoed] throughout the universe: substances and accidents and their relations,
as though fused together in such a way that what I tell is but a
simple light.)

Because of the overarching significance of this metaphor—presenting God as a specifically verbal *Deus artifex*—all the passages in the *Commedia* that call attention to the poem's bookishness work in an unexpected direction. Rather than dispelling
the illusion of verisimilitude, the literary self-consciousness of
the *Commedia* confirms it as an authentic imitation of the world
beyond the text. Its acts of literary confession accomplish the
poet's spiritual conversion; and with the "penne" of desire on
which he mounts to the Empyrean, he also writes the poem.
The references to "questa comedìa" (this Comedy; *Inf.* XVI,
128) and " 'l poema sacro" (the sacred poem; *Par.* XXV, 1), and
to the difficulties of composition,[25] strengthen the poem's close
imitation of God's book of the universe, just as its allegorical
style strengthens its imitation of God's book of history. Instead
of distinguishing between fiction and the reality it represents,
the *Commedia*'s bookish references urge the lack of distinction.
Though the poem is but a preface to the great book written by
God, the analogical relationship is very close indeed.

Dante's strategy of allegorical prefigurement and fulfillment
evades the problem of ordinary analogies, which, arising out of
the speaker rather than his subject, depend on the speaker's reliability—something we might suspect in a poem that records
a consummation so devoutly to be wished. Once again, however, the authenticating effect of Dante's allegorical language
depends on his conversion. This experience alone would give

him the knowledge of the world after death through which he travels. His claim to write allegory in the manner of the theologians is a bold move in literary fiction,[26] but one resulting in an argument about the world beyond the text that the entire structure of Christian belief would encourage his readers to accept as true. The similarity of his book to the books of God confirms the conversion which alone could give him knowledge of that world.

Allegorical analogies are a response to the often chaotic human experience of the world and time. They seek an eternally stable pattern of meaning to order the flux and mutability that so rule our affairs. This mutability conditions the world of *Troilus and Criseyde*, and the poem is about the attempts of both lovers and poet to find just the stable, immutable eternity promised by Dante's allegory. The lovers, of course, are betrayed by their desire; so is the poet by his. Chaucer's efforts to overcome time and change in his poetic language are as subject as the love affair itself to the devastations wrought by mutability. As in romance generally,[27] Chaucer moves to fix his poem in the continuous literary tradition embodied in his revered "olde bokes." He invokes the passage of time in order to lend history's authenticity to his story, and simultaneously attempts to overcome time by renewing Lollius's old book for his present audience.[28] In this poem more than in any other, Chaucer also employs the cousins of literary tradition, proverbs,[29] which are not restricted to the written transmission of language. Conventional modes of expression, whether oral or written, can provide the same kind of stay against time and change as written texts, and because proverbs represent an extreme form of convention—so petrified in form that they seem immutable—they crystallize the issue of mutability in the language of the *Troilus*, and illuminate Chaucer's use of other conventional language as well.

One might call proverbs "pseudotypology"; because they are part of the common stock of language shared by the poet and his audience, they, like Dante's allegory, are not so much invented as discovered. Yet they are not discovered in the objects they are intended to illuminate; they are applied, often without sufficiently convincing motivation, by the characters to each other and their world, and by the narrator to the distant world of Troy. Analogies of language in the *Troilus* frequently do not correspond to nonverbal analogies. Because this common stock of language is connected only very loosely to what it is meant to describe, the power of human language in general to comprehend the nature of reality comes under question. And because Dante claims this power for his allegorical language, the questionable authenticity of Chaucer's proverbs and conventions of literary love language—many of them expressed in language drawn from the *Commedia*—also questions Dante's analogical construction of reality.

Most studies of the *Troilus*'s proverbs, which concentrate on them as means of characterization, define the term so broadly as to include nearly any *sententia*.[30] Such breadth of definition, however, obscures the special character of the analogical language I wish to single out. I will focus not on the whole range of traditional *sententiae* present in Chaucer's poem, but on a narrower class: those that use metaphor to comment by analogy on their contexts.[31]

The Latin etymon of "proverb," *proverbium*, provides a key for my discussion. *Proverbium*, according to the Oxford English Dictionary a (recognized) set of words put forth, or an old saying, is in turn derived from *pro-* + *verb-* + the collective suffix *-ium*; it is thus one group of words standing for another group. The etymon suggests that the essence of a proverb lies in its recursiveness; that is, it is something like a pronoun or any other grammatical "pro-form" ("does," for instance), which shifts meaning according to the antecedent it replaces. To use the more traditional terminology of medieval grammatical theory, *proverbium*, words standing for other words, thus paraphrases Isidore of Seville's famous definition of *allegoria* as *alienoloquium*, speaking by means of other things,[32] and echoes Dante's definition of allegory in the Letter to Can Grande: "Nam *allegoria* dicitur ab *alleon* graece, quod in latinum dicitur *alienum*, sive *diversum*" (For allegory is named from Greek *alleon* [other], which in Latin is called *alienum* [other] or *diversum* [different]).[33]

Since I am arguing for a fundamental distinction between the allegorical analogies of the *Commedia* and the proverbial analogies of the *Troilus*, this consonance raises a problem. However, Isidore classifies as subcategories under allegory a number of tropes—irony, for instance—that we are accustomed to separating today. Isidore's definition is too general to be useful in distinguishing between Dante's and Chaucer's characteristic modes of analogy. I risk the charge here that I merely toss out the nearly universal medieval definition, which includes proverbs as a subclass under allegory, when it proves inconvenient for my analysis. But I think my ahistoricity is justified by two reasons. First, Dante distinguished among allegories, consciously choosing "the allegory of poets" for the *Convivio*, and consciously rejecting it in favor of "the allegory of theologians" for the *Commedia*.[34] In both works, he flew in the face of the scholastics, who held poetry in contempt and denied that it could partake of the mode whose goal was Truth; even in the *Convivio* he assumed that poets had the power to choose theological allegory as their signifying mode.[35] Second, after Dante at least, theological allegory was available to poets as a stylistic alternative; Chaucer did not choose it. Therefore, whether or not either poet would have considered proverbs to be a kind of allegory, the differences between Dante's typological allegory and Chaucer's proverbs remain significant.

The typological analogies of the *Commedia* differ from the proverbial analogies of the *Troilus* in three respects. First, they treat time differently. The scriptural allegory Dante imitates posits a historical relationship between the two terms of the analogy. The first term is a precursor to the second, and gives the second its manner of expression. The "before" and "after" of scriptural allegory gives history a linear shape, but the meaning of the whole is nonetheless present in each constituent event, as in Augustine's famous meditation on time as a sentence spoken by God.[36]

Second, although scriptural allegory functions through repetition, it is not iterative, but incremental; meaning accrues with each repetition and raises the figure to a higher level of signification. Thus Exodus in the Old Testament refers to a literal, historical salvation. When it is repeated in the New Testament, and subsequently in the life of the individual converting Christian, it is a spiritual salvation achieved by a symbolic crossing out of Egypt. Nonetheless, the original event loses none of its literal historicity when it is revealed as the typological prefiguration of its later symbolic fulfillment. The allegory retains its literal truth when the spiritual level is added to it; as a form of analogy, the first term signifies the second term, which in turn clarifies the full meaning of the first.

Dante's imitation of typological allegory in the *Commedia* also functions in this "vertical" manner; the successive Exodus crossings, from the failure of *Inferno* I to the successful passages in the *Purgatorio* and through the River of Light, exemplify this pattern of raising through repetition. The later, progressively more spiritual crossings take their form from the earlier ones (whether within or outside the poem); they also retrospectively reveal the hidden meaning of those earlier crossings. Historically, the Old Testament Exodus and its New Testament fulfillment in Christ's redemption (as well as the failed Ulyssean crossing of the prologue scene in Dante's own life) are necessary antecedents to Dante's ultimate arrival on the other side of the stream. The connection between the two terms in allegorical analogy is thus extremely close, indeed integral; for both parts are grounded in a supernatural significance imparted to history by God. The third and final difference, then, is that Dante's allegory is not "imposed" from without; rather it proceeds from the real analogical structure of the nonverbal world.

None of this can be said of proverbial analogies. They posit no history; nor do they gain incremental meaning through repetition. Rather, they function "horizontally," by substitution. The literal level of a proverb is replaced completely by the meaning it derives from its metaphorical application to the context in which it is used. To the extent that proverbs are alle-

gories at all, they are not of the typological variety we find in
Dante, but of the imposed "this-for-that" translation sometimes thought wholly to define the protean allegorical mode.[37]
The loss of the literal level of meaning in proverbs is important
in my argument, and should be kept in mind as I define more
precisely the nature of proverbial analogies.

Proverbs are crystallized statements of traditional wisdom
that posit a logical relationship "mediating between two aspects of reality, two levels of classification."[38] They possess a peculiar linguistic status derived from the fact that, although
their propositions appear specific and unambiguous, they cannot be treated as such without comic effect or reduced meaning.
Each term in a proverb—for example, "leopard" in "the leopard cannot change his spots"—is stable with respect to the rest
of the sequence, and cannot be substituted for by any ordinarily
available lexical alternative. The equally possible statement
"the Holstein cow cannot change her spots" communicates a
good deal less, in part because it lacks the weight of traditional
use.[39] A proverb must be treated as a single significant unit, fro-
zen and selected whole from the lexicon of all complete proverbial statements, rather than as an ordinary syntagm produced
by the combinative freedom of the speaker. The comforting authority of a proverb stems from its ambiguous linguistic character as a stereotypically fixed articulation.[40] Individual speakers
"invent" a proverb each time they articulate it; but because the
same articulation recurs frequently, it appears to describe a universal truth of nature which many have observed and remarked
on. Once selected, a proverb issues automatically, and hence
seems outside human influence and more objective than ordinary sentences.

Nonetheless, proverbs do allow a certain amount of combinative freedom. Because they belong to the language system independent of their articulation in any specific instance, a
speaker can say, "You know about the leopard's spots," and although he does not state the proverb in its complete form, this
does not inhibit its "automatic issue" as an essential underlying

element. The full significance of his statement depends on a double mediation, for although he refers directly only to the proverb, the proverb in turn supplies the metaphoric analogy he wishes to make. Even the statement "the Holstein cow . . ." can acquire a significance beyond the literal, if speaker and listener understand it as an allusion to the traditional proverb its structure so resembles. A proverb's form can change within limits as long as both parties understand it as the realization of a shared concept. The immutability of a proverb's form resides at the level of deep structure, a systemic concept that individual "performances" more or less realize—if less, then the speaker invokes the proverb by way of allusion, or as a proverbial phrase.

In contrast, a proverb's meaning is not immutable. Its semantic mutability results from its character as a specific, metaphoric statement describing another situation by analogy. Metaphor distinguishes proverb from maxim, which is a general, literal sententia. Both maxims and proverbs can comment on the same situation, as in the following example from Nigel Barley: Albert Smith, previously convicted of theft, has been caught stealing again. We can either invoke the maxim "once a thief, always a thief," without metaphoric mediation; or we can comment "the leopard cannot change his spots." The logical relation the proverb posits is: leopard is to Albert Smith as spots are to criminality.[41] The proverb acquires its authority by inviting us to derive, from two examples, a general law of nature. Proverb and maxim demand different responses; if we were to mistake "the leopard cannot change his spots" for a maxim, for instance, we would react as Judy Holliday did in *Born Yesterday*—"Of course not—they're right there, in his fur!" This comic failure to acknowledge the analogy disrupts the proverb's power.[42]

In this example, both maxim and proverb apply equally well to the recidivist thief Albert Smith. However, if we take the case of my own office, always messy despite my frequent resolves to reform, we can no longer say "once a thief, always a thief." The maxim refers only to those it describes literally—thieves. But we can still say "the leopard cannot change his spots," for the proverb easily encompasses both situations, even with the change in gender.[43] This is possible because, although we can manipulate a proverb's form only within limits, its meaning depends on the context that evokes it.[44]

Conversely a proverb, always available to shape thought, may create as well as describe a situation. Albert Smith may relapse into thievery because he has already identified himself as the leopard unable to change his spots. Or, if he is innocent but falsely accused on the basis of circumstantial evidence, the proverb offers a convenient, familiar—and prejudicial—framework conditioning the observer's perceptions. Belief in the proverb may cause justice to light on him as the likely suspect, and his subsequent conviction circularly confirms the authority of the old saying that influenced it. The proverb thus becomes a self-fulfilling expectation.

That a proverb's meaning varies according to context undermines the stability promised by fixed form. When we find proverbs as mutable as they are in the *Troilus*,[45] then, it is not Chaucer's peculiar invention. Proverbs by their nature betray the expectations of stability they arouse, and the regularity with which they do so here suggests that the poet consciously exploits proverbial language's semantic slippage in order to comment on language in general. In transmitting traditional forms of expression, Chaucer seeks not only to validate "truth by finding it in the past and making it live in the present,"[46] but also to warn us of the limitations of this endeavor.

Chaucer exploits this semantic slippage most clearly in the variations on a single proverb, and on a set of catalogues expressed in proverbial language. My first example appears at 1.257–58: "The yerde is bet that bowen wole and wynde / Than that that brest." These words, or allusions to the proverb they represent, recur frequently in the *Troilus*. Here the poet, considering the irresistible power of Love, offers two possible descriptions of the shortly-to-be-smitten Troilus. He can be

either the stick that breaks, if he tries to withstand Love's inex-
orable attack, or the flexible stick that survives by bending, if
he succumbs. The second alternative is clearly more desirable,
and because Troilus indeed succumbs, he defines himself as the
stick that bends.

The next reference to the proverb changes the image slightly,
but not the fundamental structure or concept:

> "And reed that boweth down for every blast,
> Ful lightly, cesse wynd, it wol aryse;
> But so nyl nought an ook, when it is cast . . ."   (II.1387–89)

The comparison between a flexible survivor and a stiff victim
remains, although a reed and an oak tree replace the two
"yerdes."[47] More important, the contextual reference has
shifted as well as the desirable alternative, for the image offers
two descriptions of Criseyde. She can either bend but never
break, never yielding to Troilus's advances; or she can seem un-
bending until she finally gives way altogether, becoming Troilus's mistress. To this point, Troilus has met with little success
in breeching the lady's defenses, and Pandarus wants the second
alternative to assure his friend that, if he perseveres, Criseyde
will eventually capitulate. Combining this with the first realization of the proverb, we can see a developing distinction:
Troilus is the reed (or "yerde") that bends and Criseyde is the
oak that falls.

Thus Pandarus. But the poet begins to have other ideas,
which complicate the facile distinction I have just made.
Shortly before Pandarus defines Criseyde in such comforting—
and wishful—terms, the poet describes the growth of Troilus's
desire with several proverbial analogies, including:

> Or as an ook comth of a litel spir,
> So thorough this lettre, which that she hym sente
> Encrescen gan desir, of which he brente.   (II.1335–37)

This is our familiar "greak oaks from little acorns grow," mod-
ified slightly to sustain the opposition between a great stiff

stick and a small flexible one. But here Troilus is an oak grown
out of his former sapling state, and through the juxtaposition
of "Thorugh more wode or col, the more fir" (II. 1332), he is an
oak threatened with conflagration. Chaucer thus qualifies the
optimistic reference to Criseyde as an oak ripe for the axe before
Pandarus makes it.

The same images reappear in Book III's consummation scene:

> And as aboute a tree, with many a twiste,
> Bytrent and writh the swote wodebynde,
> Gan ech of hem in armes other wynde.   (III.1230–32)

Though this is not precisely an allusion to the original proverb
(indeed its literary lineage is impeccable),[48] the diction—tree,
wode-, -bynde, wynde—urges us to connect it to the other related images I have cited. Here at the moment of stasis, the ze-
nith before the poem's declining action, the image also reaches
a state of equilibrium. Unlike earlier instances, it makes no opposed identifications. Instead, it is a picture of mutuality, and
thus sustains the ambiguity that arose when Troilus grew into
an oak not sixty lines before Criseyde became one too.

The final transformation of the proverb comes in Book IV.
When Troilus returns from the parliamentary decision to exchange Criseyde for Antenor, Chaucer describes him with an
image from Dante that I have discussed before in another context:

> And as in wynter leves ben biraft,
> Ech after other, til the tree be bare,
> So that ther nys but bark and braunche ilaft,
> Lith Troilus, byraft of ech welfare,
> Ibounden in the blake bark of care,
> Disposed wood out of his wit to breyde,
> So sore hym sat the chaungynge of Criseyde.   (IV.225–31)

Again, the image alludes to rather than states the proverb. But
when Troilus is thus clearly bound in a tree, it supplies a new
reference for the matrix of language initiated by "The yerde is

bet that bowen wole and wynde / Than that that brest." If Troilus has finally put down roots, then Criseyde, although the poem does not state it in so many words, becomes the bending reed, surviving each storm because of her lack of firmness. But what are we to do with the proverb, which seemed so clear and authoritative when it first appeared? Its clarity depends on isolating a moment in the narrative, but we cannot choose to see the analogy as the characters do, in terms of action in time. For us, as for Chaucer, the entire cumulative text—beginning, middle, and end—exists simultaneously, transcending the gradual unfolding of meaning.

It is worth comparing the temporal isolation on which the referential clarity of this proverb depends with the temporal relations of the *Commedia*'s analogies. There, each image depends on the cumulative meaning of all its permutations in the poem. It may change in form and local reference, even appearing antithetical to the force of its later recapitulations; this is true of the mediation of literature in *Inferno* V, for instance. But when the entire matrix is read together, as in memory, the ironic inversions of the *Inferno* do not undermine their positive revisions (the mediation of the book in Statius's life, for instance). Rather, allegorical permutations record the same progress we find in the narrative as a whole; the earlier versions, incomplete and aggressively literal, clearly indicate the spirit they lack, and thus imply the later corrections that replace them. Allegory in the *Commedia* works synecdochically, so that it is possible to read the whole from each part. Hence there is no conflict, as there is in the *Troilus*, between isolated moments in the narrative as it unfolds and the text as a whole.[49]

The trustworthy stability of meaning in the *Commedia*'s allegory contrasts sharply with the variability of proverbs in the *Troilus*. The transformations in reference they undergo cause us to distrust them, wherever they appear, as figures pretending to stability, calling upon a venerable tradition that crystallizes their structure—but not their meaning. In Chaucer's poem,

repetition leads to retraction or reversal, not completion or fulfillment. The oak-reed proverb is an example of a failed attempt
to secure stability through traditional language.

If we return for a moment to the original context of "The
yerde is bet that bowen wole and wynde / Than that that brest,"
we can see that in exposing the proverb's semantic instability,
Chaucer from the beginning invokes and undermines the im-
pulse toward eternity that gives birth to such immutable ways
of speaking. The proverb is introduced near the end of the
poem's first set of proverbs and sententiae. Here, at 1.211–66,
Chaucer interrupts his narrative of how Troilus falls in love
with a series of generalizations that link the distant world of
Troy firmly to that of his audience. Troilus becomes an "ensam-
ple" (1.232) showing the universal power of love to subject all
to the "lawe of kynde" (1.238); his case is amplified by the proverbial Bayard, who must in like manner endure "horses lawe"
(1.223).[50] With Bayard, Chaucer extends the general validity of
statements like "For kaught is proud, and kaught is debonaire"
(1.214) and "But alday faileth thing that fooles wenden" (1.216)
downward through the hierarchy of created being. With the
following stanza, he extends it to all times and places:

> That this be soth, hath preved and doth yit.
> For this trowe I ye knowen alle or some,
> Men reden nat that folk han gretter wit
> Than they that han be most with love ynome;
> And strengest folk ben therwith overcome,
> The worthiest and grettest of degree:
> This was, and is, and yet men shall it see.   (1.239–45)

The second-person "ye" subjects Chaucer's English audience as
well to the law that rules Troy. And most important, the inclusive range of past, present, and future in the first and last lines
of this stanza suggests an immutable truth that overcomes
time.

Yet by the end of the poem all has changed; the poet tells his
audience "Repeyreth hom fro worldly vanyte" (V.1837) such as

the love that binds Troilus in its traces here, for the law of grace has superseded the "lawe of kynde" and transformed history itself. The limitations thus imposed on the universal, exemplary nature of Troilus's experience add a new dimension to the dramatic irony of the taunt he aims at his lovelorn companions in the instant before conceiving his own great passion: "Ther nys nat oon kan war by other be" (1.203). And Chaucer, at the moment of introducing proverbs as a way of figuring his Trojan world, stresses all the expectations of stability and universality proverbs usually arouse—but does so in order to frustrate these desires in the end.

The attempt to secure stability through traditional language, and the failure of that attempt, are aspects of a deliberate poetic strategy in the *Troilus*. When Chaucer bids his poem farewell, he includes a plea for the preservation of his text: "So prey I God that non myswrite the, / Ne the mysmetre for defaute of tonge" (V.1795–96). Exact transmission and order of a poetic text are crucial to its meaning, but the act of making such a plea implies a recognition that change and instability in language are likely. The poet demonstrates the importance of order to meaning with a set of catalogues, once again expressed in proverbial language, that seek to establish a metaphorical relationship between fixed natural phenomena and the course of the love affair. Each catalogue comments optimistically on the ascending action. But Chaucer realizes its potential for reversal when he transposes the order of terms or shifts the context in the descending action of the last two books.

The first catalogue appears in the midst of Troilus's lovesickness for Criseyde. Here Pandarus attempts to exorcise Troilus's despair with:

> "For thilke grownd that bereth the wedes wikke
> Bereth ek thise holsom herbes, as ful ofte
> Next the foule netle, rough and thikke,
> The rose waxeth swoote and smothe and softe;
> And next the valeye is the hil o-lofte;

> And next the derke nyght the glade morwe;
> And also joie is next the fyn of sorwe."   (1.946–52)

Immediately before Troilus faints in Book III, Chaucer antici-
pates the imminent transformation of abject failure into success
with a similar list:

> But now help God to quenchen al this sorwe!
> So hope I that he shal, for he best may.
> For I have seyn of a ful misty morwe
> Folowen ful ofte a myrie someris day;
> And after wynter foloweth grene May;
> Men sen alday, and reden ek in stories,
> That after sharpe shoures ben victories.   (III.1058–64)

By offering the cycles of nature as metaphors for the course of
the love affair, this string of proverbs makes the reversal of for-
tune seem inevitable. A low point is but a prelude to a high
one. But once again, proverbial language proves treacherous; by
invoking cycles as analogues to the story, the words also imply
their own inversion. It is equally true that after day comes
night, winter follows summer, and victories—especially at
Troy—often evaporate in the renewal of strife.

What transpires later in the *Troilus* only emphasizes the double potential of these proverbs. Their apparent fixity of meaning is compromised in Book IV, when Pandarus, offering his ineffectual consolations "for the nones alle" (IV.428), uses the
same words to convey the opposite advice:

> "For also seur as day comth after nyght,
> The newe love, labour, or oother wo,
> Or elles selde seying of a wight,
> Don olde affecciouns alle over-go."   (IV.421–24)

Proverbs cannot transfer the stability of fixed natural cycles
to the love affair—a metaphorical analogy is after all nothing
more than a verbal act—but they succeed in arousing Troilus's
expectation of the immutability they seem to promise. Promising so much, they must inevitably disappoint, and when
Chaucer puts an end to the illusion he himself perpetuated, its

unreality is starkly evident: "The day goth faste, and after that
com eve, / And yet com nought to Troilus Criseyde" (V. 1142–
43). After these lines, we can no longer deny that analogies first
proposed by verbal fiat can be disposed of in the same manner.
Proverbs are apt not to describe reality as it is, but only as we
wish it to be. They function in the optative mode: the relationship Chaucer reveals in them, taking with one hand what he
gives with the other, is not between love and nature, but between love and the element of desire implicit in the language
we use to formulate reality.

In this context, let us return for a moment to the point at
which Criseyde becomes an oak, a passage extraordinary for the
conspicuousness of its rhetoric:*

> "Peraunter thynkestow: though it be so,
> That Kynde wolde don hire to bygynne
> To have a manere routhe upon my woo,
> Seyth Daunger, 'Nay, thow shalt me nevere wynne!'
> So reulith hire hir hertes gost withinne,
> That though she bende, yeet she stant on roote;
> What in effect is this unto my boote?
>
> "Thenk here-ayeins: whan that the stordy ook,
> On which men hakketh ofte, for the nones,
> Receyved hath the happy fallyng strook,
> The greete sweigh doth it come al at ones,
> As done thise rokkes or thise milnestones;
> For swifter cours comth thyng that is of wighte,
> Whan it descendeth, than don thynges lighte.
>
> "And reed that boweth down for every blast,
> Ful lightly, cesse wynd, it wol aryse;
> But so nyl nought an ook, whan it is cast;
> It nedeth me nought the longe to forbise." (II. 1373–90)

*The formulation of the oak-reed image in the last quoted stanza is the one that
most resembles Dante's, at *Par.* XXVI, 85–87: "Come la fronda che flette la cima /
nel transito del vento, e poi si leva / per la propria virtù che la soblima" (As the bough
which bends its top at passing of the wind, and then uplifts itself by its own virtue
which raises it). Like the internal workings of Chaucer's passage, however, the resemblance is verbal alone; the ideas and references could not be more different.

By introducing the first half of the proverbial comparison with "peraunter," Pandarus identifies it as a rhetorical "opposite" to be discarded when he proposes the second half. This kind of rhetorical structure arouses strong expectations; as soon as we read "peraunter," we know that "Thenk here-ayeins" will eventually follow. When Cicero writes "non solo," we know that "sed etiam" will complete his thought, and when a sonneteer begins his octave with "when," we expect the sestet to begin with "then." A poet can play with these expectations; when Shakespeare, in Sonnet 29, postpones "then" until a line and a half into the sestet, he brings our desire for rhetorical fulfillment to such a pitch that when it finally comes, our spirits, out of pure relief, soar "like to the lark at break of day arising." Here, Pandarus arouses the same expectations in Troilus, and strengthens his rhetorical structure with proverbial language, which itself expresses our desires rather than more objective reality.

What prevents the argument from convincing is its purely verbal nature. In addition to the emphatic rhetorical structure, the speech is adorned with personifications. And curiously, amidst all the words, Criseyde disappears. The bending reed clearly refers to her at first; but thereafter, not even a pronoun connects her to rhetorical fulfillment. Formally, structure and proverb mime arousal and fulfillment of desire, but this verbal process can be extended to reality outside of words only by an act of faith. Pandarus does not say, "Criseyde is an oak"; he merely suggests, "Think of it this way." Troilus believes because he wants to, but Chaucer, by stressing the fictive rhetorical nature of the passage, asks us to consider whether its formal fulfillment applies to the nonverbal world as well. And when, in an act parallel to his retraction of a relationship between natural cycles and the love affair, he makes Criseyde ultimately resemble a bending reed more than a sturdy oak, he shows that there is no necessary connection. The proverbial image Pandarus invokes does not describe Criseyde; it replaces her.

Thus the stability proverbial language promises is doubly

deceptive, because the same words can mean various things in various contexts, and because people use them to deceive themselves into believing that what they want to see is what is really there to see. These characteristics of the *Troilus*'s proverbs illuminate the use of two other kinds of "borrowed language." First, within the poem, Chaucer stresses the same elements in other conventional manners of speaking, primarily the poetic words of love, which seek to fix experience by supplying a stable context of verbal tradition. These traditions constitute a lexicon like that of proverbs. Proverbs, with their complete loss of the literal level, are perhaps the clearest examples of the poem's treatment of conventional forms of language, because in them the semantic slippage within a rigid, "borrowed" form is the greatest. They thus put into sharp focus the double nature of Chaucer's use of convention in the *Troilus*. Through conventional language, he aims both to assure the authenticity of the experience he narrates, and simultaneously to undermine the authenticity of the narration. Second, Chaucer's choice of proverbs as the chief strategy of analogical language comments on the poem from which he borrowed so much conventional love language, the *Commedia*.

The inherent mutability of proverbs also marks the conventions that appropriate the language of religion and the hunt to describe the love affair. Pandarus, who knows the "olde daunce," teaches Troilus the words that portray love as a religious experience.[51] But he finds himself suddenly out of control just as his schemes verge on success. As Troilus waits in the secret stew, Pandarus bids him make ready, "For thow shalt in to hevene blisse wende" (III.704), then adding, "this nyght shal I make it weel, / Or casten al the gruwel in the fire" (III.710–11). Troilus's response, a prayer for "hevene blisse," shows how thoroughly the parodic language of religion has shaped his conception of love. In Troilus's eyes, Criseyde is a goddess who bestows grace, and whose presence defines the meaning of his world.[52] Love becomes the Beatific Vision in his hymn at III.1254–74, a passage imitated from Bernard's prayer in *Para-*

diso XXXIII. Pandarus understands the nature of *amour courtois*: its conventions are games, fictions, or literally lies.[53] Only figuratively can a mortal woman be a goddess, and when a lover expresses his feelings in such terms, he refracts objective reality through the prism of his desire. But Troilus does not use the conventions merely in a manner of speaking; believing, as it appears, in a natural link between *res* and *verbum*, he treats the two as commutative terms. However, he is a character in a poem where this relationship is problematic, where language as convention rather than ideal is a theme.[54] In his desire for transcendence, Troilus reifies the fiction, and confounds words with the reality they only indirectly represent.

Attempting to create a reality to match the verbal image, Troilus creates instead a burden too heavy for any mortal love to bear. His religious language is a convention abstracted from its original context, and as we know from proverbs, contextual shift signals mutability. Although Troilus tries thereby to make his love transcend time and place, to seize the day and fix it eternally, the unfixed nature of his language—along with his blind trust in it—betrays him. In a sense, this traditional form of love discourse causes the tragic end of the story by arousing expectations it cannot fulfill.[55] Through his language Troilus seeks to achieve the stability of the ideal; instead, he makes the comparative inadequacy of the real stand out the more sharply.

The same reversal—poetic description confounded with the thing described—is also at work in the convention of love as the hunt. By shaping action and response after its image, this convention creates rather than describes the course of events. Troilus is a bird of prey, a noble falcon who catches his victim; and "What myghte or may the sely larke seye, / Whan that the sperhauk hath it in his foot?" (III.1191–92). Much of what goes wrong in the love affair can be traced to this attitude, arising out of conventions of artistic language, toward love. Hunt imagery determines that the men pursue Criseyde with little regard for her desires and fears; and she responds like a chased animal, postponing the inevitable for as long as possible.

In Criseyde's second courtship, Chaucer exploits the duplicities of convention by reusing the same elements in a different context. We are alerted to the similarities by repetition of a maxim, previously uttered by Pandarus: "Unknowe, unkist, and lost that is unsought" (I.809). And by Criseyde: "He which that nothing undertaketh, / Nothyng n'acheveth" (II.807–8). Diomede's version echoes Criseyde's: "For he that naught n'asaieth, naught n'acheveth" (v.784). The poet recalls the convention of love as hunt when Diomede considers

> How he may best, with shortest taryinge,
> Into his net Criseydes herte brynge.
> To this entent he koude nevere fyne;
> To fisshen hire he leyde out hook and lyne. (v.774–77)

The hunt seems embedded in the prehistory of the poem,[56] enabling Cassandra to interpret Troilus's dream correctly by establishing Diomede's descent from Meleager, the mythological slayer of the Calydonian boar.[57] Diomede's promises resemble Troilus's previous oath of service, and in this relationship as well, the lovers exchange (the same) jewelry. Language and action are essentially the same as, if speedier than, when Troilus wooed Criseyde—but for all the similarity, most readers find the two courtships very different.[58]

This difference results from a paradox of conventional language; when Troilus expresses himself with the time-honored words of *amour courtois*, we would gladly believe in the permanence he seeks to achieve by linking his love with tradition. Yet when Diomede uses the same words, precisely because they are conventional, he casts a shadow of impermanence on the stability Troilus thought to guarantee. At this point in the poem, many readers pore back over the development of Criseyde's character, searching for clues of the emotional instability that would make her infidelity comprehensible.[59] It is unlikely, however, that Chaucer intended it to be fully comprehensible, or for Criseyde to be an open book for us to read. In her second courtship, he deliberately withdraws from full psychological realism. This withdrawal should alert us to other concerns in the text. Criseyde's betrayal was in the story Chaucer found; to it he adds a second betrayal, that of the conventional language of love. Because of this second betrayal, the narrator breaks off in his report of Diomede's love talk immediately after the Greek assumes what Muscatine calls "an air of Troilus": "What sholde I telle his wordes that he seyde? / He spak inough for o day at the meeste" (v.946–47).[60] The narrator cannot bear the retrospective effects of Diomede's love language on Troilus's.

In giving Troilus and Diomede the same words to woo Criseyde, Chaucer confronts us with the impossibility of Troilus's idealist treatment of language. The words of love are conventions meaning only what we can agree they mean. Just as with proverbs, their significance is relative to context—speaker, listener, the worsening political circumstances in Troy—and their fixed form derives not so much from true semantic stability as from our desire for such an absolute relation to reality: *ut nomina consequentia rerum sint*.

Troilus and Criseyde thus expresses a profoundly ambivalent attitude toward conventional love language. On the one hand, religious parody exalts the love affair, embellishing it with the lovely poetic fictions of *amour courtois*; the use of convention in general, because of its history of repetition, mimes timelessness. But on the other, Troilus's use of convention to seek the ideal and the timeless imperils an inevitably imperfect human love, for then conventional language must shape his vision of what is possible. Mistaking the flexible reed of poetry for a sturdy oak, he expects his love to take its nature from the words of love. On this level, the *Troilus* is about both the desire to fix an inherently mortal, transitory love permanently, and the impossibility of fulfilling that desire. When Chaucer proclaims his purpose to help lovers to "pleyne," he means the information and "usage" he will pass on to his audience about the steps of the "olde daunce." But he also means the traps that await us if we begin to believe literally that love is the same thing as conventional love language.

Proverbs illuminate a second sphere of "borrowed language," Chaucer's Dantean usages. The *Troilus* owes a good deal of its love language to the *Commedia*, and the manner in which it appears comments directly on the original context. The irony characterizing the proverbs of the *Troilus* offers a more sweeping, if more elusive, critique of Dante's poem and its poetic typology.

Because the language borrowed from the *Commedia* supports the plot borrowing from *Inferno* v, we should seek an underlying strategy to account for Chaucer's Dantean usages in a manner consonant with the poem's profound ambivalence toward the way language represents experience. That Chaucer's intent in borrowing does not match Dante's original intent can be seen from the jumbled order of the echoes. Chaucer has Troilus mix infernal and paradisal elements without distinguishing between them; Troilus uses them both to express the ideal of transcendent love he seeks. He lives the plot of *Inferno* v while speaking words from the *Paradiso*.[61] Furthermore, Chaucer consistently presents the change of heart Troilus undergoes when he falls in love with Criseyde as a conversion. But Troilus is a pagan; he has no access to the grace that would allow him to convert in Dante's terms. So he cannot gain the knowledge he needs to distinguish properly directed from misdirected love, the love of Beatrice from the love of Francesca.

In a sense, Troilus is an "unconverted" reader of the *Commedia*;[62] it is as if he read Dante's poem and, in his idealistic ignorance, found not the fine distinctions within parallels Dante had labored to build, but only language of the most exalted sort with which to express his experience and expectations of human love. Chaucer perhaps equivocates by locating his response to Dante in a story set in pagan Troy; but he had Dante's own precedent of Ripheus, Virgil's just Trojan mysteriously become a Christian *ante litteram*.[63] And the equivocation allows Chaucer to show the dangers of the *Commedia*'s language of love without thoroughly undercutting the admirable idealism of his protagonist.[64] For the *Commedia* expresses true and false transcendence in the same terms, the language of human love. And in the reading by someone who, like Troilus, does not share Dante's conversion and the knowledge that proceeds from it, the two poles of infernal and paradisal love converge. When Chaucer appropriates the words of the *Paradiso* for the new context of Troilus's hymn praising human love, their stable grounding in the divine is lost; and they become subject instead to the shifting sands of human contextual signification. Dante's reformed poetry proves in the *Troilus* as treacherous as any other form of borrowed language—proverbs, conventional literary love language, or even the story Chaucer retells from his sources. It merely arouses expectations and desires for transcendence, which cannot be fulfilled in the sublunary world of mutability we share with Troilus.

The deceptive nature of proverbs makes them an ideal vehicle through which to counter the manner in which the *Commedia*'s analogical language represents reality. I call them pseudo-typologies for this reason: their odd linguistic status, as a stable sequence selected whole from the lexicon of proverbial language, leads to their automatic issue even when their actual performance is fragmentary or distorted. They seem outside human influence and hence more objective—less subject to the distortions that might arise from the speaker's personal perspective—than ordinary, freely combined sentences. In this respect they mime the nonhuman origins of the *Commedia*'s typological allegory, a system of signification written into human history and the created world by God. Divine in origin, typological allegory is stable in meaning and does not depend on the intentions of the speaker who utters the human words that express it; it too issues automatically. Hence it subsumes even infernal irony, which affirms the very meaning it seems to deny. The sacrifice Ugolino's sons offer their father, however literally Ugolino himself understands it, refers ultimately to the reenacted sacrifice of the eucharist; and the negation of the sacrament's spiritual sustenance of its communicants magnifies the horror of his "fiero pasto." The allegory of the *Commedia* works because its integral relation to an allegorical *seculum*, in which the whole of history and the world proceeds from God and points back to him, fuses the true nature of reality with human ways of understanding and speaking it.

Chaucer's proverbs are inherently ironic. They promise stability, yet deliver only flux; they seem to offer an objective description of the world, yet reflect the speaker's desires as much as they do any reality independent of desire. Indeed, they point more to the gaps and failures of human understanding that call proverbs forth in the first place; their analogies are imposed on the world, and the resemblances they seek to define are accidental, not substantial. There is no necessary difference in the ontological assumptions about the world made in allegorical and proverbial analogies; but there is a vast epistemological difference. Proverbs stress the distance between the human knowing subject and the world he seeks to understand.

Thus the traditional definition of proverbs as "little allegories" is misleading. They are not subsumed under allegory; rather, they parody it, and Chaucer's irony is thus not as affirmative as Dante's.[65] This is *not* to say that it denies meaning. To the extent that Chaucer's ironic proverbs expose the false claims of a pagan world, they affirm the superiority of the Christian world; and indeed Chaucer ends his poem with a Dantean prayer to the Trinity and Mary. However, Chaucer does not include his own poem, as Dante did his, in the affirmation afforded by the only Word that can offer a stable ground of signification. The Christian poet of the *Troilus* is as deeply implicated as Pandarus in flawed analogies, both in his proverbs and in the very act of making fictions. The enterprise of mimetic fiction rests on an analogy between the invented world of the poem and the real world outside it. We ask that our fictions point in some way to reality; hence the poet's desire for authenticity.[66] Chaucer's participation in analogies influenced by his desires suggests that we cannot limit the ironies to Troy. The

failed typology of proverbs not only exposes the falseness of a
pagan construction of the world, but questions the claims of a
Christian poet as well.

The proverbs of the *Troilus* betray the capacity of human analogical language to point beyond itself to nonlinguistic analogies as well.[67] Because the critique is so general, we should no
more confine it to the *Troilus* than to Troy. Instead, we should
extend it to the supremely analogical poem whose poetic typology is parodied by proverbs. Through them, Chaucer questions Dante's claim that his allegorical language describes, but
in no way invents, the allegorically structured reality of a logocentric universe, and that it does so without the distortions of
desire inherent in human analogies. Despite the internal stability of God's allegorical significations, the act of making an
analogy between his manner of writing and any human poet's
literary efforts remains optative.

The *Commedia*'s authenticity rests finally on our faith that,
because he has converted, Dante's knowledge and intentions toward us are trustworthy. Still, because the literal level of the
Commedia is a fictive analogy to the central narrative of Christian history, the possibility remains that the narrator, desiring
conversion and salvation so strongly, deludes himself into believing his wish to be reality. Perhaps more important, the language of desire in which Dante phrases his transcendent experience may well mislead readers whose wills are not yet justified. They might then believe that they, following the pilgrim
through the poem, have achieved the supreme object of desire
as well—a formulation even more likely to be rankest wish fulfillment. Through the antitypology of proverbs in the *Troilus*,
Chaucer probes the authenticity of Dante's poetic typology,
and lays open the possibility that the truth of Dante's analogies
may well be as illusory and evanescent as the permanence Troilus sought in loving Criseyde.

5. Circumscribing the World

The ending of the *Troilus* is a fitting culmination of all that has gone before: the gaps in understanding that characterize Chaucer's analogies between two worlds; his effort to narrate true history; his intimacy with his characters long dead. When the ending rends the tense accord of witness and history, it also dispels any illusion of "true" fiction. Chaucer's ending could not be more different from Dante's, with its reunification of the "I" and final union with God. Yet borrowings from the *Commedia* ask us to see a relationship between Dante's poetic treatment of transcendence and Chaucer's.

Through the first borrowing, from the scenes in which Dante looks down at earth from the Heaven of Gemini (*Par.* XXII, 133–38, and XXVII, 82–84), Chaucer renders the pagan Troilus's soul journey in partially Dantean terms, thus suggesting that Troilus's final vision resembles Dante's. The second borrowing, the Dantean prayer to the Trinity (*Par.* XIV, 28–30), ends the poem. These borrowings imply a criticism of the *Commedia* achieved by foregrounding significant differences defined against the concern common to both endings, the relationship between poetic language and transcendence. Chaucer departs from Dante by making Troilus's transcendence depend on a death that is real, not metaphorical. Moreover, Troilus's transcendence leads to a silence that cannot generate the poem; it can only end it. The ending of the *Troilus* accomplishes a series of disjunctions separating Troilus from the world, pagans from Christians, and the poet from Troilus;[1] these disjunctions answer the *Commedia*'s final transcendent union. By combining them with the Dantean borrowings, Chaucer questions the authenticity of Dante's rendering of transcendence in poetic language.

In order to understand Chaucer's final departures from poetry in the Dantean vein, we must trace the relations between language and transcendence in the *Paradiso*. Although the ending of the *Commedia* is marked by the joining of the autobiographical "I"'s, and the union of Dante with God, the final *cantica* also chronicles the failures of sense, memory, and expression: in other words, of everything upon which the journey and the poem have depended thus far. Paradoxically, however, these failures attest to the reality of Dante's experience of transcendence.

Dante models the flight of the *Paradiso* on Pauline vision and its exegetical tradition.[2] Paul's *raptus* to the third heaven (in 2 Corinthians 12:2–4) exemplified for Augustine the highest means by which human beings could regain "paradise" in this life: a direct, unmediated intellective vision of God.[3] Later, Richard of St. Victor transformed Augustine's visionary taxonomy into a dynamic ladder by which the contemplative could mount toward God.[4] Glossing the opening lines of the *Paradiso* with a truncated version of 2 Corinthians in the Letter to Can Grande, Dante refers also to the Transfiguration as it is treated by Richard and others.[5] Like Dante, Richard associated the Transfiguration with Paul's *raptus*; both events characterize the highest levels of contemplation, at which vision exceeds sense and reason and instead attains a direct intuition of the highest mysteries of the faith. When the three disciples at the Transfiguration fall on their faces and can report no more, they represent for Richard the threefold failure of sense, memory, and reason at the sight of God in his essence.[6] These failures result in the inexpressibility to which Paul referred as "arcana verba, quae non licet homini loqui" (secret words, which it is not granted to man to utter; 2 Corinthians 12:4).

Dante opens the *cantica* with the failure of knowledge, memory, and tongue:

Nel ciel che più de la sua luce prende
   fu' io, e vidi cose che ridire
   né sa né può chi di là sù discende;
perché appressando sé al suo disire,
   nostro intelletto si profonda tanto,
   che dietro la memoria non può ire.   *(Par. I, 4–9)*

(I have been in the heaven that most receives of His light, and
have seen things which whoso descends from up there has neither the knowledge nor the power to relate, because, as it draws
near to its desire, our intellect enters so deep that memory cannot go back upon the track.)

Though his "trasumanar" may not be signified in words (*Par.*
I, 70–71), Dante still needs some way of expanding Paul's spare
reference to "arcana verba" in order to write the poem at all.
Had Dante followed Paul's inability or refusal to speak, the *Paradiso* would be characterized chiefly by inarticulateness. Instead, it is filled with the speaking silences of inexpressibility
by which Dante circumscribes what he cannot describe. The
Pauline visionary tradition provides him with a framework to
map radical inexpressibility onto the writing of a poem. The
failures of sense, memory, and reason join with Paul's silence,
and transform Dante's inability to represent his vision into a
unique authenticating strategy.

The levels of the *Paradiso* are demarcated by periodic lapses
in Dante's ability to see and hear; indeed, he is drawn upward
as much by defect of vision as by vision itself. Ordinary human
reason, based on sensory perception, cannot explain the moon-
spots; Beatrice tells Dante that his wings of reason are inade-
quate (*Par.* II, 56–57). Reason's greatest inadequacy occurs at
the most transcendent level of vision, in canto XXXIII. Richard
describes this kind of contemplation as above and contrary to
reason; it is immediate intuition.[7] Although we are not accustomed to thinking in these terms, human reason seems a contingent faculty in the *Paradiso*. The faculty by which we demonstrate the evidence of things we believe, reason, would be
superfluous—just as faith and hope are superfluous to the

blessed—were we able to see them directly. In the last series of visions, when Dante sees the image of man inscribed in the Trinity, reason avails him not at all. He sees but fails to understand the mystery, for the wings of reason do not suffice. Dante represents the failure of reason with a simile from the sublimely rational science of mathematics:

> Qual è 'l geomètra che tutto s'affige
>   per misurar lo cerchio, e non ritrova,
>   pensando, quel principio ond' elli indige,
> tal era io a quella vista nova . . .   (*Par.* XXXIII, 133–36)

(As is the geometer who wholly applies himself to measure the circle, and finds not, in pondering, the principle of which he is in need, such was I at that new sight . . .)

That sense and reason should fall short at the highest levels of vision is a truism of contemplation. It is the other failures, of memory and expression, that pose the most interesting problems in a literary work that represents itself as a book of memory. A large part of both the poignancy and the exultation of the *Paradiso* stems from these failures and from Dante's efforts to circumvent them.

From the outset Dante presents memory's failure as an aspect of Pauline inexpressibility. Forgetting presupposes a prior experience of vision or intellect; hence this failure shares the paradoxical quality of most inexpressibility topoi—the manner in which an experience is absent from the text confirms its reality more resonantly than could a description predicated on full memory. Twice at the summit of his vision, Dante clings to joy as the only vestige of the highest heaven. Both times he circumscribes his experience with visual images of dissolution and scattering in order to intimate the primal unity he saw but cannot recover, for himself or for us. The second image is a figure for the entire poem:

> Nel suo profondo vidi che s'interna,
>   legato con amore in un volume,
>   ciò che per l'universo si squaderna:

sustanze e accidenti e lor costume
  quasi conflati insieme, per tal modo
  che ciò ch'i' dico è un semplice lume.
La forma universal di questo nodo
  credo ch'i' vidi, perché più di largo
  dicendo questo, mi sento ch'i' godo.   (*Par.* XXXIII, 85–93)

(In its depth I saw ingathered, bound by love in one single volume, that which is dispersed in leaves [disquartoed] throughout the universe: substances and accidents and their relations, as though fused together in such a way that what I tell is but a simple light. The universal form of this knot I believe that I saw, because, in telling this, I feel my joy increase.)

Memory grapples with the hopeless task of translating eternity into temporal terms. Ordinarily, this faculty overcomes the limitations of space and time, recalling to mind things no longer present corporeally. Memory is thus our simulacrum of eternity and immortality. Dante's poetry, both in the *Vita nuova* and here, is quintessentially memorial; yet he presents it as a book whose binding has been rent by its descent into the realm of time where it may be read. As a perfect memorial of Dante's experience, the *Commedia* fails; but by failing it attains greater authenticity in the measure that it points beyond itself to the eternity human memory cannot capture.

Memory both preserves and severs Dante's connection to transcendence. This results from the paradox of recording eternity with a temporally defined faculty. As Boethius lucidly explains, eternity is the eternal present; God's perspective does not distinguish past, present, and future into separate temporal moments.[8] Augustine writes that we perceive the present moment only after it is over, in memory, much as we understand syllables and words in retrospect, when contrastive sounds succeed one another to form intelligible utterances.[9] Human memory depends on interruption and contrast. Hence that memory exists at all in the *Paradiso* chronicles Dante's loss. For memory in the eternal regions does not resemble the human faculty, so wedded to time and change. Beatrice explains angelic memory thus:

> "Queste sustanze, poi che fur gioconde
>   de la faccia di Dio, non volser viso
>   da essa, da cui nulla si nasconde:
> però non hanno vedere interciso
>   da novo obietto, e però non bisogna
>   rememorar per concetto diviso . . ."   (*Par.* xxix, 76–81)

("These substances, since first they were gladdened by the face of God, have never turned their eyes from It, wherefrom nothing is concealed; so that their sight is never intercepted by a new object, that therefore they have no need to remember by reason of interrupted concept . . .")

Angels and the blessed souls do not remember by interrupted concept, but Dante does; his experience of paradise differs from that of its inhabitants. Conversion, spiritual death, and resurrection are not quite equivalent to the anagogical salvation of which they are a foretaste.

Hence despite the remembered joy, Dante cannot recover the rest of the vision as long as he remains timebound, and

> Un punto solo m'è maggior letargo
>   che venticinque secoli a la 'mpresa
>   che fé Nettuno ammirar l'ombra d'Argo.   (*Par.* xxxiii, 94–96)

(A single moment makes for me greater oblivion than five and twenty centuries have wrought upon the enterprise that made Neptune wonder at the shadow of the Argo.)

Although the direct comparison here is between 2,500 years and a single instant without temporal dimension (hence represented spatially; "un punto solo" also recalls the "solo un punto" at which Paolo and Francesca ceased reading, *Inf.* v, 132), Neptune's gaze is the more evocative part of the simile. Reversing the order of enlightenment in Plato's cave, the sea god here recognizes, at the moment of loss, the uninterrupted sunlight that had bathed his realm until the first ship broke its rays. Henceforward, though he can still remember that unbroken light had once shone, he can no longer recall what it had been. From his loss are born awareness, memory, and longing, the three movements of the human soul described in *Purgatorio* xxv, 83.

Because Dante has earlier represented himself as a new Jason (*Par.* II, 16–18), a *galeotto* steering the ship of his poem through seas never before attempted (*Purg.* I, 1–3; *Par.* II, 1–18), the simile captures in little the representative status of the *Paradiso*. The poem is a shadow cast by the solid body of paradise, and by its interruption of the light we may know that light exists. Dante's book of memory is a vain endeavor from the outset, yet it is precisely because the concept has been interrupted that he transcribes it at all. In human memory, as in Augustine's sentence, the contrastive sound ensuing upon the previous syllable generates meaning. Dante's single moment of oblivion likewise generates his poem of desire, always longing for return to the heavenly nest. Had he remained in the Empyrean, circling with the object of his desire, the poem would not have been written; for the love poet writes only in times of separation.

Dante's failure to express his unimaginable experience confirms its authenticity. Augustine linked the ontogeny of language with frustrated infantile desires,[10] and Dante in the *Paradiso* also associates the failure of language with a return to childhood, the primal state of innocence before separation from the maternal breast creates unfulfilled desire.[11] Having undergone the death of the old self, Dante now completes his conversion through a series of similes in which he follows Christ's edict: "Amen dico vobis, nisi conversi fueritis, et efficiamini sicut parvuli, non intrabitis in regnum caelorum" (Amen I say unto you, unless you be converted, and become as little children, you shall not enter into the kingdom of heaven; Matthew 18:3). The child similes of the *Paradiso* chart Dante's regression to a state of innocence before the buffetings of desire engender language. The first describes him as a sick infant:

> Ond' ella, appresso d'un pïo sospiro,
>   li occhi drizzò ver' me con quel sembiante
>   che madre fa sovra figlio deliro . . .   (*Par.* I, 100–102)

(Whereupon, after a pitying sigh, she turned her eyes on me with the look that a mother casts on her delirious child.)

In order to rise to the highest vision, Dante must become

> come fantolin che 'nver' la mamma
> tende le braccia, poi che 'l latte prese,
> per l'animo che 'nfin di fuor s'infiamma . . .
>
> (*Par.* XXIII, 121–23)

(. . . as an infant which, when it has taken the milk, stretches its arms toward its mother, its affection glowing forth . . .)

He achieves this condition, in two stages, in the Empyrean. The first comparison illustrates his desire:

> Non è fantin che sì sùbito rua
>   col volto verso il latte, se si svegli
>   molto tardato da l 'usanza sua,
> come fec' io . . .   (*Par.* XXX, 82–85)

(No infant, on waking far after its hour, so suddenly rushes with face toward the milk, as then did I . . .)

The final child simile of the poem records the bliss of his reunion with God:

> Omai sarà più corta mia favella,
>   pur a quel ch'io ricordo, che d'un fante
>   che bagni ancor la lingua a la mammella.
>
> (*Par.* XXXIII, 106–8)

(Now will my speech fall more short, even in respect to that which I remember, than that of an infant who still bathes his tongue at the breast.)

This *terzina* seals the inverse relationship between language and fulfilled desire. By the last canto, filled with disclaimers that his attempts to express transcendence are but pale similitudes of the real vision, Dante has indeed become the little child of which Beatrice speaks earlier (in language that should be compared to that of the confession scene at *Purg.* XXXI, 58–75):

"Fede e innocenza son reperte
  solo ne' parvoletti; poi ciascuna
  pria fugge che le guance sian coperte.
Tale, balbuzïendo ancor, digiuna,
  che poi divora, con la lingua sciolta,
  qualunque cibo per qualunque luna;
e tal, balbuzïendo, ama e ascolta
  la madre sua, che, con loquela intera,
  disïa poi di vederla sepolta."   (*Par.* XXVII, 127–35)

("Faith and innocence are found only in little children; then each flies away before the cheeks are covered. One, so long as he lisps, keeps the fasts, who afterward, when his tongue is free, devours any food through any mouth; and one, while he lisps, loves his mother and listens to her, who afterward, when his speech is full, longs to see her buried.")

One might expect the consequence of Dante's transformation into a stuttering infant (which etymologically means "not speaking") to be silence. But like the memory that depends on interrupted concept, the language of transcendence itself reveals the poet's poignant loss. Returning to the world and time, he retains only traces of his vision in his memory. If silence results from the fulfillment of desire, the words of the poem represent the renewed flight of language written with the wings ("penne") of desire. Only by writing can Dante feel his joy renewed; but as in any love poem, the words that renew his joy result from his separation from the object of his desire.

Nonetheless, the shortcomings of language also index the reality of Dante's pilgrimage to God. The similes that record his diminishing ability to express his eternal vision in temporal terms also transform him from a full-bearded man in his middle years into the child Christ says he must resemble to attain the kingdom of heaven. The suckling infant that Dante comes to resemble by the last canto has as little desire as he has speech; remaining at his mother's breast, he needs no words. Because language originates out of frustrated desire, inexpressibility in the *Paradiso* demonstrates the truth of the vision it can only cir-

cumscribe. Dante may be unable to express the traditionally silent experience of paradise, but he can suggest, through the
failure of expression and through the inverse relationship between language and fulfilled desire, that it indeed took place.
The poem's representational failure before a vision beyond human words thus authenticates the conversion upon which all
else depends.

The child similes through which Dante obliquely portrays
the stilling of all desire suggest the completion of his conversion, and so does the grammar of the last canto. If the death of
the old self was before manifested by the *passato remoto*, the narrative tense of histoire, now Dante's verbs imply the other half
of his metamorphosis, and substantiate the rebirth of the "I"
hitherto recorded only indirectly in simile. Suddenly, in *Paradiso* XXXIII, the present tense predominates. The single passage
of direct discourse, Bernard's address to Mary, is not a narrative
but a prayer. Asking Mary to grant Dante the final vision, Bernard generally uses the present tense with future relevance.[12]
The rest of the canto contains seven similes, two of which refer
to incidents in the remote past, expressed in the *passato remoto*;
and five of which are expressed in the present tense. There are
several apostrophes, also in the present tense.

Moreover, Dante frequently describes his vision in the "eternal present," as in the last line: "l'amor che move il sole e l'altre
stelle" (the Love which moves the sun and the other stars; *Par.*
XXXIII, 145). Presumably Dante could have availed himself of
this stative present throughout, for the otherworldly landscape
does not cease to exist when he ceases to describe it. However,
elsewhere he generally chooses the descriptive tense of histoire,
the *imperfetto*. His otherworld is thus usually presented not ontologically but cognitively, as filtered through the consciousness of one who has seen it in the past. Here, the grammatical
difference is minimized, for the final source of the present tense
in the last canto is Dante's emphasis on the twin efforts to remember and record his vision: in other words, on the moment
of composition rather than on the past experience he tries

thereby to recreate. Five of the seven similes illuminate the poet's present rather than the pilgrim's past, and Dante adds to these comparisons by directly describing his difficulties. This passage contains both modes:

> Da quinci innanzi il mio veder fu maggio
> che 'l parlar mostra, ch'a tal vista cede,
> e cede la memoria a tanto oltraggio.
> Qual è colüi che sognando vede,
> che dopo 'l sogno la passione impressa
> rimane, e l'altro a la mente non riede,
> cotal son io, ché quasi tutta cessa
> mia visïone, e ancor mi distilla
> nel core il dolce che nacque da essa.
> Così la neve al sol si disigilla;
> così al vento ne le foglie levi
> si perdea la sentenza di Sibilla.   (*Par.* XXXIII, 55–66)

(Thenceforward my vision was greater than speech can show, which fails at such a sight, and at such excess memory fails. As is he who dreaming sees, and after the dream the passion remains imprinted and the rest returns not to the mind; such am I, for my vision almost wholly fades away, yet does the sweetness that was born of it still drop within my heart. Thus is the snow unsealed by the sun; thus in the wind, on the light leaves, the Sibyl's oracle was lost.)

Finally, Dante subordinates the past to the present by subordinating his narrative passages to verbs in the present tense: "Io credo, per l'acume ch'io soffersi / del vivo raggio . . ." (I believe that, because of the keenness that I endured from the living ray . . . ; *Par.* XXXIII, 76–77).

As a result of prayer, similes, and emphasis on the moment of composition, there is very little in the last canto that can be called narrative. Only ten verbs are first-person *passato remoto*, six concentrated in one passage beginning and ending with verbs in the present tense (ll. 76–93). Partially because Dante describes his vision as stative or as ongoing action, he often expresses even definitely past parts in the imperfect. Consequently, there are also only twelve verbs in the third-person *passato remoto*. The role played by the tense associated so strongly with the death of his former self and the disjunction of pilgrim from poet thus shrinks to nearly nothing. What stands out here is not the difference between the two "I" 's, but their identity. The canto brings the pilgrim out of the past and into the present, so to speak, and the vision reported here reunites him with the poet struggling to recover his remembered experience.

The reunification generates the poem, both in its success and in its failure. To the extent that the pilgrim's conversion into poet succeeds, it provides the subject of the poem and Dante's capacity to write it. Because the "I" has been united, the pilgrim's experience is treasured up in the memory of the poet, who can report it authentically in the first person. To the extent that reunification fails, it gives Dante the reason to write the poem. For now, no longer circling in the Empyrean, his desire is stilled no more. It moves the words with which Dante seeks to renew the joy he feels in remembering the traces of his transcendence. The final lines of the *Commedia*, which unite "il mio disio e 'l *velle*" (the object of my desire and my will; *Par.* XXXIII, 143), join Dante for a moment to God. Like the infant nestled at his mother's breast, in this moment he has no need of the language that can express only separation and unfulfilled desire. The ending of the *Commedia* mimes the superfluity of words in the face of union with God; there is no more to say.

Yet because Dante voyages to the Empyrean while still in this life, he cannot sustain the moment of perfect peace. Inevitably, he must relinquish it until he joins for all eternity the ranks of the blessed in the celestial rose. Meanwhile, he must return to time; and the loss of his moment of eternity leads to the memory, founded on interrupted concept, and the language, predicated on loss and separation, that generate the poem. Dante's only consolation for loss is the writing of the *Commedia*: both for the private joy he feels when he gets it right; and for the community of author and readers—the inclusive "nostra" of the poem's first line—that he establishes when he can convince us, if not of what he saw, then that it is there to see. Dante's separation from God becomes the means, in his rhetorical love poem, by which he joins himself to us.

Though they are also founded on the relations of silence, speaking, and transcendence, the disjunctions at the end of the *Troilus* are of another order. Chaucer's separation from Troilus is prefigured by Pandarus's departure. When Pandarus is confronted with the final proof of Criseyde's faithlessness and with his own inability to console Troilus, he stands "As stille as ston; a word ne kowde he seye" (v.1729). He momentarily breaks his silence to say "What sholde I seyen? I hate, ywys, Cryseyde;/ And, God woot, I wol hate hire evermore!" (v.1732–33). However, his final speech begins and ends with speechlessness; his last words are "I kan namore seye" (v.1743). With this announcement, Chaucer's surrogate poet within the text departs.

Chaucer, of course, does not lapse into speechlessness upon separation from Criseyde. However, silence enters the poem at Troilus's departure. His transcendence is marked by silence; he does not speak, but only "in hym self . . . lough" (v.1821). His silent transcendence creates a parallel (limited by the difference between symbolic and literal death) to the *Commedia* at the level of narrative action; the poet's silence in the face of his protagonist's transcendence definitively breaks with the *Commedia* at the level of narrative authentication.

Chaucer's silences begin with his farewell to "litel myn tragedye" at v.1786–98; here, he consigns the *Troilus* to a modest place at the steps to a house of fame, reverently subject to its great forebears but also exalted by association with such illustrious pillars of narrative poetry as Virgil, Ovid, Homer, Lucan, and Statius.[13] In fact, the figure echoes the *Thebaid*'s envy-postscript: "vive, precor; nec tu divinam Aeneida tempta,/ sed longe sequere et vestigia semper adora" (O live, I pray! nor rival the divine *Aeneid*, but follow afar and ever venerate its footsteps).[14] Chaucer explicitly links his poem to a tradition that will help preserve it from the silence of oblivion; in the next stanza, he prays that the *Troilus* will also survive the ravages of linguistic variation and textual corruption. Behind both stanzas lies the concern that the same forces that destroyed the love affair—time and mutability—might also conspire to silence Chaucer as a poet who seeks to communicate to a comprehending audience.

Comprehension is the key here, for Chaucer follows his plea with a case in point: the short-circuited insight into whatever knowledge Troilus gains from his posthumous flight to the spheres.[15] The odd sequence of the ending has often troubled readers: first a plea for the survival and understanding of the text; next the final events of the narrative; then the summary of the poem's action and moral; and finally the dedication to Gower and Strode, and the subdued prayer to the Trinity and Mary.[16] One problem is the presence of the "litel bok" stanzas before the report of Troilus's death and soul journey. These two stanzas shift the focus of the following eight (until Chaucer's next mention of the "forme of olde clerkis speche / In poetrie"; v. 1854–55) to include, in addition to the story, the dynamics of narrative rendering.[17] We must try to ascertain not only the nature of Troilus's final understanding, but also the relationship between his perspective and Chaucer's. The difficulties of these eight stanzas make a great deal of sense if we approach them, with an eye toward narrative discourse, as Chaucer's strategy to illustrate the problem of communicating unshared experience. What we have here is silence, not in the strict sense of wordlessness, but in the more suggestive sense of a failure to understand. Throughout the *Troilus* there has been a tension between two mutually exclusive truth-claims, that of objective history and that of personal experience. Each alternately compels our belief, and each undermines the other. The sequence at the end exposes the inauthenticity of a narrative rendered either as distant history or through the narrator's personal implication. The analogies between worlds—pagan then and Christian now, fictive and real—held together by the narrator, crumble in the face of otherworldly experience.

The first stanza reports Troilus's death, and the next three his flight to the sphere of the fixed stars:[18]

And whan that he was slayn in this manere,
His lighte goost ful blisfully is went
Up to the holughnesse of the eighthe spere,
In convers letyng everich element;
And ther he saugh with ful avysement
The erratik sterres, herkenyng armonye
With sownes ful of hevenyssh melodie.

And down from thennes faste he gan avyse
This litel spot of erthe that with the se
Embraced is, and fully gan despise
This wrecched world, and held al vanite
To respect of the pleyn felicite
That is in hevene above; and at the laste,
Ther he was slayn his lokyng down he caste,

And in himself he lough right at the wo
Of hem that wepten for his deth so faste,
And dampned al oure werk that foloweth so
The blynde lust, the which that may nat laste,
And sholden al oure herte on heven caste;
And forth he wente, shortly for to telle,
Ther as Mercurye sorted hym to dwelle.   (v. 1807–27)

Chaucer's primary source for this passage is the *Teseida*, XI. 1–3, which records Arcita's similar translation; but the flight has analogues in the *Somnium Scipionis*, Boethius, Lucan, and, of course, Dante.[19] The language in which Chaucer reports Troilus's understanding is quite faithful to Boccaccio's, and where it is not, the differences can be accounted for as echoes of Dante's first glance down to earth from the Heaven of Gemini. Troilus "despise[s] / This wrecched world" in terms stronger than "e ogni cosa da nulla stimare / a rispetto del ciel" (and held everything as nothing in comparison to heaven),[20] but no stronger than in Boccaccio's passage as a whole.[21] In the third stanza, Boccaccio has Arcita smile,

> . . . la vanitate
> forte dannando dell' umane genti,
> li quai, da tenebrosa cechitate
> mattamente oscurati nelle menti,

> seguon del mondo la falsa biltate,
> lasciando il cielo . . .
>
> (Teseida, XI, 3)

(. . . strongly condemning the vanity of human beings, who, dimly obscured in their minds by dark blindness, follow the false beauty of the world, leaving heaven.)

From this description, one can easily read the attitude that informs Troilus's "and fully gan despise / This wrecched world" (v. 1816–17).

But Chaucer weakens Boccaccio's repudiation of the world in three ways. First, he moves "del mondo la falsa biltate" to the "Swich fyn" stanza; I will discuss this later. Second, he reduces Boccaccio's powerful description of human blindness to one word, "blynde." Finally, there is an important modal distinction between the two passages. On the one hand, Boccaccio tells what human beings erringly follow ("la falsa biltate"), why they do so ("da tenebrosa cechitate"), and the implications of doing so ("lasciando il cielo"). Thus his vision is entirely descriptive, and does not offer a more positive alternative. Chaucer, on the other hand, adds to the joy of heaven; Troilus's ghost "ful blisfully is went" to the "pleyn felicite" of heaven (v. 1808, 1818). And Chaucer adds a word of advice to counteract the error of humankind: "And sholden al oure herte on heven caste" (v. 1825). Thus he supplies a positive alternative to the blindness of this wretched world.

Two of the changes associated with Troilus's insight are Dantean echoes. From Dante's vision of earth's "vil sembiante" (vile semblance; *Par.* XXII, 135) comes the verb "despise," which in Latin and Italian is *vilificare*. Dante responds to his vision with a *terzina* that is modally similar to Troilus's advice:

> e quel consiglio per migliore approbo
> che l'ha per meno; e chi ad altro pensa
> chiamar si puote veramente probo.
>
> (Par. XXII, 136–38)

(and that counsel I approve as best which holds it for least, and he whose thought is turned elsewhere may be called truly upright.)

To "despise" the world suggests a philosophical detachment also connoted by "avyse," and quite different from Boccaccio's "dannando," condemning, a word that matches the sharp rhetorical opposition of "la falsa biltate," the false beauty. Both Dante and Troilus, then, place the world and its love in the same hierarchical synthesis; the world is not wholly negative, as it is in Boccaccio, but rather a place that offers the opportunity to cast one's eyes upward.

Thus Chaucer renders the pagan Troilus's soul journey as at least partially parallel to Dante's flight, especially in the understanding Troilus gains from the spheres. Does this mean that Chaucer endorses Troilus's insights? The answer is a qualified "yes." Chaucer reports them in the subjective mode he has used throughout the poem to bring us close to his story. He intermixes his own perspective with Troilus's; though the bulk of this section reports Troilus's actions and inward perceptions in the preterite tense ("saugh," "gan avyse," "gan despise," "held," "caste," "lough," "dampned"), the substance of what Troilus saw and understood is rendered in the present tense of general truth. Thus Chaucer not only reports the nature of Troilus's final understanding, but also tells us that his perceptions are generally valid: "the pleyn felicite / That is in hevene above" (v. 1818–19) is still true for Christians now, and "oure werk" still "foloweth so / The blynde lust, the which that may nat laste" (v. 1823–24). And Troilus's advice, that we "sholden al oure herte on heven caste" (v. 1825) is still good advice for Chaucer and his audience.

Thus Chaucer renders Troilus's transcendent insights as if he shared them. The shared perspective of the poet and his hero is given the strongest expression in this stanza:

> Swich fyn hath, lo, this Troilus for love!
> Swich fyn hath al his grete worthynesse!
> Swich fyn hath his estat real above!
> Swich fyn his lust, swich fyn hath his noblesse!
> Swich fyn hath false worldes brotelnesse!
> And thus bigan his lovyng of Criseyde,
> As I have told, and in this wise he deyde.　　　(v. 1828–34)

The poet concurs with Troilus's repudiation of "false worldes brotelnesse," which substitutes for Boccaccio's "del mondo la falsa biltate." This is a powerful expression of disdain for the world, stronger perhaps even than Troilus's. Chaucer has resolved the tension of Boccaccio's sharp opposition, but his phrase introduces an ambiguity. Does "false" modify the world, or its "brotelnesse"? Whichever it is, Troilus does indeed seem to have joined the narrator, across the abyss of time and religion that separates them.[22]

But the "Swich fyn" stanza, by calling attention to two gaps in the poet's record of transcendence, demonstrates that Chaucer cannot share either the perspective or the insight of his translated hero. With these gaps in narrative rendering, Chaucer aims the irony of the stanza, not so much at Troilus and the validity of his final understanding, as at his own understanding, and indeed at his whole project of writing a poetic Trojan history.

First, Chaucer widens a gap of perspective between himself and Troilus when he refers to "his estat real above." This may only emphasize Troilus's high social rank; as a member of the Trojan royal family, he was certainly "above" Chaucer. But "above" also recalls its appearance a few stanzas before, in the "pleyn felicite / That is in hevene above" (v. 1818–19). The word appears three times in these eight stanzas; the third use, referring to Christ who "sit in hevene above" (v. 1844), parallels the first. In the second two cases, "above" is clearly anchored in Chaucer's perspective; Troilus is "above" him either socially or in some other way, and Christ is clearly "above" the earthbound poet. It is therefore likely that the first "above" in Troilus's flight is also anchored in Chaucer rather than in his translated hero. The word thus tells us nothing about Troilus's position with respect to the music of the spheres; rather, it tells us that both Troilus and heaven are above the poet, who does not, then, share Troilus's perspective at all. The present tense of general truth with which Chaucer reports Troilus's insights implies a much fuller participation in his understanding than the speaker-anchored "above" permits.

Troilus could also be "above" Chaucer in v. 1830 in exactly the same sense as in v. 1819 (and as Christ is in v. 1844); the line would then refer to "swich fyn" Troilus's royal estate has above in the heavens. And this possibility calls attention to the second gap in narrative rendering, one that cuts Chaucer and us off from Troilus's posthumous understanding. We cannot ascertain the validity of this understanding because we don't know what "fyn" Troilus had. On earth, it was death. But intervening between death and the "Swich fyn" stanza is the narrative of his translation, which ends indeterminately: "And forth he wente, shortly for to telle, / Ther as Mercurye sorted hym to dwelle" (v. 1826–27). The indeterminacy of Troilus's final destination recalls Chaucer's inability to tell us whether Criseyde had any children (I. 132–33).[23] There, his frankness assured us of both the existence of a history independent of his report, and his commitment to transmitting it accurately. The third-person separation of the narrator from his character thus authenticated the *Troilus* as history uninfected by the speaker's personal involvement, his desire that his history be complete. Chaucer's ignorance about where Troilus's shade went after death also appeals to impersonal history. Yet here, the gap in knowledge concerns not an extraneous detail, but an event crucial to our understanding of the insight Troilus attains.

The poet introduces the vagueness apparently demanded by strict objectivity immediately after having suspended those self-imposed limits in his report of Troilus's flight. The knowledge Troilus gains in the spheres is predicated on his death, from which he, unlike Dante, cannot return. Furthermore, he says nothing; he only looks and laughs to himself. Nonetheless, Chaucer reports the substance of an insight no earthbound reporter, separated by death from his character, could have shared—and then passes over in silence the crucial objective fact that might have substantiated his claim to share Troilus's insight. It is unsettling that Chaucer should retreat from "seeing with" his hero at this point. By reimposing strict disjunction of narrator from character at the end of a passage in which his report apparently overcomes the silence of history, Chaucer reveals the untenability of objective history. It cannot tell us the most important thing about the transcendent insights that apparently move Troilus out of his pagan world and closer to Chaucer's Christian one: did they lead to salvation? Is Troilus like Dante's "Riphëo troiano"?

The effect of Chaucer's failure to know and report Troilus's destiny indicates that such complete separation between a historian and his history, accurate and honest though it may be, leads to meaninglessness.[24] Once the issue of final things is raised, we need the Christian historian's interpretative intelligence to make sense of the bare events. The retrospective imposition of a salvific order onto history, from the Christian present onto a pagan past, is necessary in order to salvage Troilus's story for Chaucer's Christian audience. Without such an imposition, the silence of the past leads only to incomprehension.

The limits on Chaucer's knowledge render the objective report of Troilus's end inauthentic. Yet this gap in knowledge is only the most extreme example of a characteristic running throughout the poem. The disjunction between Chaucer and his characters has resulted in similar gaps at nearly every important moment of the story. The enigma of Criseyde is well known;[25] every time we need solid, objective information about her, Chaucer dodges us, hiding behind his books or his ignorance, giving us instead opinions, conjectures, or inconclusive statements.[26] We do not finally know, for example, what moral valence to assign Criseyde's decision to love Troilus. Her internal debate, which is cast in the terms of moral choice,[27] ends in a dream as inconclusive as the meditation that precedes it:

> And as she slep, anonright tho hire mette
> How that an egle, fethered whit as bon,
> Under hire brest his longe clawes sette,
> And out hire herte he rente, and that anon,
> And dide his herte into hire brest to gon—
> Of which she nought agroos, ne nothyng smerte—
> And forth he fleigh, with herte left for herte.   (II.925–31)

Howard interprets this psychologically as evidence that whether or not Criseyde consciously wishes to fall in love, in fact a decision has already been reached at a more fundamental level beneath that of conscious consent.[28] But I don't think the dream gives us such unequivocal answers. The eagle figures not only the attraction Criseyde feels for Troilus, but also her sense of helplessness. He certainly seems a regal bird, and causes her no fear or pain; but his color is "whit as bon."[29] This sepulchral image, along with the violence of his heart rending, makes the eagle an ominous portent of the power of circumstances over Criseyde's actions. As elsewhere in the poem, any reader's interpretation of this passage depends not on what we know, but on what we want to believe about her.[30] The ambiguity of the dream hinders our certain knowledge about whether or not Criseyde makes a choice, and if she does, of what kind. In this gap of knowledge, so crucial to moral judgment, Chaucer instead foregrounds our own unavoidable interpretative act. The same bit of information, the conditions and extent of Criseyde's final choice, is missing from the parallel Diomede sequence; the narrator, refusing to guide our interpretation firmly, says only "Men seyn—I not—that she yaf hym hire herte" (V. 1050).

Such gaps in knowledge also affect what we know of Troilus before the end. In this regard, it is instructive to set the incomparable inexpressibility topoi of the *Paradiso* against their counterparts in the *Troilus*. Here, they are not nearly so arresting; nor do they serve the same purpose. Chaucer's inexpressibility is not, properly speaking, about the inability to speak the ineffable at all; one might more accurately label it "unknowability." The centrality of such passages to Chaucer's authentication derives from their open admission of lacunae, which interfere with the narrator's attempts both to report his distant Trojan history, and to insinuate himself into the experience of his characters. Both impulses underlie his long interjection in the consummation scene (III. 1310–37), which begins:

> Of hire delit, or joies oon the leeste
> Were impossible to my wit to seye;

> But juggeth ye that han ben at the feste
> Of swich gladnesse, if that hem liste pleye!
> I kan namore, but thus thise ilke tweye
> That nyght, bitwixen drede and sikernesse,
> Felten in love the grete worthynesse.   (III.1310–16)

He can neither transmit the words of his "auctour" with the slavish fidelity to which he aspires, nor, since he is no adept at love, imagine the lovers' experience fully enough. Consequently he leaves it, as always, to the judgment of his readers and to their capacity for imaginative interpretation.

By the time we arrive at Troilus's second sorrow in Books IV and V, unknowability has become a topic of considerable thematic weight. The limit on knowledge becomes the most important issue in Troilus's despairing speech on free will, determinism, and foreknowledge, at IV.958–1082.[31] He fallaciously concludes that, just as the fact of a man sitting causes one to see and know of his sitting, if one can foresee future events, then they too must of necessity occur. Troilus's characteristic leap to certitude here errs logically; he thinks that if he vividly imagines what he fears, it will happen. This error in part causes his passive acceptance of Criseyde's exchange. Chaucer himself makes no such leap; quite the opposite:

> Who koude telle aright or ful discryve
> His wo, his pleynt, his langour, and his pyne?
> Naught alle the men that han or ben on lyve.
> Thow, redere, maist thiself ful wel devyne
> That swich a wo my wit kan nat diffyne;
> On ydel for to write it sholde I swynke,
> Whan that my wit is wery it to thynke.   (V.267–73)

Under the comic pose of incompetence lies an important point. The narrator clearly shares some of the anguish Troilus feels at Criseyde's departure from Troy, but here as elsewhere, Chaucer stresses the limits of his empathy. The gap between speaker and subject can be bridged only partially, and that only with the equal imaginative participation of the audience.

This unknowability prefigures the manner in which Chaucer seeks to circumvent the vague objectivity with which he reports Troilus's final journey with Mercury. By mixing his perspective into Troilus's in the flight stanzas and in the "Swich fyn" stanza, Chaucer strives to bridge the abyss of silence with the means he has used throughout the poem to make history come alive: his ahistorical vicarious involvement in the experience of his characters. But if Troilus does not entirely leave his pagan context and join the poet in the Christian present, then this too is inauthentic. Chaucer's closeness to his hero and endorsements of his insights would constitute moving toward the limited, non-Christian insights Troilus might have gained; his closeness to his character would achieve fictive realism in defiance of the great split between past and present that brought ordered Christian meaning to history. Thus the manner in which Chaucer first renders Troilus's translation, and then apparently adopts his hero's repudiation of earthly love and all the other transitory things this world has to offer, constitutes the final crumbling of the poem's authentication. Both objective history and subjective involvement, Chaucer shows us, are equally inauthentic. The bare facts (which are in any case based on the fiction of Lollius) are meaningless; the participation with which Chaucer makes them come alive with realism and meaning is markedly fictional because it involves adopting a perspective he does not and cannot authentically share.

In the next three stanzas, as Bloomfield says, Chaucer leaps to a new distance from his story.[32] Addressing his audience in the stanza "O yonge, fresshe folkes, he or she" (v.1835), he advises them to repair "hom from worldly vanyte" (v.1837). His perspective here and in the next stanza adumbrates the falseness of sharing his perspective with Troilus.[33] It may resemble Troilus's distanced "dampnacioun" of this "wrecched world" (v.1817), but it is not the same—not because Troilus's attitude is so bitter, but because Chaucer does not try to express his own final understanding by insinuating it into the perspective of a character who could not wholly accommodate it. Troilus cast his glance *down* at "This litel spot of erthe" (v. 1815), and concluded that humankind should "on heven caste" their hearts (v. 1825); Chaucer here advises young lovers "And of youre herte *up* casteth the visage / To thilke God" (v. 1838–39) who "sit in hevene *above*" (v. 1844; my italics). Unlike Troilus, he remains earthbound. Thus when he tells us that all is vanity, he does so from an earthly perspective. He does articulate "vanity fair" sentiments, but the world seems neither wholly wretched nor wholly distant: "Al nys but a faire, / This world that passeth soone as floures faire" (v. 1840–41). The flowers, though they pass, are fair, and his regret is unmistakable.[34]

This and the following stanza most strongly assert the superiority of "love celestial" over "feyned loves," and also most clearly separate Chaucer from his Troilus. Urging the "yonge, fresshe folkes" of his audience to prefer Christ's love to any love lesser and more liable to betray them, Chaucer invokes the difference between pagan Troy, under the Law of Nature, and Christian England, under the Law of Grace—a difference hitherto present largely through irony. Indeed, one prominent instance of overt Christianity in the story before this stanza articulates the opposite sentiments:

> O blisful nyght, of hem so longe isought,
> How blithe unto hem bothe two thow weere!
> Why nad I swich oon with my soule ybought,
> Ye, or the leeste joie that was theere?
> Awey, thow foule daunger and thow feere,
> And lat hem in this hevene blisse dwelle,
> That is so heigh that al ne kan I telle!   (III. 1317–23)

The stanza from Book III comes at the height of the narrator's vicarious involvement in the story, where the strength of his imaginatively personal reading works most effectively to make the *Troilus* vivid, immediate, realistic—in a word, authentic. Consequently, when Chaucer so firmly disjoins himself from Troilus, and indeed, from the entire world of the poem, he retracts his effort to authenticate it as shared experience relevant not only to himself but also to his audience of lovers, for whose benefit he had originally undertaken to recount his tale.

The separation between the poet and his subject is presented in these two stanzas as the result of historical processes, the passage of time and the great scission the Incarnation made between pagan Troy and Christian England; and as the result of the differences between transcendent and worldly perspectives. The sufficiency of both subjective and objective means of authentication has by now been thoroughly undermined. In the rhetorically climactic stanza that ends this sequence, Chaucer withdraws not only from his story, but from fiction making in general. He apparently designates the kernel of the *Troilus* with:

> Lo here, of payens corsed olde rites!
> Lo here, what alle hire goddes may availle!
> Lo here, thise wrecched worldes appetites!
> Lo here, the fyn and guerdoun for travaille
> Of Jove, Appollo, of Mars, of swich rascaille!   (v.1849–53)

Very little in the poem has prepared us for this attack. The thematic emphasis has not been on "payens corsed olde rites," propitiating rascal gods—unless those gods are Venus and Cupid, significantly absent from this stanza. In fact, the machinations of the gods mentioned here are part of the material Chaucer explicitly excludes as "a long digression / Fro my matere" in his disingenuous *occupatio* at I.141–47 (an exclusion he reiterates at v.1765–71). Moreover, in the last two lines Chaucer appears to condemn, along with all the consequences of paganness, his own effort to transmit "the forme of olde clerkis speche / In poetrie" (v.1854–55). Since he bade farewell to his book in the most affectionate terms not 100 lines before, and expressed his regard for his "makyng" precisely in measure that it follows in the footsteps of the five great narrative poets of the pre-Christian era, this is possibly the most bewildering withdrawal of all. His change in attitude must be engendered by the events intervening between that eloquent farewell and this disappointed consignment of his poem to the dump heap of failed religions and broken ideas. And what intervenes is, of course, preeminently the transcendence of Troilus. This experience he could neither share imaginatively nor report objectively with any sufficiency. The state of souls after death[35] and insight brought back from the realms of the dead are beyond the scope of this poem; instead they definitively rend the always questioning, tentative authenticating endeavor beyond repair. With these lines, Chaucer places his fiction among the things of this world: like the "feyned loves" and the "floures" (of rhetoric as well) a fair thing indeed, but one he exposes as illusory.

Thus the order of the ten stanzas from v. 1786–1855 shows Chaucer's withdrawal from his fiction. After the dedications to "moral Gower" and "philosophical Strode," he ends the *Troilus* with the second Dantean borrowing, a prayer in the hortatory subjunctive petitioning for Christian transcendence for himself and his audience:

> Thow oon, and two, and thre, eterne on lyve,
> That regnest ay in thre, and two, and oon,
> Uncircumscript, and al maist circumscrive,
> Us from visible and invisible foon
> Defende, and to thy mercy, everichon,
> So make us, Jesus, for thi mercy, digne,
> For love of mayde and moder thyn benigne.   (v. 1863–69)

For this poet, unification with a transcendent ideal—his own Christian glory or Troilus's possible apotheosis—lies, like the certitude proceeding from it, outside the province of poetry. Final certainty is quite literally "uncircumscript" in the *Troilus*, and the poet cannot imitate the only being who "al maist circumscrive." The terms in which Chaucer describes the Trinity are not solely geometric; they also refer to the stable source of meaning in a logocentric universe—the Divine Word. Chaucer affirms the comprehensive supremacy of the Word, but he does not include his own poetry in this affirmation. His words, incapable of circumscribing ultimate realities, remain in comparison inauthentic. They partake of an ironic disjunction from the ideal; poets, like lovers, cannot escape from the deceptions of human language. The end is a prayer—and silence.

The ending of the *Troilus* is difficult to accept because it reveals the inauthenticity of the poem and because it circumscribes the place of Chaucer's poetry. However, with the Dantean prayer and the Dantean echoes in Troilus's flight, Chaucer also turns his ending to a much broader critique of the capacity of human poetry to render transcendent experience authentically. It is significant that Chaucer assigns Dantean transcendence to a pagan. Troilus's transcendence exalts him, but it also reduces the claims of Dante's poem by exposing the extent to which the *Commedia* is "pagan." Chaucer first stresses the paganness of the ending in his catalogue of poets; as Alfred David suggests, this may be another Dantean echo.[36] Chaucer substitutes Statius (for whom Dante invented a conversion to Christianity) for Horace, the only poet from *Inferno* IV's pantheon who does not appear in V.1792. With this refusal of Dante's authority, Chaucer also denies an integral part of Dante's scheme; Statius's conversion by reading the pagan poet Virgil had countered the ill effects of reading literature in *Inferno* V, and supplied a paradigm for Dante's own Virgilian conversion. The positive effects Virgil has on the two poets is in turn an essential element of Dante's poetic typology, with its grand reconciliation of pagan literature with Christian allegory.[37] This, for Dante, was "going beyond" Virgil, an act crucial to transforming Virgilian fictional "tragedìa" (*Inf.* XX, 113) into a Christian "comedìa,"[38] and crucial therefore also to the unique claim of the *Commedia*: to write the allegory of theologians with the language of poets. By assigning Dantean transcendence to a pagan, and separating this transcendence from his own Dantean prayer to the uncircumscript Word, Chaucer shows his skepticism of Dante's claim for the inclusiveness of poetry.

The gap between the ideal of transcendence and the actuality of mundane existence is the stuff of Chaucer's irony, and this too constitutes a reaction against Dante's unitive allegory written in imitation of the form and content of God's Book. For all the inadequacies of human language to describe the ineffable experience of beatitude, the scattered leaves of Dante's poem are still those of God's Book, bound into one volume at the end of the vision and at the end of our reading. Dante's analogical, liturgical universe is unified by the Incarnation then, now, and always, as it is repeated each year in the Paschal season and in the life of each person who undergoes conversion; and it is possible to describe (or at least to circumscribe) such a universe and such a conversion in the incarnational language of the *Commedia*.

Chaucer, however, shows the ideal of transcendent experience reported in language to be attainable only inauthentically— that is, as a figment of reified desire. His analogies are optative; and showing this painful gap between desire and fulfillment in the experience of his characters, he cannot blind himself to the same gap, and the same pain, in his own poetic efforts. His final prayer uses Dante's words to set limits on the place of poetry in this world; for Chaucer, these limits cannot be circumscribed by any inexpressibility topos or by any analogical, allegorical mimesis. The final certain truths of religion cannot be captured by poets, Christian though they may be. Circumscription for Chaucer means something very different from Dante's circumscription.

Placing such limits on the province of poetry does not, how-ever, make Chaucer the lesser poet. It merely makes him turn back to the world, to see how he, his characters, and his audi-ence may struggle toward knowledge and moral vision within the strictures of experience unfolding in time before death.[39] Chaucer is, pace Auerbach, more strictly the secular poet.[40] Within the limits of temporal experience in this world, I think, he saw a moral equivocation in the reading of the *Commedia* for anyone not sharing Dante's intimately personal experience of grace. For in human language there is little distinction between the words of a falsely transcendent earthly love—as in the canto of Paolo and Francesca, and in Troilus's religious language of courtly love—and the words of the truly transcendent love of the *Paradiso*. Like Troilus, the unconverted reader would confound the words of *Inferno* and *Paradiso* because of an overwhelming desire—and this is a laudable intention hardly to be distinguished from Dante's own—to attain the highest good. The danger is that the inevitable failure of insufficient objects to fulfill surpassing desire makes it more difficult to endure the life in this world, which is all we have for the moment. We cannot live retrospectively—forward, as it were, from death. We can only write retrospectively. Dante's poem, by holding out such large promise, increases the anguish of the human condition for those who do not follow him. Better to remain silent, as Paul did, since the rest of us are not likely to be "stellyfyed" as yet.

The elusive reward in limiting poetry so that it does not encompass final things is Chaucer's "compassioun." He introduces "compassioun" at the end of the opening proem, a context that recalls Dante in so many ways that it might indeed serve as an epitome of the differences between the two poets:[41]

> For so hope I my sowle best avaunce,
> To prey for hem that Loves servauntz be,
> And write hire wo, and lyve in charite,
>
> And for to have of hem compassioun,
> As though I were hire owne brother dere.
> Now herkneth with a good entencioun,
> For now wil I gon streght to my matere,
> In which ye may the double sorwes here
> Of Troilus in lovynge of Criseyde,
> And how that she forsook hym er she deyde. (1.47–56)

"Compassioun" is a near English equivalent of "pietà," a word that Dante uses four times in his account of Paolo and Francesca to signal his sympathetic involvement in their story.[42] Because Virgil and Dido are present in this canto, "pietà" also recalls Aeneas's *pietas*, the civic virtue that led him to abandon Dido and embrace instead his providential destiny to found Rome.

Thus the pity that seizes the pilgrim Dante here is a serious danger, a blind passion at strife with his own providential journey toward transcendent knowledge and "quella Roma onde Cristo è romano" (that Rome whereof Christ is a Roman; *Purg.* XXXII, 102).[43]

But though Chaucer may have translated the word from Dante, his "compassioun" is not the discredited romantic sentimentality of *Inferno* v. As with other instances in which Chaucer's use of a Dantean passage offers a glimpse at Virgil, I am unsure how much we can see here. Certainly Chaucer, in *The House of Fame* and elsewhere, repeatedly sided with Dido against Aeneas; he seems to have regarded her as a particularly luminous emblem of the difficulties and uncertainties of historical poetry. He used her in *The House of Fame* to demonstrate his antitypological vision of history as mere stories and his unsettling awareness of stories as fame: what people say regardless of what is true. That the uncertain capacity of historical poetry to capture truth again concerns Chaucer in the proem to the *Troilus* is suggested by his reference to the same canonized "tydynges" which traduced his Dido; here he asks his audience to pray "for hem that falsly ben apeired / Thorugh wikked tonges, be it he or she" (*TC*, 1.38–39). Within the story, this prayer applies most immediately to Criseyde and the "wikked tonges" of her literary past and future. Separated as reports are from events, however, the truth of human history is indeterminate, and the poet needs another guide to meaning to supplete the firm knowledge he cannot attain. That guide is his "compassioun," a "pietà" redefined as something close to the "charite" to which Chaucer links it here. In the *Troilus*, "compassioun" is not an impediment to knowledge but a spur to understanding.

The proem in which "compassioun" appears challenges the foundation of Dantean transcendence. By telling us the end of his story at the outset, Chaucer achieves a "view from the end" resembling that of both the autobiography and the allegory of Dante's historical poem.[44] For Dante, the vantage outside narrative and historical time allows him to inscribe a transcendent mode of knowledge into his poem. Chaucer, however, uses this view from the end for different purposes. Its effect on the quality of suspense is clear enough: because we know from the beginning that Criseyde forsook Troilus before she died, our desire to know is shifted from the *what* to the *hows*: how, in the inner story, love "Yelt bittre fruyt, though swete seed be sowe" (1.385);* and how, in the frame, the story is rendered. The structure of knowledge the proem creates is that of rereading a book, or of retelling a known history, both of which inform Chaucer's doubled narrative pose.

Like that pose, and like the proverbs of the *Troilus*, the proem's view from the end does not suffice to understand the story that follows. It isn't true to human experience as it is known in its temporal unfolding, to participants who don't know what happens next (their efforts to know result in their pagan fatalism, a sort of transcendent knowledge manqué), and who cannot always foresee or realize the consequences of their intentions. It's true rather of books; in the terms *The House of Fame* proposes, the view from the end is a shape characteristic of tidings rather than of historical events themselves. The apparently Dantean perspective Chaucer evokes at the beginning of the *Troilus*, then, stresses not Dante's truth, but rather the made, fictional qualities of his poem or any poem—the critical effect of authorial shaping. It enables Chaucer to build his poem around the contrast between two ways of knowing, each inauthentic in its own way: transcendent knowledge because it is unattainable, no matter how much one might wish for it; and temporally defined knowledge because it is so painfully incomplete. In such a context, the literal "suffering with" of Chaucer's "compassioun" measures the extent to which he shares

---

*Dante uses this proverb as well, though in an utterly different context, at *Par.* VIII, 91–93: "e così mi fa chiaro, / poi che, parlando, a dubitar m'hai mosso / com' esser può, di dolce seme, amaro" (and so now do you make clear to me [since in speaking you have raised the question in my mind] how from sweet seed may come forth bitter). The image is applied to the differences among members of the same lineage.

with his characters the temporal limitations on human knowledge rather than Dante's transcendent perspective.

In *The House of Fame* the only overt guide Chaucer offered to aid us in our interpretation of his wonderful dream was his curse against those who would "hyt mysdemen in her thoght / Thorgh malicious entencioun" (*HF*, 92–93). That is, Chaucer directed our wills rather than our rational faculties. He does so again in the proem to *Troilus and Criseyde*: "Now herkneth with a good entencioun" (1.52). The "compassioun" that guides his understanding also defines the "good entencioun"—a word linked to desire and interpretation as well as to attention[45]— with which he asks his audience to listen to the voices from the past. We may not know of a certainty what fills the gaps in knowledge so crucial to Chaucer's rendering of his Trojan history, but if we attend with good will—and to our own good will—we will understand as well.

If transcendence and its accompanying knowledge are impossible poetic ideals, then the poet cannot damn anyone, any more than he can know Troilus's final destination. One of the greatest difficulties of Dante's claim to otherwordly knowledge is his judgment of historical contemporaries and near contemporaries. Whatever epic machinery he uses to distance himself from the act of judgment, it is still Dante who designed and populated this hell. For many characters, the only evidence of the sin for which they stand condemned is the *Commedia* itself. No contemporary record mentions any love between Paolo and Francesca, for example.[46] Others were still alive in 1300, or at the time Dante wrote them into the *Commedia*.[47] And for many, notably Brunetto Latini and Ugolino, Dante invented metaphorical sins in order to fit them into the framework of his poem.[48]

Dante himself seems concerned about the propriety of such judgments, for he writes his own defense in two cantos of the *Paradiso*. When he meets his ancestor Cacciaguida, Dante obliquely asks whether he should divulge the secrets he has learned:

"ho io appreso quel che s'io ridico,
    a molti fia sapor di forte agrume;
e s'io al vero son timido amico,
    temo di perder viver tra coloro
    che questo tempo chiameranno antico." (*Par.* XVII, 116–20)

(". . . I have learned that which, if I tell again, will have for many a savor of great bitterness; and if I am a timid friend to the truth, I fear to lose life among those who shall call this time ancient.")

This is an incipient defense of his judgments, since cowardice is the only reason he offers for a failure to reveal them. Cacciaguida further legitimates them by ordering Dante to publish his otherworldly tidings: "tutta tua visïon fa manifesta; / e lascia pur grattar dov' è la rogna" ("Make manifest all that you have seen; and then let them scratch where the itch is"; *Par.* XVII, 128–29). How does Dante reconcile this with Thomas Aquinas's warning (*Par.* XIII, 130–42) against presuming to know the mystery of God's judgments? By including both warning and judgments, I think, Dante means to distinguish his true knowledge of God's intentions from less well-grounded opinion.

Chaucer's "compassioun" is another matter. As aware as Dante of literature's power to award praise and blame, Chaucer responds to the responsibility of exercising it by redefining the exemplary nature of his historical poem. This is most apparent in his treatment of Criseyde. Before Chaucer, she had existed solely for her infidelity; in *Il Filostrato* she was merely the means by which Boccaccio evoked sympathy for Troiolo. Without changing any of the "facts" of his story, Chaucer works around them to complicate our response to her.[49] By elaborating the power of extenuating circumstances—her pagan world, the destructive ideology of courtly love, the pressure of Pandarus's manipulations, the vicissitudes of Trojan politics, and always the plain fact of war—he makes it extraordinarily difficult to condemn her with the absolute judgment of the *Commedia*. She no longer exemplifies a moral failing seen from a final perspective. Rather, she adumbrates a set of truths about the process of human experience: that we know too little and only too late fully to control our lives; that our freedom to act is both more and less constrained than we can know or like to admit; that our moral responsibility for our actions is therefore, in this world, not wholly decipherable. Such definition is reserved to a view from the end sub specie aeternitatis, and for Chaucer belongs authentically only to God. We, however, share with Chaucer the temporality of his characters, and only by reading through the "paynted proces" (II.424) of their experience with the sympathy he enjoins can we make the analogy to the moral conditions of our own lives. By attending to the process of love joined and torn apart, rather than only to the monitory result, we can escape Troilus's anti-exemplary sentiment, uttered in the instant before he falls in love: "Ther nys nat oon kan war by other be" (I.203).

In Dante, the superiority of fiction over history lies in its capacity, as ethical analysis, to put a certain, final construction on events and causal relations.[50] Chaucer's construction of the *Troilus* story, however, bears a closer resemblance to casuistry.[51] By emphasizing the constant necessity of interpretation, he writes a fiction that questions our own acts of moral judgment. The implicated poet shares the sufferings of his characters, and cannot bring himself to "unloven" Criseyde. Though he must finally admit her betrayal, he sorrows rather than condemns: "Iwis, I wold excuse hire yet for routhe" (V.1099). Though he does not interpret or judge finally—his effort to ameliorate Criseyde's fame does not entirely succeed—most of his readers probably do. Yet Chaucer makes it impossible for us to do so without an unsettling awareness of our own judgmental acts.

Chaucer sorrows also for the limitations the world imposes on his craft of poetry; since he uses human language, he cannot escape the specter of the Sicilian bull, whose maker was its first victim. His poem is "a yerde / With which the maker is hymself ybeten" (I.740–41). To claim otherwise would be for

Chaucer a failure to recognize human limitations. Yet when he limits the realm of poetry to nontranscendence, it throws him back upon the world to find, by way of consolation, what good it does contain. The way of the world cannot satisfy: "Swich is this world, whoso it kan byholde:/In ech estat is litel hertes reste" (v.1748–49). But though "al nys but a faire,/This world that passeth soone as floures faire" (v.1839–40), it *is* fair while it lasts, and as long as we expect no more from it than its nature allows, we can be happier with the brief intimations of immortality it does afford: "God leve us for to take it for the beste!" (v.1750).

Troilus and Criseyde is, among other things, a sustained dialogue with Dante on the circumscription of human fictions. After the *Troilus*, Chaucer no longer argues against Dante as openly as he does here. He pays a compliment here and picks a quarrel there; but for the most part he silently assimilates what he can use, and ignores the rest. If his subsequent engagement with Dantean poetry is not as sustained as it is here, however, Chaucer does not shy from taking Dante on again. When he reappears in fulfillment of his promise at the end of the *Troilus* "to make in some comedye" (v.1788), it is, as Howard writes, as a practitioner of a comically exaggerated Augustinian charity: to hate the sin and love the man.[52] In *The Canterbury Tales*, Chaucer's unqualified, myopic approval of his not-so-perfect traveling companions is absurd, but the ironic double vision of the General Prologue invokes the ideal at the same time that it suspends judgment on the people who compromise it; they are capable of change while they yet live. It enables us to laugh rather than weep at the endemic corruption of a world no visionary poet can convert.

Reference Matter

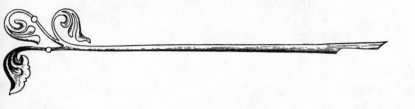

Notes

Complete authors' names, titles, and publication data are given in the References, pp. 263–82. A key to the abbreviations of Chaucer's works is in the Note to the Reader, p. ix.

Introduction

1. "Daunt in Inglissh" is Lydgate's enigmatic phrase in *Fall of Princes*, Prol. 303. For the first position, see Hammond, *Chaucer*, p. 82; and more recently, Schless's reference work, *Chaucer and Dante* (based on his still useful dissertation, "Chaucer and Dante: A Reevaluation"), which discusses nearly all the passages in the Chaucerian canon in which Dantean influence has been detected. For the second position, see especially Tatlock, "Chaucer and Dante"; Lowes, "Chaucer and Dante"; Koonce, *Chaucer and the Tradition of Fame*; and more recently, Shoaf, *Currency of the Word*; and Wetherbee, *Chaucer and the Poets*.

2. This is the force of Boitani, "What Dante Meant to Chaucer," an essay that fits into neither of the above categories, and instead treats Chaucer as a poet who admired and used Dante, but did not follow him uncritically. See below, Ch. 2.

3. Howard, in *Idea of the Canterbury Tales*, p. 88, considers the imagined feat of memory of the *CT* probably Chaucer's greatest debt to Dante.

4. Kittredge, *Chaucer and His Poetry*, p. 180. I concur fully with Kellogg's evaluation of the Pardoner, as well as with his comparison of him to Troilus and Arcite: "Of the ultimate end of the Pardoner, Chaucer, who refused to follow Troilus and Arcite to their last abode, tells us nothing. The Pardoner has fulfilled virtually every requirement for damnation, but like all human beings, he is to Chaucer somehow not quite damnable" ("Augustinian Interpretation," pp.

475, 481 n. 65). Kirkpatrick, in "Wake of the *Commedia*," pp. 221–24, also discusses how Chaucer differentiates himself from Dante by his nonjudgmental stance toward the Pardoner.

5. Howard, *Idea of the Canterbury Tales*, pp. 35–36. For the view that the *Troilus* changes at this point from a tragedy into a comedy, see Middleton, "Chaucer's 'New Men,'" p. 35; and Wetherbee, *Chaucer and the Poets*, p. 225. See also Boitani, "What Dante Meant to Chaucer," p. 128, for discussion of this passage.

6. Most consider *TC* a tragedy; see Kittredge, *Chaucer and His Poetry*, pp. 112–17; Root's commentary in his edition of *Troilus and Criseyde*, p. xlix; Root, *Poetry of Chaucer*, esp. pp. 125–27; Curry, "Destiny"; Robertson, "Chaucerian Tragedy" and *Preface to Chaucer*, pp. 472–502; and Howard, *Three Temptations*, pp. 149–53. Some have seen it as a mixture of tragedy and comedy; see David, "Hero of the *Troilus*" and "Chaucerian Comedy and Criseyde"; Corsa, *Chaucer*, pp. 40–70; Erzgräber, "Tragik und Komik"; Steadman, *Disembodied Laughter*, pp. 88–93; McAlpine, *Genre*, pp. 35–45 and chs. 5–6 (pp. 148–217). Others find *TC* a romance; see Lewis, "What Chaucer Really Did"; Young, "Chaucer's *Troilus*"; Kirby, *Chaucer's Troilus*; and Boitani, *English Medieval Narrative*, pp. 192–226. Other generic labels include epic (see, e.g., Boughner, "Elements of Epic Grandeur") and drama and novel. For a convenient summary of the genre issue, see Kaminsky, *Chaucer's Troilus*, pp. 74–83.

7. In this I am inclined to agree with Jauss ("Alterity and Modernity," esp. pp. 208–22) that we should look for smaller generic units within a work rather than try to designate one genre for the entirety.

8. Dante calls the *Aeneid* "l'alta . . . tragedìa" at *Inf.* XX, 113; he calls his own poem "comedìa" at *Inf.* XVI, 128, and *Inf.* XXI, 2. On the implications of *tragedìa* and *comedìa* in Dante, see Barolini, *Dante's Poets*, pp. 211–56, 277–82.

9. Those with suggestions include Jordan, who in discussing cosmic perspective in the *Troilus* applies Dante's description of the *Commedia* to Chaucer's poem as well: "The work ends in God himself" (*Shape of Creation*, p. 107). He quotes the Letter to Can Grande (Epistola X.xxxiii). McAlpine's "Boethian comedy" approaches Dantean comedy; see *Genre*, pp. 23, 181. See also Rowe's neoplatonic reading in *O Love O Charite*, pp. 147–51 and 172. None of these readers thoroughly develops the Dantean parallels found. Boitani's

"What Dante Meant to Chaucer" has a very good general approach to the Dante-Chaucer relationship, though his comments on the *Troilus*, pp. 126–30, are quite brief.

10. Shoaf, *Currency of the Word*, pp. 107–57; see also a condensed version of his argument in "Theory of Mediation."

11. Wetherbee, "Descent from Bliss," p. 309. See also his *Chaucer and the Poets*, esp. pp. 145–78. Wetherbee's reading includes many other Dantean influences; I cite the central sequence as one example, and will have occasion to cite others below.

12. Wetherbee, "Descent from Bliss," p. 307; *Chaucer and the Poets*, p. 146.

13. The phrase is from Traugott and Pratt, *Linguistics*, p. 272 *et passim*.

14. Benveniste, *Problèmes*, pp. 238–50.

15. Weinrich, *Tempus*, p. 32, citing Bühler, *Sprachtheorie*, on the etymological relationship between pointing and saying.

16. Example and analysis from Fillmore, *Deixis*, p. 39.

17. For a more complete discussion, see Traugott and Pratt, *Linguistics*, pp. 272–82.

18. Ibid., pp. 228, 287–88; Genette, *Narrative Discourse*, p. 260.

19. Weinrich, *Tempus*, pp. 223–36.

20. Benveniste, *Problèmes*, pp. 235, 256.

21. Thus *I* and *you*, like locatives and verbs anchored in the speaker's perspective, are "shifters." See Jakobson, "Shifters"; Traugott and Pratt, *Linguistics*, pp. 272–75; and Fillmore, *Deixis*.

22. Even the present tense does not always indicate a deictic proximity to the speaker; it can indicate habit, or, in the present of definition ("water boils at 100 degrees centigrade"), timelessness. This timelessness might be seen as *modal* proximity, however; the tense presents the content as universal fact, but the certainty originates in the speaker. Consequently, although Benveniste includes this use of the present tense in histoire, as not anchored in the speaker's perspective (*Problèmes*, p. 239), Weinrich includes it in his *besprochene Welt* (world of commentary), since it depends on the subjective mode of certainty originating in the *I* (*Tempus*, p. 57). Genette also doubts whether such use of the present tense can be severed from all connection with discours (*Narrative Discourse*, p. 212). The "historical present" also indicates modal rather than temporal proximity; it expresses

a distant event in the present tense in order to make it more vivid to *you* or to indicate that it is vivid to the *I*. Tense can also express modal distance, as in the English present subjunctive, which is morphologically past but semantically unreal: "If I were king . . ."

23. Here I leave out all the finer points, such as the double temporal anchoring of the future perfect, the aspectual differences between simple and progressive tenses, and the "relief" function of tense to distinguish between foreground action and the background against which it takes place, as in "The rain was falling hard when he finally arrived," with the foreground preterite and the background past progressive. In French and Italian, the relief function is expressed by the *passé composé / passato prossimo* alternating with the stative imperfect in discours, and by the *passé simple / passato remoto* alternating with the imperfect in histoire. For temporal sequencing in French, see Benveniste, *Problèmes*, pp. 238–50; in French, Italian, English, and German, see Weinrich, *Tempus*, esp. pp. 21–22, 64–87, 222–26. The best study available for all the semantic uses of tense to indicate information other than time is Weinrich.

24. Barthes, in "Introduction à l'analyse structurale," muddies the waters here considerably when he distinguishes "personal" and "apersonal" narration. While claiming to base his distinction on Benveniste, he actually reverses Benveniste's categories. According to Barthes, personal narration obtains if one can rewrite its sentences substituting first-person pronouns for third-person pronouns; thus a sentence like "He entered a tobacco shop" is personal because one can rewrite it as "I entered a tobacco shop" without having to change any other element to avoid anomaly. But "He seemed pleased at the distinguished air his uniform gave him" resists such rewriting; to substitute "I" for "he" would result in the incongruity I have discussed. Barthes thus terms such a sentence "apersonal" (p. 20). For a critique of Barthes's terminological confusion, see Culler, *Structuralist Poetics*, pp. 199–200, from which I have borrowed these examples. I think the confusion runs deeper than terminology, for verbs like "seem" contain an inherent speaker-anchored perspective whatever person is realized; verbs like "enter" do not automatically raise the question "who sees?" and can be used in either discours or histoire. Thus the real distinction, as with verb tense, is whether or not a verb is limited to the speaker-oriented focus of discours and thus is excluded from histoire. This does not, however, mean that "he entered" and "I en-

tered" refer in exactly the same way; for one thing, the second refers to my past, but the first may not.

25. Benveniste, *Problèmes*, p. 242; Weinrich, *Tempus*, pp. 33–39. Most discourse analysis has focused on spoken conversation, but discours is not limited in this way; see Coulthard, *Discourse Analysis*, p. 180.

26. Benveniste, *Problèmes*, p. 24.

27. Ibid., p. 239; Hamburger, *Logic of Literature*, p. 311.

28. Genette, *Narrative Discourse*, p. 213.

29. Ibid., pp. 243–45.

30. Banfield, in *Unspeakable Sentences*, makes an elegant distinction between "self" and "speaker" in written fictional discourse. In her description, when there is a fictional self in a sentence, there can be no real speaker; hence "unspeakable sentences."

31. For more thorough discussions, see Booth, *Rhetoric of Fiction*; Stanzel, *Narrative Situations*; Friedman, "Point of View"; Romberg, *Studies in Narrative Technique*; and Genette, *Narrative Discourse*, pp. 185–211, 243–54.

32. This group corresponds to Friedman's seventh and eighth categories, the "dramatic" and "camera" styles of objective or behaviorist narrative; to Romberg's third category of objective narrative; and to Genette's narrative of "external focalization," in which the narrative voice knows or says less than any of its characters.

33. Thus what Barthes has called the "reality effect," from things mentioned not because they are relevant but simply because they are there, is very strong. See Barthes, "L'Effet de réel"; Culler, *Structuralist Poetics*, pp. 193–94; and Genette, *Narrative Discourse*, pp. 165–66.

34. In "The Killers" and similar objective narratives, the only remaining traces of the generating instance are the preterite verb tense, which places the story in a relative past, and the attached name of the author, whom we know to be a maker of fictions. Even the former is purged from some *nouvelles romans*, such as Robbe-Grillet's early works, which are narrated in the present tense; see Genette, *Narrative Discourse*, pp. 218–19.

35. This group thus corresponds roughly to Hamburger's "epic genre" with objective narration taken out (*Logic of Literature*, pp. 94–159); to Stanzel's omniscient and focalized narration; to Friedman's omniscient narration with or without authorial intrusion, as well as

to his two varieties of "selective-omniscient" narration, with single or multiple focalization; to Romberg's omniscient narration and narration with point of view; and to Genette's two heterodiegetic categories—nonfocalized narration, in which the narrator says more than any of the characters know, and the various forms of focalized narration (fixed, variable, and multiple) in which the narrator says what one or more of his characters know (but excluding first-person narration).

36. For the neutralization of empirical time in this manner, see Hamburger, *Logic of Literature*, esp. pp. 59–64; and Weinrich, *Tempus*, pp. 46–48, and examples, as on pp. 71, 241. For the representation of inner speech and inner action, see Hamburger, pp. 81–98; and Genette, *Narrative Discourse*, pp. 169–85.

37. Banfield, *Unspeakable Sentences*. She offers a cogent discussion of the peculiarities of language in fiction as they have developed in European languages since the seventeenth century. She argues that in these relatively modern works written narration and represented speech differ from speech itself because they have no real speaker (author) and arise instead from a fictional subjectivity "speaking" to an equally fictional audience. Hence "it is writing, by making possible the sentence of narration and the sentence representing consciousness, which allows the literary work to take on an objective life independent of its author" (p. 253). Since Dante and Chaucer write premodern rhetorical narration, however, the "death" of the speaker cannot apply to either.

38. On the lucid reflector, see the collected prefaces to James's novels in *Art of the Novel*; on free indirect style, characterized by direct representation of inner speech with deictics anchored in the character but past tense and third person anchored in the narrator, see Traugott and Pratt, *Linguistics*, pp. 299–302. See also Banfield, *Unspeakable Sentences*, pp. 183–224.

39. For the distinction between "showing" and "telling," see Booth, *Rhetoric of Fiction*, pp. 3–20. This distinction, basically Aristotelian, is particularly important in Lubbock, *Craft of Fiction*, which argues (with James) that the novelist must show his story in such a way that it will tell itself, without the help of the narrator's interpolations (p. 62).

40. Genette, *Narrative Discourse*, pp. 163–69.

41. Banfield describes this in its most extreme form as the absence of the narrator (*Unspeakable Sentences*, pp. 222–23).

42. This group corresponds to Stanzel's *Ich-Erzählung*, Friedman's I-witness and I-protagonist, Romberg's first-person, and Genette's homodiegetic narrations.

43. Vance, "Augustine's *Confessions*," p. 4.

44. Vitz, " 'I' of the *Roman de la rose*," p. 49.

45. Benveniste, *Problèmes*, p. 239; Hamburger, *Logic of Literature*, p. 311.

46. See Bauer, *System und Gebrauch der 'Tempora'*; and Burnley, *Chaucer's Language*, pp. 39–58, for Chaucer's verbal system.

47. These terms are Weinrich's equivalents of histoire and discours.

Chapter 1

1. I follow the traditional order of Chaucer's works, dating *HF* probably in the late 1370's and before *PF*, which also shows Dantean influence. See Benson, " 'Love-Tydynges,' " which concludes from astronomical and literary evidence that 1379 is the most likely date.

2. *HF*, 1095. The most productive readings have followed Chaucer's suggestion in the third invocation and considered the poem an *ars poetica*; I depend heavily on those who have preceded me in treating *HF* as a statement about Chaucer's poetic practice. To my knowledge, the first to suggest this was R. Allen, "Recurring Motif." Over the last 20 years or so, a consensus has developed supporting the *ars poetica* reading; see esp. David, "Literary Satire"; Payne, *Key of Remembrance*, p. 128; J. A. W. Bennett, *Chaucer's Book of Fame*; Shook, "*House of Fame*"; Howard, "Flying Through Space" and "Chaucer's Idea of an Idea"; Dane, "*Rota Virgilii*"; Miller, "Writing on the Wall"; Boitani, "Chaucer's Labyrinth"; and Jordan, "Lost in the Funhouse of Fame."

3. Howard, "Flying Through Space," p. 5, calls *HF* "the greatest statement in the English language about the nature of poetic influence."

4. Wetherbee, *Chaucer and the Poets*, p. 21.

5. I do not quarrel with the conclusions of Braswell, "Architectural Portraiture," and Kendrick, "Palais de Justice," that the three

settings of the poem—the Temple of Venus in Book I, and the palace of Fame and the House of Rumor in Book III—are modeled on the three parts of the Palais de Justice in Paris, respectively Sainte-Chapelle, the Great Hall, and the connecting Gallery of Haberdashers. I merely suggest that the original setting, like the books to which the poem alludes, underwent a thorough transmogrification in significance as the poem took shape. Though it might seem apparent that the dream vision form would afford insights into the workings of the mind, it is only since Howard's two essays on the *HF* that critics have focused on the interiority of the poem. Howard quite properly insists that the setting is Chaucer's mind; see esp. "Flying Through Space," p. 6.

6. A view still argued with qualifications by Clemens, *Early Poetry*, pp. 111–12; and Leyerle, "Chaucer's Windy Eagle," p. 257.

7. Kendrick, "Palais de Justice," suggests that the eagle lectern and the "griffon (vulture) claw with talons that hung from the ceiling in the middle of the nave of the upper chapel" of Sainte-Chapelle (p. 131) also informed Chaucer's choice of a guide in Book II; see also Leyerle, "Chaucer's Windy Eagle," p. 254. Other Dantean aspects of *HF* include the division of the poem into three books, each prefaced by an invocation (the second and third echoing Dante verbally); and numerous local imitations. For a relatively complete list and discussion, see Schless, *Chaucer and Dante*, pp. 29–78. See also Boitani, "What Dante Meant to Chaucer," pp. 118–25, for an insightful discussion of the transformations Chaucer worked on his Dantean invocations. Gellrich, *Idea of the Book*, argues that *HF* follows Dante in subverting the "book of culture" of the Middle Ages; see pp. 27, 167–201. Gellrich's argument, however, elides the differences between secular and religious writing; and in adopting Kermode's opposition of "secrecy" and "sequence" (see "Secrets and Narrative Sequence") to explain the narrative jumpiness of *HF*, he makes it into a divine poem on the order of the *Commedia*.

8. Ruggiers, in "Unity," p. 264, suggests that both Dantean eagles go into the making of Chaucer's eagle. I disagree, however, with the inference he draws from the combination, that the meaning of the dreamer's flight parallels that of the flight in the *Paradiso*: a journey to the mysteries of divine judgment beyond human knowledge. Boitani, "What Dante Meant to Chaucer," p. 118, also suggests that

Chaucer's eagle includes a trace of the eagle in the Heaven of Justice in his genealogy.

9. Chiampi, in *Shadowy Prefaces*, p. 169, writes that "the Eagle of the Heaven of Jupiter is simply an anagogical version of the visible speech . . . of Purgatory, since it transforms itself from letters into a speaking sign."

10. For a lucid description of the representational issues of Dante's ecphrasis here, see Barolini, *Dante's Poets*, pp. 274–75. See also K. Taylor, "From *superbo Iliön*," and "Chaucer Reads the *Divine Comedy*," pp. 19–20.

11. On the LVE acrostic of *Par.* XIX, 115–41, see below, Ch. 3, and K. Taylor, "From *superbo Iliön*."

12. I draw the following brief description of allegory primarily from Auerbach, "Figura"; and Singleton, *Dante's 'Commedia,'* pp. 88–92. The description goes back to Augustine, *On Christian Doctrine*, I.ii.

13. The idea that the images of Book I should be connected to Dante's *visibile parlare* was originally suggested by Thomas C. Moser, Jr., in a seminar on *HF* in 1980. The connection between the terrace of pride, which is in part about artistic fame, and *HF* deserves much fuller treatment than I can give here. Boitani, in *Imaginary World of Fame*, pp. 87–88, has made a beginning by investigating the words Dante uses for fame (e.g., "mondan romore," "fiato di vento," "nome," "voce," "nominanza," all of which have counterparts in *HF*). Another connection I would add (by way of preliminary suggestion) is the "architectural" purgation undergone by the souls here. They are bent into shapes that remind Dante of columns or corbels supporting ceilings or roofs (*Purg.* X, 130–35); this may have given Chaucer the idea for the poet-pillars supporting Fame's hall in Book III. See also Kendrick, "Palais de Justice," pp. 121–24, for the influence of the statuary in the Great Hall of the Palais de Justice.

14. The best discussion of Book I's debt to the visual arts is ch. I of J. A. W. Bennett's *Chaucer's Book of Fame*. The suggestion that the scenes may be bas-reliefs is his, pp. 13–14.

15. The phrase "shortly for to tellen" recurs throughout Book I (e.g., in ll. 239–44) as Chaucer abbreviates those parts of the story he does not wish to stress; the long section from l. 269 through l. 426, largely Chaucer's addition, is a classic *amplificatio* in its senten-

tiae and its references to comparable exempla from other books (see esp. ll. 388–426). These bookish references are further evidence that the art of Book I is originally verbal rather than visual. For the "word-paintings" of *HF* and their origins in Ovid (*Metamorphoses* IX.137–43 and XII.39–63), Virgil (*Aeneid* IV, 173–97), and Boethius (*Consolation*, II.pr.7 and III.pr.7), see Hanning, "Chaucer's First Ovid," pp. 141–46.

16. J. A. W. Bennett treats the images in almost exclusively visual terms; Delany, in *Chaucer's House of Fame*, pp. 50–58, discusses them in exclusively literary terms. Perhaps the best account is R. Allen, "Recurring Motif," p. 396: "In fact, when one considers the words (engraved on brass) with which the story of Aeneas begins, it is easier to see the pictures, involved as they are with sound and movement, as imaginative reactions to a written text than to see the story emerging from a series of wall-paintings." My account of the images, below, largely follows up on this idea.

17. Augustine, *In Ioannis Evangelium*, XXIV, 2, *PL* 35, col. 1593 (trans. mine). See Freccero's comments on this passage and its implications for representation in the *Commedia*, in "Infernal Irony," p. 95. This essay drew my attention to the passage.

18. Augustine, *Confessions*, XI.xviii; ed. Watts, vol. 2, p. 248; *PL* 32, col. 818. I thank Marie Borroff for her help with the translation. McGerr, in "Retraction and Memory," p. 105, discusses this passage in terms that prove useful for *HF* as well; she writes, "The key to this process is that the words conceived by means of images recreate those images in the mind of the hearer as *they* pass through *his* senses. The words, in fact, have replaced the original events."

19. For thorough discussions of Augustine's verbal cognition and its influence on medieval theories of psychology, see Bundy, *Theory of Imagination*, chs. 8–9; and Colish, *Mirror of Language*.

20. See Virgil, *Aeneid* I, 1–7; ed. Fairclough, vol. 1, p. 240.

21. For the purpose of the narration in the *Aeneid*, see Wetherbee, *Chaucer and the Poets*, p. 92, citing Patterson, "'Rapt with Pleasaunce,'" pp. 455–57.

22. Ovid, *Heroides*, VII.

23. Jerome, *Adversus Iovinianum*, I.43, *PL* 23, col. 310.

24. See J. Taylor, *Ranulf Higden*, p. 77, citing *Polychronicon*, I.166 and II.432.

25. Boccaccio, *Comento alla Divina Commedia*, *Inf.* v, senso lette-rale, 65–83; ed. Guerra, vol. 2, pp. 119–24.

26. Boccaccio, *De mulieribus claris*, xvii, "De Didone seu Elissa Cartaginensium regina."

27. Boccaccio, *De genealogie deorum gentilium*, ii, 60. For modern discussions of the dual tradition, see D. C. Allen, "Marlowe's *Dido*"; and Fyler, *Chaucer and Ovid*, pp. 34–35. In addition, Zaccaria's notes to his edition of Boccaccio, *De mulieribus claris*, pp. 514–15, are in-valuable.

28. Jordan, "Lost in the Funhouse of Fame," p. 107, discusses the thematic function of *HF*'s disjunctiveness; Delany, in *Chaucer's House of Fame*, p. 56, also says that the contradictoriness of the tra-dition is the main point of Book I.

29. See Bundy, *Theory of Imagination*, ch. 9.

30. See Delany's excellent discussion of "fantome" and "illusion" in *Chaucer's House of Fame*, pp. 58–67.

31. Mazzotta, *Dante*, p. 180.

32. Hanning, "Chaucer's First Ovid," p. 146, also suggests "reading backwards" as the proper approach to the narrative structure of *HF*.

33. Howard, "Chaucer's Idea of an Idea," p. 45, citing the OED.

34. See ibid., pp. 44–45, for a discussion of the labyrinth as a symbol of human craftsmanship and of the world.

35. Obviously memory is a crucial part of the combinative func-tion; see, for example, Augustine, *Confessions*, x.viii; ed. Watts, vol. 2, pp. 94–99. See also Bundy, *Theory of Imagination*, ch. 9; and for a brief, clear description (following Albertus Magnus), C. S. Lewis, *Discarded Image*, pp. 161–64.

36. Rowland, "Artificial Memory," has interpreted the *HF* as an artificial memorial structure of the sort described by Yates in *Art of Memory*. More recently and convincingly, Carruthers, "Italy," sug-gests that both Dante and Chaucer knew the thirteenth-century mne-monic of Bono Giamboni; she too connects speaking images, *Purg.* x and Fame's hall of poet-pillars.

37. Howard, "Chaucer's Idea of an Idea," p. 46. Howard sug-gests that this aspect of the poem shows that Chaucer thought of po-etry as "made up of reports whose objective truth is neither here nor there." If I understand correctly, I disagree; such an attitude would

not produce a poem of such deep concern with the issue of "trouthe." See Delany (*Chaucer's House of Fame*, pp. 56–57), who demonstrates what a knotty problem it is in Book I.

38. Ruggiers, in "Words into Images," suggests *Par.* III, 29, as the source of this passage. Here Dante mistakes spirits for reflections; the mistake illustrates the representational mode of this *cantica*, in which the poet tries to render heaven visible and at the same time expose its visibility as a benign fraud designed to accommodate heaven to human understanding. For Ruggiers, the borrowing exemplifies the difference between the two poets, for Chaucer borrows the device but strips away the philosophy. Clearly I agree with the first part, but not the second: *HF* is relentlessly cerebral, and Chaucer borrows the device of visible speech in order to turn it to his own equally theoretical purposes. J. A. W. Bennett, in *Chaucer's Book of Fame*, p. 98, suggests that Chaucer's tidings "correspond to those shades in Dante that embody the mental state of men in life."

39. See Spitzer, "Poetic and Empirical 'I.'"

40. J. A. W. Bennett, in *Chaucer's Book of Fame*, pp. 178–79, suggests a link between tidings and the *CT* tales; Leyerle, in "Chaucer's Windy Eagle," pp. 264–65, also suggests a close relationship between the House of Rumor, with its tale-telling pilgrims and pardoners, and the *CT*. The argument for a relationship between the two poems, however, does not depend on such things as the conjunction he identifies between the size of the House of Rumor and the distance to Canterbury from London (60 miles).

41. Howard, "Chaucer's Idea of an Idea," esp. p. 46. Howard suggests that Chaucer points "to the basic relation of poetry to the spoken language." By "spoken language," Howard does not mean oral speech so much as "the stream of speech as it exists in our thoughts." For two different views, each distinguishing the oral from the written in fundamental ways, see Nykrog, "Rise of Literary Fiction"; and Banfield, *Unspeakable Sentences*.

42. John of Salisbury, *Metalogicon*, 1.13, quoted and translated by Clanchy in *From Memory to Written Record*, p. 202. The entire passage in question reads: "Littere autem, id est figure, primo vocum indices sunt; deinde rerum, quas anime per oculorum fenestras opponunt, et frequenter absentium dicta sine voce loquuntur." On *vox*, cf. Irvine, "Medieval Grammatical Theory."

43. Augustine, *Confessions*, VI.iii; ed. Watts, vol. 1, pp. 272–75.

44. Clanchy, *From Memory to Written Record*, pp. 202–30, esp. p. 230. See also Howard, *Idea of the Canterbury Tales*, pp. 63–67.

45. This is the meaning of the word in the *Troilus* envoi (V.1789), where Chaucer forswears any rivalry with the great masters of narrative poetry. In the prologue to *A Treatise on the Astrolabe*, however, "envie" seems to refer to doubt of the author's authority: "But considre wel that I ne usurpe not to have founden this werk of my labour or of myn engyn. I n'am but a lewd compilator of the labour of olde astrologiens, and have it translatid in myn English oonly for thy doctrine. And with this swerd shal I sleen envie" (ll. 59–64). The Middle English verb "envye" had two meanings, corresponding to two etymological pathways: (1) [OF *envier*, from ML *invidiare*] to feel ill will, to envy, to be jealous; and (2) [OF *envier*, from L *invitare*] to contend or vie. See Davis, et al., *Chaucer Glossary*, pp. 47–48, which, however, glosses "envye" in *HF*, 1476, as "enmity" rather than "competition" or "contention."

46. I think here particularly of those occasions upon which Dante "corrects" Virgil; good examples are *Inf.* XX, 52–99, where Virgil tells a story of the founding of Mantova at odds with *Aeneid* X, 185–203 (see Barolini, *Dante's Poets*, pp. 214–17); and *Purg.* XXII, 40–41, where Statius "mistranslates" *Aeneid* III, 56–57 (see Shoaf, "'Auri sacra fames'").

47. Leyerle, "Chaucer's Windy Eagle," p. 253, suggests that in creating the eagle Chaucer "transformed a metaphor into a palpable eagle; the figure of speech is father to the bird." Leyerle means Boethius's metaphor of the wings of thought in *Consolation*, IV.pr.1, with influence also from *Purg.* IX and *Metamorphoses* X. I mean something slightly different: that the eagle's words quite literally (in the fiction of the poem) create their speaker. It seems to me that this is a fundamental insight on Chaucer's part into the creation of literary fiction and characters, and to attribute the metaphor reified by the eagle to Chaucer's sources misses the real excitement of the passage.

48. See Stevenson, "Endings," which after discussing all the proposed endings suggests that Chaucer, had he finished *HF*, would not have resolved the oppositions previously set up in the poem.

49. This is very close to the medieval understanding of fame, both as rumor and as renown. See (in addition to Virgil and Ovid)

Dante, *Convivio*, I.iii.11. Festus, *De verborum significatu*, ed. Lindsay, p. 76, derives *fama* from the verbs *fari* and *loqui* (both mean "to speak"); Isidore picks this definition up in *Etymologiarum*, V.27.26–27. For a good discussion of *fama*, see Boitani, *Imaginary World of Fame*, pp. 40–41.

50. See Horace, *Satires* I, x, 33, and Ovid, *Heroides*, XIX, 195–96.

51. See Epistola VII, written to Henry in May 1311; Dante salutes him with the words "Ecce Agnus Dei, ecce qui tollit peccata mundi!" (Behold the Lamb of God, behold him who taketh away the sins of the world; Dante, *Opere latine*, ed. Giuliani, vol. 2, pp. 22–26).

52. Bloomfield, "Authenticating Realism," pp. 177–84.

53. Ibid., p. 178.

54. Aquinas, in his commentary on Aristotle's *Metaphysics*, called poets liars: "Sed poetae non solum in hoc, sed in multis aliis mentiuntur" (But not only in this, but in many other things, poets lie; Thomas Aquinas, *In Metaphysicam Aristotelis commentaria*, ed. Cathala, p. 21, no. 65, quoted in Curtius, *European Literature*, p. 218; trans. mine). Curtius's discussion of the scholastic attack on poetry, pp. 214–27, is excellent; see also Wetherbee, *Platonism and Poetry*, for a sense of the struggle in France; and Hollander, "Dante *Theologus-Poeta*," for a discussion of Boccaccio, Dante, and the other trecento defenders of literature. Hollander's bibliographical notes are indispensable.

55. Bloomfield, "Authenticating Realism," pp. 180–81, speculates that the need for authentication arose with the demise of oral performance. With respect to the oral performance of Chaucer's works—the nature of his real audience and the circumstances under which they may have been performed—we can be sure of little. Many discussions of this issue have centered around the idealized frontispiece to the Corpus Christi manuscript (Cambridge MS 61). On the frontispiece, see Brusendorff, *Chaucer Tradition*, pp. 19–22; Galway, "*Troilus* Frontispiece"; Williams, "*Troilus* Frontispiece"; Kean, *Chaucer*, vol. 1, pp. 25–26; David, *Strumpet Muse*, pp. 9–10; Howard, *Idea of the Canterbury Tales*, pp. 63–64; and Pearsall, "*Troilus* Frontispiece." While Galway and Williams try to identify the people in the miniature, the more recent studies emphasize the idealized portrait of the poet and its unrealistic depiction of Chaucer's relation

to the audience. Howard introduces the concept of "voiceness," which is, I think, related to authentication: the portrait is an imagining of the intimate relationship between author and audience that helps to guarantee truth. For the implied audience in the text, which replaces the real audience of oral performance, see esp. Ong, "Writer's Audience"; Mehl, "Audience of Chaucer's 'Troilus'"; Reiss, "Chaucer and His Audience"; and Strohm, "Chaucer's Audiences."

56. See Wetherbee, *Chaucer and the Poets*, pp. 24–25; and Minnis, *Chaucer and Pagan Antiquity*, pp. 22–29.

57. *Mandeville's Travels*, ed. Seymour, p. 234. For the authentication of *Mandeville's Travels*, see Josephine Bennett, *Rediscovery*, pp. 26–53; and Howard, "*Mandeville's Travels*," pp. 2–6.

58. Bloomfield, in "Authenticating Realism," p. 184, comments on the role of the dream to make the narrative seem more, not less, true.

59. For a convenient summary of the common metaphor of nature as a book written by the hand of God, see Curtius, *European Literature*, pp. 311–32 and 544–46.

60. See Singleton, *Dante's 'Commedia'* and "In exitu Israel de Egypto."

61. "Embryology" is Freccero's word; for his excellent discussion of the relation between procreation and poetic creation, see "Manfred's Wounds," pp. 201–5.

62. Again, see Barolini's superb discussion of Dante's poetic *imitatio Dei*, in *Dante's Poets*, pp. 89–91 and 274–75.

63. Bloomfield, "Distance and Predestination."

64. Bloomfield, "Authenticating Realism," pp. 186–87.

65. Guido delle Colonne, *Historia destructionis Troiae*, Prologue; trans. Meek, pp. 1–3, and Meek's introduction, pp. xi–xvii. Minnis's discussion of Guido's historical authentication is also helpful; see *Chaucer and Pagan Antiquity*, pp. 23–26.

66. Pratt, "Chaucer's Lollius." Minnis, *Chaucer and Pagan Antiquity*, p. 25, interprets Lollius as a straightforward claim to ancient authority; Wetherbee, *Chaucer and the Poets*, pp. 25–26, 111, makes the intriguing suggestion that for Chaucer Lollius was a figure for the incomplete and ambiguous transmission of the classics (especially the history of Thebes) in such sources as the Vatican mythographers and the *Ovide moralisé*.

67. In *BD*, which shows no trace of Dante, the authenticating

devices include the "I," the circumstantial realism of the frame, and the very dreamlike dream itself; see Bloomfield, "Authenticating Realism," pp. 184–86.

Chapter 2

1. The most notable example is Amis in the *Roman de la rose*; Gallehault in the Old French prose Lancelot is also relevant. On Pandaro, Pandarus, and the *Roman de la rose*, see Lewis, "What Chaucer Really Did," esp. pp. 68–73, and *Allegory of Love*, pp. 192–93; Muscatine, *Chaucer and the French Tradition*, pp. 137–53; and Wetherbee, *Chaucer and the Poets*, pp. 54–76.

2. Howard, in "Literature and Sexuality," p. 447, points out that we are never told that Pandarus leaves the room. He must leave at some point in order to come back in the morning, but here all it actually says is that Pandarus "leyde hym to slepe" (III.1189). According to Howard, pp. 446–47, the possible presence of the sleeping Pandarus (along with the dissociation of the narrator) forestalls the danger of the reader's voyeurism.

3. Howard, "Literature and Sexuality," p. 447. Helterman, "Masks of Love," p. 20, also suggests that Pandarus both reads and watches, but goes too far in tentatively identifying the romance he reads as the Lancelot romance. Chaucer seems careful to avoid such easily identifiable anachronisms; the only other "romaunce" he mentions in *TC* is that of Thebes (II.100), also an ancient story, and one rather more about war and history than love.

4. On the pairing of Pandarus and the poet here, see Howard, "Literature and Sexuality," pp. 446–48.

5. For amplification, see, among others, Coghill, *Poet Chaucer*, pp. 75–76; Bloomfield, "Distance and Predestination," p. 26; Howard, *Three Temptations*, p. 144; Donaldson, "Chaucer's Three 'P's'"; Zimbardo, "Creator and Created," pp. 286–87, 292; K. Taylor, "Proverbs"; Fyler, "Fabrications of Pandarus"; and Wetherbee, *Chaucer and the Poets*, p. 63.

6. Cf. Geoffrey of Vinsauf, *Poetria nova*, ll. 43–48; ed. Faral, p. 198; trans. Kopp, p. 34. For two points of view on this passage, see Howard, "Chaucer's Idea of an Idea," pp. 42–43; and Wetherbee, *Chaucer and the Poets*, pp. 78–79. Howard discusses the differences between Geoffrey of Vinsauf's neoplatonic original and Chaucer's

variation, in which Pandarus wins his purpose by "lucky accident," as if he were catching his purpose rather than realizing a mental archetype; Wetherbee nicely contrasts Geoffrey's process of preconception with Pandarus's process of "reconnaissance."

7. See Fyler's excellent treatment of Pandarus's fictions in "Fabrications of Pandarus."

8. See Lewis, "What Chaucer Really Did"; and Payne's summary of rhetorical changes in *Key of Remembrance*, p. 178. For Chaucer's treatment of *Filostrato*, see Meech, *Design*; Wallace's very fine study, *Early Writings of Boccaccio*, esp. pp. 106–40; and Windeatt, "Chaucer and the *Filostrato*," and his extremely useful parallel-text edition of *Troilus and Criseyde*.

9. Schless, "Transformations," p. 220 n. 1. His opinion is also reflected in his chapter on *TC* in *Chaucer and Dante*, pp. 101–47; the present chapter is meant partly as a response to Schless. For differing arguments, see K. Taylor, "Text," and Wetherbee, *Chaucer and the Poets*, pp. 37–41.

10. See Schless, "Transformations," p. 218, where he concludes that "many of the posited ascriptions to Dante . . . more likely come from common knowledge or a common source." He includes any echoes of *Inf.* V in this highly doubtful category; see *Chaucer and Dante*, pp. 108–12, though the discussion of *Inf.* V, 100, is limited to a response to Bethel's ascription of influence on *TC*, 1.897–903— which, I agree, is highly doubtful. I have not been able to consult directly Bethel's unpublished Harvard dissertation, "Influence of Dante."

11. Mazzotta, *Dante*, pp. 147–91, is the best discussion of the Dante-Virgil relationship as an act of reading. See also Barolini, *Dante's Poets*, pp. 201–56; and Gellrich, *Idea of the Book*, whose argument that Dante's allegory is an "allegory of reading" depends on both Mazzotta and de Man, "Rhetoric of Temporality."

12. For the sequence, see Singleton's commentary in Dante, *Divine Comedy*, vol. 2, pt. 2, pp. 734–37, 740–41. The direct quotation at *Purg.* XXX, 21, is from *Aeneid* VI, 883: "O, manibus date lilia plenis!" (O, give lilies with full hands!); cf. ed. and trans. Fairclough, vol. 1, pp. 568–69. This is the passage in which Anchises laments the (future) premature death of Marcellus, who would have led Rome back into a Golden Age had he lived long enough. Here it mourns Virgil's "prematurity" in a backward glance; in a forward

glance, however, the lilies of mourning become the lilies of resurrection, the passage a celebration of Beatrice's Christlike advent. The close translation—"conosco i segni de l'antica fiamma" ("I know the tokens of the ancient flame"; *Purg.* XXX, 48)—is of Dido's words as she falls in love with Aeneas at IV, 23: "agnosco veteris vestigia flammae." The oblique allusion is the threefold repetition of Virgil's name in Dante's farewell to his mentor: "Ma Virgilio n'avea lasciati sceme / di sé, Virgilio dolcissimo patre, / Virgilio a cui per mia salute die'mi . . ." (But Virgil had left us bereft of himself, Virgil sweetest father, Virgil to whom I gave myself for my salvation; *Purg.* XXX, 49–51). This echoes the anaphora of *Georgics* IV, 523–27: "tum quoque marmorea caput a cervice revulsum / gurgite cum medio portans Oeagrius Hebrus / volveret, Eurydicen vox ipsa et frigida lingua, / a miseram Eurydicen! anima fugiente vocabat. / Eurydicen toto referebant flumine ripae" (Even then, while Oeagrian Hebrus swept and rolled in midcurrent that head, plucked from its marble neck, the bare voice and death-cold tongue, with fleeting breath, called Eurydice—ah, hapless Eurydice! "Eurydice" the banks re-echoed, all adown the stream; ed. and trans. Fairclough, vol. 1, pp. 232–33). Just as Orpheus had lost Eurydice with a backward glance after bringing her out of the underworld, so too Dante looks back only to find that Virgil has returned to his place among the pagans of the first circle. Dronke, in "Francesca and Héloïse," p. 123, suggests that Dante may see himself as a Christlike Orpheus.

13. See Barolini, *Dante's Poets*, pp. 256–69.

14. Statius translates *Eclogues* IV, 5–7: "Magnus ab integro saeclorum nascitur ordo. / iam redit et Virgo, redeunt Saturnia regna; / iam nova progenies caelo demittitur alto" (The great line of the centuries begins anew. Now the Virgin returns, the reign of Saturn returns; now a new progeny descends from heaven on high; ed. and trans. Fairclough, vol. 1, pp. 28–29).

15. See Singleton's commentary in Dante, *Divine Comedy*, vol. 2, pt. 2, p. 530. The reference is to Statius's *Thebaid*, VII.424–25: "Iam ripas, Asope, tuas Boeotaque ventum / flumina" (Already they were come to thy banks, Asopus, and the Boeotian streams; ed. and trans. Mozley, vol. 2, pp. 504–5). For a provocative discussion of Dante's Christian reading of Statius and its source in the *Thebaid*, see Wetherbee, *Chaucer and the Poets*, pp. 134–41.

16. It seems likely that Dante was rereading the *Aeneid* at the

time he abandoned the *Convivio*; see Leo, "Unfinished *Convivio*." Hollander, in a note to "Dante *Theologus-Poeta*" (p. 136), writes: "I would suggest this much: that in his own life it was his rereading of the *Aeneid* that brought Dante back to Christianity, to the great poem with Beatrice at its center, that, for Dante, Virgil the prophet (of Christ and of Empire) was the voice he heard crying in the wilderness of the philosophically oriented *Convivio*."

17. The most famous of the "romantic" readers of *Inf.* v is probably De Sanctis, who in an 1869 essay celebrated her "spontaneous" involuntary yielding to Paolo; see *Nuovi saggi critici*, pp. 4–8. For excellent critiques of the romantic reading, see Poggioli, "Tragedy or Romance?" (an essay to which I am deeply indebted); and Girard, "Mimetic Desire."

18. Poggioli, "Tragedy or Romance?," p. 342.

19. I follow Poggioli's close analysis here, ibid., p. 338. See also Dronke, "Francesca and Héloïse," pp. 124–25. For Guinizelli's canzone, see Contini, ed., *Poeti del duecento*, vol. 2, pp. 460–64.

20. Dante also alludes to this incident at *Par.* XVI, 15, comparing Beatrice's withdrawn smile to the cough with which the Dame of Malehout signaled her presence to the illicit lovers "al primo fallo scritto di Ginevra" (at the first fault that is written of Guinevere). See, for example, Toynbee, "Dante and the Lancelot Romance." Hatcher and Musa conveniently summarize the literature on this issue in "Kiss," p. 99.

21. See Dronke, "Francesca and Héloïse," p. 129; Meyer-Lübke, *Wörterbuch*, pp. 311–12, entry 3642; Battaglia, *Grande dizionario*, vol. 6, pp. 548–49. *Galeotto* derives from medieval Latin *galeottus*, steersman, from medieval Greek *galaia*, a kind of ship. See also Toynbee, *Dictionary*, p. 257: "The name of Gallehault came to be used . . . as a synonym for pander; hence D. makes Francesca da Rimini . . . say of the Romance of Lancelot, which she and Paolo were reading, 'Galeotto fu il libro e chi lo scrisse.'" Toynbee thus implies (as does Singleton in Dante, *Divine Comedy*, vol. 1, pt. 2, p. 95) that the pun was already well known before Dante used it, but he does not adduce any evidence; I have been unable to find any either. Boccaccio calls Gallehault a "mezzano" (go-between) and glosses *Inf.* v, 137: "E così vuol questa donna dire che quello libro, il quale leggevano Paolo ed ella, quello uficio adoperasse tra lor due, che adoperò Galeotto tra Lancellotto e la reina Ginevra" (and so this lady wishes to say

that that book, which she and Paolo were reading, performed the same function between these two as Gallehault performed between Lancelot and Queen Guinevere); *Comento alla Divina Commedia*, ed. Guerra, vol. 2, p. 145, lecture 21 (trans. mine). Boccaccio also refers to the *Decameron* as "prencipe Galeotto," and although Gardner believes that he was invoking Gallehault's reputation as a faithful friend (see "'Matière de Bretagne,'" p. 16), I see no reason why he could not also have had Dante's passage and Gallehault's role as go-between in mind when he named his book "Galeotto." The absence of any debased meaning for *galeotto* when Dante used it, however, does not exclude the possibility that semantic pejoration may have taken place *because* of Boccaccio's use of the word in the *Decameron*; see Wallace's suggestion ("Chaucer and Boccaccio's Early Writings," p. 159) that Chaucer may never have named Boccaccio in his works because of the semantic and moral degeneration of the latter's treatment of romance language and ethos apparent in his works.

22. Poggioli, "Tragedy or Romance?," p. 358.

23. D'Ovidio, *Nuovi studii danteschi*, app. 5, p. 531.

24. Hatcher and Musa, "Kiss," p. 109.

25. Augustine, *Confessions*, VIII.xii; ed. Watts, vol. 1, pp. 462–67. For the parallel, see Swing, *Fragile Leaves*, p. 299; Hollander, *Allegory*, pp. 112–14; and Dronke, "Francesca and Héloïse," p. 129 n. 32.

26. Augustine, *Confessions*, I.xiii; ed. Watts, vol. 1, pp. 38–43. See Mazzotta, *Dante*, pp. 165–70.

27. Mazzotta, *Dante*, p. 170. Dante's disagreement with Augustine involves the appropriation of Virgil's providential shape to history. Augustine saw it as an apology for secular empire, but Dante turned it to Christian purposes.

28. For the hyperbolic treatment of Troilus's courtly behavior, both serious and comic, see Muscatine, *Chaucer and the French Tradition*, pp. 133–38. For a view of Troilus's behavior as wholly serious, see J. Mann, "Troilus' Swoon"; Mann maintains that Troilus's diffidence, especially his swoon, is not ridiculous, ineffectual, or passive. Rather, it illustrates his good intentions and refusal to assert unwanted power of the kind Criseyde so fears, and thus makes him the ideal lover for her.

29. Young, "Chaucer's *Troilus*."

30. Toynbee's text and trans. in "Dante and the Lancelot Romance," pp. 18 and 33.

31. Ibid., pp. 20 and 35.

32. See Young, *Origin and Development*, pp. 43–66, comparing Boccaccio's Pandaro to Gallehault and other courtly "friends" as a go-between. Kirby, *Chaucer's Troilus*, pp. 110–17, adds a comparison on the basis of friendship; both feel that any relationship between Chaucer's Pandarus and the "galeotto" of *Inf.* v is at best indirect, through Boccaccio. On Pandarus as a good friend, see Slaughter, "Chaucer's Pandarus." As a bad friend, see Gaylord, "Friendship"; R. Cook, "Chaucer's Pandarus"; and Freiwald, "Swich Love of Frendes."

33. *HF*, 342–60. Both this and Criseyde's lament should be compared to the twelfth-century French *Roman d'Eneas*, ll. 1539–1604; see *Eneas*, trans. Yunck, pp. 87–88.

34. Chaucer, *Troilus and Criseyde*, ed. Root, p. 445; *Complete Works*, ed. Robinson, p. 819. Stephen A. Barney, in Chaucer, *Riverside Chaucer*, ed. L. Benson et al., p. 1033, prefers the explanation of metaphorical intoxication.

35. Speirs, *Chaucer the Maker*, p. 62; and Howard, "Experience," p. 176, both suggest this reading. For the argument that Criseyde's question (and state of mind) is considerably less ambiguous and more openly passionate, see Donaldson, "Briseis," pp. 8–9.

36. Patterson has edited the relevant portion of the *Disce mori*, "The Seven Tokens of Carnal Love," in "Ambiguity and Interpretation," pp. 301–7. The *Disce mori* quotes the first stanza of the "Canticus Troili" (1.400–406) in ll. 64–70 (p. 304 in Patterson's edition); and summarizes its treatment of carnal love with "So be þei confedered in ille as a þeef to a þeef and dronken of þis sweet poison: 'Of which poison is you lust more to rede, / Seeþ þe storie of Troilus, Criseide, and Diomede'" (ll. 148–51, pp. 306–7) in Patterson's ed.).

37. *Roman d'Eneas*, ll. 810–14; ed. Salverda de Grave, vol. 1, p. 25. *Eneas*, trans. Yunck, p. 72.

38. See Mieszkowski's treatment of the tradition of Criseyde in "Reputation of Criseyde."

39. For a catalogue of what we don't know about Criseyde from this portrait, see Donaldson, "Four Women of Style," pp. 53–54.

40. Wetherbee, in *Chaucer and the Poets*, p. 55, speaks of how dif-

ficult it is to condemn the characters of *TC*; nonetheless the force and tone of his discussion suggest that he does condemn both Criseyde and Pandarus. His attitude seems to spring from his argument that Troilus is a Dante-figure; this casts Criseyde into the role of a siren or a false Beatrice, and Pandarus into the role of a false Virgil. The need to keep Troilus sexually innocent and pure results in charged, overly negative readings of the other two main characters. See below, Ch. 3.

41. See *Inf.* III, 112–17, and *Aeneid* VI, 309–12; for a valuable discussion of Dante's borrowing from Virgil, and Chaucer's borrowing from *Inf.* III here, see Wetherbee, *Chaucer and the Poets*, pp. 38–40, 174–76.

42. See *Inf.* XIII, 22–108, and *Aeneid* III, 22–48. With the tree as Polydorus-Pier-Troilus rather than God, the Christian perspective of the leaf simile is subverted.

43. See Spitzer, "Speech and Language."

44. Particularly with the punning "wood." See Wetherbee, *Chaucer and the Poets*, p. 175.

45. Boethius, *Consolation*, III.m.9. See also *Par.* I, 103–26.

46. "Benigna donna d'ogni gentil core" (kind lady of every gentle heart; Boccaccio, *Filostrato*, III.74).

47. The best studies of Chaucer's historicism in *TC* are Bloomfield, "Chaucer's Sense of History," which shows that despite the poem's anachronisms it still gives a sense of a time past and very different; McCall, "Trojan Scene," which shows how thoroughly the pagan Troy setting informs the poem's tone and acts as a parallel to Troilus's fortunes; and Minnis, *Chaucer and Pagan Antiquity*.

48. This is part of Howard's argument in "Fiction and Religion," esp. pp. 313–14. The paganness lies mainly in the sensuality of Boccaccio's depiction of love. Meech argues that Boccaccio condemns this sensuality in the strongest terms; see *Design*, esp. pp. 4–17. But apRoberts believes the Boccaccio endorses the love of *Filostrato*, which is perfect precisely because of its high sensuality; see "Love in the *Filostrato*." For a less exalted view, of love in Boccaccio as a debasement of courtliness, see Wallace, *Early Writings of Boccaccio* and "Chaucer and Boccaccio's Early Writings," esp. p. 159.

49. Robertson, in "Chaucerian Tragedy," p. 114, interprets this as "idle talk" and self-deceiving irony: "It shows what might have been if Criseyde had actually been interested in 'vertu' rather than in 'his persone, his aray, his look, his chere.'" But see J. Mann, "Troi-

lus' Swoon," a powerful argument for the positive role of Troilus's considerate virtue in overcoming Criseyde's real fears of love.

50. Utley, "Troilus's Love."

51. On Aeneas's treachery, see Guido delle Colonne, *Historia destructionis Troiae*, XXIX; trans. Meek, pp. 209–19. For Troilus's resemblance to Dido, see Donaldson, "Ending," p. 93.

52. Mazzotta, *Dante*, p. 191. Most of the examples are of reading Virgil; to this Mazzotta contrasts Francesca's narcissistic reading of the Lancelot romance.

53. As Bloomfield writes in "Distance and Predestination," p. 17, the vivid reconstruction of the past in all its detail makes the past unique and therefore transient and distanced; it also makes the present evanescent. See also Ganim, "Time and Tone."

Chapter 3

1. On the character contrasts, see Muscatine, *Chaucer and the French Tradition*, pp. 153–57. The scene between Troilus and Pandarus invites as much disagreement as that between Criseyde and Pandarus. Robertson, in "Chaucerian Tragedy," p. 100, interprets Troilus's response (to offer Pandarus his sister in return for Pandarus's aid with Criseyde) as an indication of just how perverting the love affair is; the reading depends on the notion that Troilus is a paradigm for "every mortal sinner" (p. 118). Howard, in *Three Temptations*, p. 137 n. 86, believes that Troilus's offer is an exaggerated declaration of friendship; it should not be taken literally because friends do not ask so much of one another. Wetherbee, in *Chaucer and the Poets*, p. 72, referring to both Robertson and Howard, suggests that Troilus, in his innocence, probably doesn't understand the implications Pandarus is at such pains to lay out for him; he is "awed and moved by Pandarus's act of friendship, an act he sees as different in its essential nature from common pandering," and wishes to reciprocate with true "love of frendes."

2. Wetherbee, *Chaucer and the Poets*, p. 163.

3. Lewis, *Allegory of Love*, pp. 193–94; and Mizener, "Character and Action"; both are also cited in Wetherbee, *Chaucer and the Poets*, p. 164.

4. Wetherbee, *Chaucer and the Poets*, p. 163.

5. Howard, *Idea of the Canterbury Tales*, p. 251, discussing these

and related lines from the Wife of Bath's Prologue, writes: "We may suspect her of being an adulteress, but it is part of Chaucer's game that we cannot come up with any evidence."

6. Wetherbee, *Chaucer and the Poets*, pp. 156–57, 163–64.

7. Ibid., p. 164.

8. This reflects good scholastic literary theory: one of the charges brought against poetry was that it appealed to the will and the passions rather than solely to reason. The effect could be for good or for ill. On the one hand, when the wing of reason falls short in *Paradiso*, Dante flies on the wing of desire; in the end his *velle*, or affective faculty, unites him with God. On the other, the anonymous fourteenth-century "Tretys of Miraclis Pleyinge" regards the appeal to the will and the emotions as dangerous. For the related Arabic theory that poetry consisted mainly in image making and depended on the imagination, see Averroes, *Middle Commentary* (translated into Latin by Hermann the German), trans. Hardison. For discussions of Averroes' influence, see Hardison, "Place of Averroes' Commentary"; Murphy, *Rhetoric*, pp. 90–91; J. B. Allen, "Hermann"; and Minnis, *Medieval Theory of Authorship*, pp. 131–45.

9. See, for instance, Steadman, *Disembodied Laughter*; and Wetherbee, *Chaucer and the Poets*, pp. 17, 28.

10. See, for instance, Donaldson, "Ending"; and Robertson, "Chaucerian Tragedy." But Donaldson has a different account of the narrator in *The Canterbury Tales*; see his comment, in "Chaucer the Pilgrim," p. 12, that even after distinguishing Chaucer into three aspects—man, poet, and narrator—we cannot always be sure at any given point which has the last word. Bronson, *In Search of Chaucer*, p. 26, warns against separating the narrator from the poet. In response, Jordan has revised his view of the narrator, first published in "Narrator"; writing in *Shape of Creation*, p. 67, he says that "the narrating 'I' *is* Chaucer—Chaucer mischievously posturing by adopting roles divorced from a poetic sensibility." Jordan's revised view brings him into line with Howard in "Chaucer the Man," which argues that much of the interest of Chaucerian narrators lies in seeing through them to what they all have in common: the poet Chaucer. I am in basic agreement with this view of the *CT* narrator; we are still, I think, left with the problem of deciding to what ends Chaucer dons his poses in the *Troilus*.

11. Freccero, "Introduction," p. 4.

12. For deixis, see Fillmore, *Deixis*; Jakobson, "Shifters"; and Traugott and Pratt, *Linguistics*, pp. 272–82. See also Weinrich, *Tempus*, p. 32, on the etymological relation between pointing (Greek *deiknymi*) and saying (Latin *dicere*). For a brief discussion of deixis, the grammar of narrative, and authentication, see my Introduction.

13. For autobiography as discours, see Benveniste, *Problèmes*, p. 239; and Hamburger, *Logic of Literature*, p. 311. For the division of self in earlier narratives, see Vance, "Augustine's *Confessions*," where the split is described epistemologically as the "I-as-subject" and the "I-as-object" (p. 4); and Vitz, " 'I' of the *Roman de la rose*," where the split in the narrator is described in temporal terms—"the *me* to whom this *I* refers is indeed someone who no longer exists, a past self" (p. 49).

14. For other treatments of the addresses, see Auerbach, "Dante's Addresses," concerned primarily with their relation to classical invocation, from which they derive the vocative case and the imperative mood; and Gmelin, "Die Anreden an den Leser," a typology of the addresses and their local functions.

15. Epistola x.14, in Dante, *Dantis Allegherii epistolae*, ed. and trans. Toynbee, pp. 287–92.

16. A good example of this use of simile is *Purg.* ii, 124–33. For the constraints on report of inner speech and action, and the ways in which fiction neutralizes them, see Hamburger, *Logic of Literature*, pp. 81–98; and Genette, *Narrative Discourse*, pp. 169–85. The "novelist's alibi" is Spitzer's happy term; see "Zum Stil Marcel Prousts."

17. Benveniste, *Problèmes*, p. 239.

18. Romans 6; 1 Corinthians 15:22, 45; and Ephesians 4:22–25; and Freccero, "Introduction," p. 5.

19. Singleton translates the *ci* as the oblique form of the first-person plural *noi*; in his reading, Beatrice speaks in a sort of imperial (or perhaps only imperious) "we." But *ci* could just as well mean *qui* (here); this demonstrates nicely the relationship between person and place in the proximate complex *I–here–now*.

20. Stammerjohann lists ten aspects of the *passato remoto* in "Strukturen der Rede," p. 314: (1) an action in the distant past; (2) an action in the past that has no connection to the present anymore; (3) a single action in the past; (4) an action in the past seen in its totality (perfective); (5) an action at a precise time in the past; (6) a sententious generality; (7) an action in the past interposed into another

action already under way in the *imperfetto*; (8) a foregrounded action in the narrated past; (9) what happened (not what was); and (10) generally, the narration of the past. Fourteenth-century Italian is not strikingly different; see Ronconi, "Aoristi e perfetti in Dante."

21. Hence Weinrich, *Tempus*, p. 104, speaks of the past absolute in Romance languages as a tense designating time that is truly dead.

22. For summaries of the commentary amassed on the grammar of this passage (much of it on l. 63 and the referent of "cui"; Singleton's translation, which I have retained, indicates Virgil, and the other possibility is Beatrice), see Singleton, "Inferno X"; and Cerisola, "'Disdegno' di Guido Cavalcanti." For the most recent argument that "cui" refers to Beatrice, see Barolini, *Dante's Poets*, pp. 144–46. One argument in favor of Beatrice is the opposition of the distanced "là" and the proximate "qui"; but finally it makes little difference for my purposes whether Beatrice or Virgil is the referent of "cui," especially since in the chain of intercession Beatrice has engaged Virgil as her agent.

23. Singleton, "Inferno X," pp. 58–60.

24. Guido died in August, 1300, from malaria he contracted during his exile from Florence, which began in late June of that year, while Dante was serving as prior. Given the great influence of Dante's *primo amico*, we must wonder why he is so systematically denied his due in the *Commedia*; the timing of his death (for which Dante was, as prior, indirectly and partially responsible) may indeed have been a determining factor of the fictional time of the poem's journey. For a good discussion of Guido in the *Commedia*, see Barolini, *Dante's Poets*, pp. 123–53.

25. Singleton, "Inferno X," p. 57 n. 9.

26. In *Purg.* XXXI; see also *Purg.* XXX, 55–63, where Dante names himself and defends this unusual practice as necessary. Here we have no "impersonal I"; the "I" of the confessional is as personal as can be. See Spitzer, "Poetic and Empirical 'I'"; and Dante's statement in the *Convivio*, I.ii.3, that a writer ought not to speak of himself unless it is necessary.

27. Augustine, *De doctrina christiana*, I, 19; *On Christian Doctrine*, trans. Robertson, p. 17.

28. Freccero, "Medusa." For the *rime petrose*, see Dante, *Rime*, ed. Barbi, pp. 103–9.

29. Idem, "Casella's Song"; and Barolini, *Dante's Poets*, pp. 31–40.

30. See Aristotle, *Rhetoric*, 1.2, 1355b–56a, and 1.9, 1367b.

31. For Dante's critique of the *Convivio*, see Mazzeo, *Medieval Cultural Tradition*, pp. 174–204; Gilson, *Dante and Philosophy*, pp. 83–161; and Nardi, *Saggi di filosofia dantesca*, pp. 3–39.

32. For Ulysses, Dante, and the *Convivio*, see Nardi, *Dante e la cultura medioevale*, pp. 153–54; Padoan, "Ulisse"; Freccero, "Dante's Prologue Scene"; and Thompson, "Dante's Ulysses." The *Convivio*'s Aristotelian opening sentence, "Sì come dice lo Filosofo nel principio de la Prima Filosofia, tutti li uomini naturalmente desiderono di sapere" (As saith the Philosopher in the First Philosophy, "All men by nature desire to know"; 1.i.1; trans. Wicksteed, p. 1), lies behind Ulysses' speech at *Inf.* XXVI, 112–20.

33. See the nautical language associating Dante's pilgrimage with Ulysses' voyage, at *Purg.* I, 1–3; *Par.* II, 1–6; and *Par.* XXXIII, 94–96, for instance. Other passages recalling Ulysses include *Purg.* I, 130–32; *Purg.* XIX, 19–24; and *Par.* XXVII, 82–83.

34. Nardi, in *Dante e la cultura medioevale*, pp. 153–54, shows that the source of Dante's allegorical siren is Cicero's *De finibus bonorum et malorum*, V, xviii, where the siren stands not for the temptations of fleshly delight, but rather for those of worldly knowledge. Elsewhere in the medieval mythographic tradition, the sirens were consistently treated as fleshly delight; see Fulgentius, *Opera*, ed. Helm, p. 48; *Fulgentius the Mythographer*, trans. Whitbread, p. 73; *Scriptores rerum mythicarum*, II.101 and III.11.9, ed. Bode, pp. 108–9 and pp. 233–34; *Ovide moralisé*, l. 3488, ed. de Boer, vol. 2, p. 262; Bersuire, *Metamorphosis Ovidiana moraliter*, pp. 92–95v.

35. See Padoan, "Ulisse," and the mythographic sources of the preceding note. The Third Vatican Mythographer includes an etymology in his interpretation: "Idem Ulixes quasi ὅλων ξένος, omnium peregrinus dici meruit, quia sapientia a rebus mundaris peregrinos facit" (Also Ulysses deserved to be called a sort of ὅλων ξένος, a stranger from all things, for wisdom makes men strangers to worldly things; *Scriptores rerum mythicarum*, III.11.9, ed. Bode, p. 233, ll. 31–33; trans. mine).

36. Aristotle, *Politics*, 1.2. Thus Ulysses is damned also on grounds suggested by Greek philosophy, not just those of Christian

dogma. Augustine too makes language central to the human community in *De civitate Dei*; see especially XIX.5–7. "Frati" echoes Aeneas's "O socii" address to his fellow exiles in *Aeneid* I, 198–203.

37. For the association of Virgil and his epic style with Ulysses and his duplicitous use of language, see Barolini, *Dante's Poets*, pp. 228–34.

38. See esp. *Purg.* XXII, in which two different Virgilian texts are read against authorial intention: the "prophecy" of Christ's birth in the Fourth Eclogue at *Purg.* XXII, 70–72, and *Aeneid* III, 56–57, at *Purg.* XXII, 40–41. See Shoaf, "'Auri sacra fames.'"

39. See above, pp. 23–25, for fuller discussion of the VOM acrostic. For the general context of artistic pride in *Purg.* X–XII, see Simonelli, "Canto X del *Purgatorio*"; and K. Taylor, "From *superbo Iliön*."

40. Chiampi, *Shadowy Prefaces*, p. 169.

41. The only other solution (besides the one I offer here, and in fuller form in "From *superbo Iliön*" proposed for this acrostic, *lue* (pestilence), makes it legible but not particularly meaningful. See Santoro, "Due acrostici"; and Valli, "Canto XIX nel *Paradiso*."

42. See also Dante's reference to his "versi brevi" (brief lines) and the address to "tu che sol per cancellare scrivi" (you who write only to cancel) in the preceding canto; *Par.* XVIII, 87, 130.

43. Superimposed on one another, I and M also suggest the graphic shape of the eagle, whose creation demonstrates God's "star writing." Originally lights that successively form letters, words, Scriptural quotation, and then from one letter, M, the image of a lily before taking on final shape as the image and spirit of justice, the eagle's elongated "neck" suggests an I. Singleton's commentary has helpful illustrations (Dante, *Divine Comedy*, vol. 3, pt. 2, p. 310).

44. This etymology was known to the Middle Ages; see Isidore of Seville, *Etymologiarum*, XI.1.4.

45. See Mazzeo, *Medieval Cultural Tradition*, p. 204.

46. Singleton, *Dante's 'Commedia,'* p. 62. The distinction between poet and pilgrim can be drawn too sharply, particularly if all capacity for change is assigned to the pilgrim. Freccero writes, "It should be stressed . . . that the distinction we have made between an experience and the expression of that experience is purely logical. . . . Ontologically, or even phenomenologically, they are one. The experience of conversion for Dante is at the same time the experience

of writing the novel of the self" ("Introduction," p. 5). Perhaps a better distinction would be to separate Dante's experience into two aspects, one a fictional otherworldly journey exemplifying conversion, the other a poetic journey in which the poet changes as well. The second aspect of conversion is experientially real in the sense that we can ourselves observe it in the changing process of representation (the movement from VOM to LVE); we do not have to take Dante's word for it.

47. Spitzer, "Addresses to the Reader," p. 584.

48. See also *Inf.* XVI, 124–36; *Purg.* XXXI, 124–26.

49. For Geryon and his role in defining the truthfulness of the *Commedia*, see Hollander, "Dante *Theologus-Poeta*," p. 112; Ferrucci, *Poetics of Disguise*, pp. 66–102; and Barolini's excellent discussion in *Dante's Poets*, pp. 213–14. Ferrucci uses the passage in support of his contention that the poem is fundamentally metaphoric; Hollander and Barolini believe (as I do) that Dante here asserts the truthfulness of his poem. I would add that, as with Spenser's treatment of Archimago in the *Faerie Queene*, part of the truthfulness lies in emphasizing the fictional approach to truth, and in not allowing any reader to mistake its potentially deceptive power. This emphasis seems a common trait of narrative allegory, and may arise from the attitude Augustine expresses in *Soliloquiorum* II.10 (*PL*, 32, col. 893), that the greater verisimilitude is the greater lie.

50. Hollander, "Dante *Theologus-Poeta*," p. 112.

51. The description comes from Friedman, "Point of View."

52. This corresponds (with qualifications) to the creation of a fictional self as described in Banfield, *Unspeakable Sentences*; see esp. pp. 61–63 and all of ch. 2, pp. 65–108.

53. See Bloomfield, "Distance and Predestination"; and Howard, *Three Temptations*, p. 113. Like the *Commedia*, the *Troilus* is what Weinrich would call a frame narrative, a category in which he includes not only works like *The Canterbury Tales* and the *Decameron* but also autobiography, retrospective first-person narrative in general (e.g., Mann's *Doktor Faustus*), and history writing. All of these present a distanced narrative of events as mediated by a first-person commentator who orders and interprets them for us. See *Tempus*, pp. 33–39.

54. See Jordan, *Shape of Creation*, esp. pp. 70–71.

55. Muscatine, *Chaucer and the French Tradition*, p. 129.

56. See Pratt, *"Roman de Troyle,"* for the suggestion that Chaucer made (likewise silent) use of a French prose rendition of *Filostrato*. For a detailed analysis of Chaucer's debt to Boccaccio, see Meech, *Design*. For the relation of the *Troilus* to Benoît and Guido, see Young, *Origin and Development*, pp. 6–139; and R. Gordon, *Story of Troilus*. Both believe that Benoît is more important, and Gordon simply skips Guido. For a comparison that does not assume Benoît's primacy, see Lumiansky, "Story of Troilus and Briseida." For Guido alone, see C. David Benson, " 'O Nyce World.' "

57. For a brief description of the narrator as both detached and sympathetically participating, see Bethurum, "Chaucer's Point of View," esp. p. 223. Though her description of the conflict between these roles is astute, the *Troilus* is not, as she asserts, "straight narration." For a more thorough description of Chaucer's dual role, see Bloomfield, "Distance and Predestination"; and for the narrator's attempts to suppress information, see Donaldson, "Criseide and Her Narrator."

58. As I. Gordon writes of the narrator, as he appears in the proem to Book II, "He will make no fundamental changes in the *historia* itself." See *Double Sorrow*, p. 73.

59. I do not construe ll. 393–98 as I. Gordon does in *Double Sorrow*, pp. 77–78. She sees the passage as a joke in which the narrator renders the precise wording of a song of which the author gives only the "sentence." It is indeed playful, since Chaucer got the lyric from Petrarch, not Lollius; but I read the interrupted syntax as meaning that Chaucer will report not only the "sentence" as Lollius wrote it, but also the words of Troilus's song as Lollius wrote them, except for the difference in language. The passage implies that Lollius recorded Troilus's words exactly, and that Chaucer follows suit.

60. Jordan, *Shape of Creation*, p. 69.

61. On the narrator's feat of memory, see Howard, *Idea of the Canterbury Tales*, pp. 137–58.

62. See the very different discussion of this passage in ibid., pp. 185–86: "And it is understood that we can tell true from false. The old idea, part of the neoplatonic heritage of Christianity, was that the truth is one but the expression of it varies in various 'sentences.' When the Host demands of Chaucer that he tell 'in prose somewhat, at the leeste / In which there be some mirthe or some doctrine' (VII: 934–935), Chaucer drolly has himself state this idea in a pompous,

circumlocutious, bumbling way. But what he says so ineptly was true all the same." Though it may be true of the gospels, the analogy does not hold well for the tales, where the emphasis is shifted to the multifariousness "in hir tellyng." See also Minnis, *Medieval Theory of Authorship*, p. 167, where he sets this claim beside that of the General Prologue (1.725–46) but does not note the conflict that arises when the claim of transparent mediation is carried to its extreme.

63. See Cooper, "Girl with Two Lovers."

64. For recent accounts of voice in *The Canterbury Tales*, see Green, "Voices of the Pilgrims"; Leicester, "General Prologue"; and Nolan, " 'Poet Ther Was.' "

65. See Kittredge, *Chaucer and His Poetry*, pp. 117–21; Minnis, *Chaucer and Pagan Antiquity*, pp. 61–107; and esp. McCall, "Trojan Scene in *Troilus*," which describes the Trojanization of the story and then argues that the detailed historical setting illuminates the tragedy of Troilus as the tragedy of Troy. One might add, the tragedy of pagandom. For Chaucer's historical consciousness, see Bloomfield, "Chaucer's Sense of History." Bloomfield remarks that, for a Christian, greater historicity makes greater symbolic significance possible (pp. 13–14).

66. Boccaccio pays little attention to historical authentication after a perfunctory and skeptical mention of "old stories" in the proem: "se fede alcuna alle antiche lettere si può dare" (if any faith may be put in old stories; *Filostrato*, Proemio, 28; trans. mine).

67. The exceptions are all in Book V, and all very general; even here he has altered *Filostrato* to some extent. See the description of Diomede at v.799–805 (*Filostrato*, VI.8, 10–11, 24, 33); the reference to Troilus's woe at v.1562–68 (*Filostrato*, VIII.1–5); and the summary of Troilus's death at v.1751–60 (*Filostrato*, VIII.6–26). See Barney's notes (from Robinson) in Chaucer, *Riverside Chaucer*, ed. L. Benson et al., pp. 1024–25, comparing *TC* to *Filostrato* line by line; and Windeatt's parallel-text edition of *Troilus and Criseyde*.

68. Henryson, *Testament of Cresseid*, l. 64; ed. Fox, p. 113.

69. See v.946–51. Distance and intimacy are part of the perspective of discours, and correspond to one aspect of what Genette calls "mood"; as such they are part of narrative rendering rather than of the story itself (see *Narrative Discourse*, pp. 162–85). The best study of the dialectic of distance and closeness in the *Troilus* remains Bloomfield, "Distance and Predestination," where he discusses how

Chaucer alternates between presenting the past as if present to us, and presenting it as very far from the world we share with the narrator; see esp. pp. 16–20. Payne, *Key of Remembrance*, p. 62, argues that the presence of the narrator constantly distances us from action. I think this is very often true, but not consistently and not in consistent degree. We should remember that the narrator is present in his narrative as well as in his intrusions, and this is the point that the varying aesthetic and emotional distance in the two courtships illustrates.

70. Donaldson argues that the comment is the only thing that makes readers think this might be true; the narrator's protestation is so weak that it makes us wonder why he takes such pains to refute the interpretation. See "Criseide and Her Narrator," pp. 65–67. Speirs, in *Chaucer the Maker*, p. 62, denies the associations of the love-potion tradition, as I discuss above on pp. 65–66. Howard, in "Experience," p. 176, suggests the "perfect ambiguity" of the scene; Criseyde's feelings could be love at first sight, or simply a heady feeling as from strong wine. Howard then discusses Criseyde's subsequent monologue as her fantasies about what it might be like to be in love with Troilus. The internal debate suggests that her love is indeed not instantaneous. Mizener, "Character and Action," pp. 70–71, takes the narrator's comment at face value, as confirming the deliberate speed with which Criseyde falls into love. Mehl, "Audience of Chaucer's 'Troilus,'" p. 179, finds the narrator's intervention at first humorously pointless, but then an effective appeal for the audience's cooperation in constructing the fiction.

71. See above, p. 66; and the *Disce mori* edited by Patterson in "Ambiguity and Interpretation."

72. Both eyes and heart are involved at II.649–50. At II.677 most editors have adopted the reading of some inferior MSS: "made love withinne hire herte for to myne" (Robinson). See Barney's textual note in Chaucer, *Riverside Chaucer*, ed. L. Benson et al., p. 1166. "Herte" is not well attested, but when it appears it suggests the power this convention exerted over scribes eager to clarify the text they copied.

73. I. Gordon, *Double Sorrow*, pp. 80–83, takes this position wholeheartedly and, I believe, too certainly, by asserting that the implications of the narrative are "fact," that the narrator's purpose is to discount this "fact," and that Chaucer's purpose in including both is

to point to the "enigma" of Criseyde's long resistance to Troilus. This strikes me as a curious distortion of Gordon's approach, the study of ambiguity. Donaldson, in "Criseide and Her Narrator," p. 69, also dismisses the narrator's comment as specious, while allowing for puzzlement, not worry, on the part of the reader over the behavior of the narrator at this point. But he, of course, does not interpret the window scene as a sign of instantaneous love, only strong attraction. See also "Briseis," pp. 8–9, where he strengthens his argument for Criseyde's powerful attraction.

74. Boccaccio, *Filostrato*, II.65–66.

75. Donaldson, "Criseide and Her Narrator," p. 66.

76. See Bloomfield's comment in "Authenticating Realism," pp. 186–87, that the narrator's imaginative involvement is in large measure what makes the story realistic and therefore believable.

77. Thus, for example, *erlebte Rede* (free indirect style), which presents a character's inner speech more immediately than in direct or indirect discourse, but at the same time retains traces of the narrator's own perspective in pronouns and tense, is hence more openly fictional than styles that conform more to the strictures of everyday conversation. See Genette, *Narrative Discourse*, pp. 169–85. For Banfield, in *Unspeakable Sentences*, pp. 183–224, this more than anything suggests that there is no narrator, only a fictional self-consciousness that does not speak for itself.

78. For a sensitive description of the interplay among speech, thought, and emotion in this scene, see Howard, *Three Temptations*, pp. 127–30.

79. See idem, "Experience," esp. pp. 184–85.

80. Howard sees the scene as an objective rendering; ibid., p. 176.

81. Both Howard, ibid., p. 187, and I. Gordon, *Double Sorrow*, pp. 98–99, point out that Criseyde and the narrator share this simile; but Gordon argues that such consonance is an ironic illusion, pointing to antithetical states of mind brought into pointed contrast by use of the same image. I must admit I don't understand her point; Criseyde's mind in this scene indeed seems like March weather, brightened and darkened as she considers her feelings about Troilus and about love in general. It would be a mistake to limit her consciousness to a single moment that traps her day in shadow while the narrator's sun shines.

82. Curtius, *European Literature*, pp. 128–30, lists a large number of nautical metaphors for poetry. The most significant, probably, is that from Statius's *Thebaid*, XII.809, which occurs just before the envy topos Chaucer imitates at V.1789–92.

83. For a good discussion of the narrator's foot-dragging, see Donaldson, "Criseide and Her Narrator," pp. 68–83.

84. See idem, "Ending," p. 91.

85. I follow Donaldson's excellent discussion of these lines in "Criseide and Her Narrator," p. 70; "how that she was unkynde" is a euphemism, and euphemism works only if it replaces the blunter alternative, "how Criseyde Troilus forsook." But "when it follows the stronger statement it purports to replace, it accomplishes no more than anticlimax. Criseide's forsaking of Troilus is emphasized, rather than palliated, by the narrator's attempt to minimize it." Cf. the Merchant's Tale, IV.2350–63, where blunt statement followed by euphemistic alternative again appears, to devastating effect.

86. In the "olde bokes" passage of the *PF*, ll. 22–25, and the "keye of remembraunce" passage of the *LGW*, ll. 17–28 of the F text. See Payne, *Key of Remembrance*, p. 175.

87. Cf. I.547–1064 with II.505–88; on this and other Pandaric fictions, see Fyler, "Fabrications of Pandarus."

Chapter 4

1. Auerbach's essay "Figura" is central to this chapter and to the idea of allegory in the *Commedia* generally. Other works I have found particularly useful on allegory in Dante are Charity, *Events and Their Afterlife*; Hollander, *Allegory*; Mazzotta, *Dante*; and Singleton, *Dante's 'Commedia.'* See also Wetherbee, *Platonism and Poetry*.

2. See above, pp. 6–10; on comparisons as *discours*, see Benveniste, *Problèmes*, p. 241.

3. For the terminology, see Lansing, *From Image to Idea*, p. 30. Lansing gets the terms from Dante, *La Divina Commedia*, ed. Porena and Pazzaglia, p. 86, which I have not been able to consult. The concept of the pseudosimile is well known; characteristic examples are *Inf.* X, 100; *Inf.* XIII, 45; and *Purg.* II, 54.

4. For the causal implication of the comparative formula *come colui che* in older Italian, see Rohlfs, *Grammatica storia*, vol. 3, p. 191.

5. See Spitzer, "Poetic and Empirical 'I,'" p. 416.

6. As with Spitzer's "novelist's alibi." See above, p. 90.

7. Auerbach, *Dante*, pp. 132–33.

8. Gilson shows that St. Bonaventure's similes, too, are not merely verbal categories, but discovered structural characteristics of the universe; see *Philosophie de saint Bonaventure*, p. 169.

9. For this framework of vision, see Newman, "St. Augustine's Three Visions," which argues persuasively that the poem's tripartite structure is matched by corresponding visionary modes derived from Augustine's hierarchy in the twelfth book of *De Genesi ad litteram*. Here, Augustine discusses corporeal, imaginative, and intellective vision as the means by which human beings can regain Paradise in this life. For the differences in stylistic representation, see Freccero, "Infernal Irony" and "Manfred's Wounds"; and Chiarenza, "Imageless Vision."

10. The three features of allegory come from Auerbach's "Figura"; the term *Urbild des Geschehens* is Auerbach's as well (p. 81 in *Gesammelte Aufsätze*; p. 58 in Manheim's trans.).

11. Ibid., pp. 80–82 in *Gesammelte Aufsätze*; pp. 58–60 in Manheim's trans.

12. See Romans 1:20.

13. In Singleton, "In exitu Israel de Egypto." See also the Letter to Can Grande, which explains the "polysemous" style of the poem with the example of Psalm 113; Epistola X.vii. Singleton's seminal essay primarily compares *Purg.* I to *Inf.* I; the following discussion is an effort to synthesize it with subsequent studies, both by Singleton and by others, of the role of Exodus in the *Commedia*. My only contribution is the material on the River of Light.

14. See Freccero, "River of Death," for the identification of the "fiumana" with the River Jordan, which is greater than the sea because of its role in Christ's baptism.

15. Ibid., p. 29, cites Bonaventure, *Collocationes in Evangelium Joannis*, XIII, col. xlviii, for the three stages of the Exodus narrative: the (Red) sea of contrition, the desert of religion, and the Jordan of death. See also Mazzotta, *Dante*, for the role of the desert in the poem. Singleton, "In exitu Israel de Egypto," cites Gregory's *In moralium*, PL 76, col. 301, to connect individual conversion with the Old Testament narrative. See also Singleton, *Journey to Beatrice*, for the continuation of the Exodus motif through the end of the *Purgatorio*.

16. See also *Par.* XXII, 94–96.

17. On Matelda and natural justification, see Singleton, *Journey to Beatrice*, pp. 204–21.

18. Augustine, *De Genesi ad litteram*, XX.27.55; ed. Zycha, p. 460 (trans. mine).

19. See Hollander's discussion in *Allegory*, e.g., pp. 119–20, where he draws together the various voyage images: "Historically, the images make an imposing string: the ill-fated ships in *Aeneid* I, which are answered by the shipwrecked but safe Aeneas; the damned voyage of Ulysses; the voyage that is Dante's poem; the pilgrim ship that arrives safely at the shores of Purgatory, an angel on its poop; and now also, on a poop, Admiral Beatrice, who is Supreme Commander of the fleet of which Dante's bark is one."

20. Thus Dante retracts his admiration for Bertran as a vernacular poet of arms, expressed in *De vulgari eloquentia*, II, ii, 9.

21. I am much indebted to Freccero, "Bestial Sign," and W. R. Cook and Herzman, "*Inferno* XXXIII," for the eucharistic language here.

22. For the view that Dante did not mean to suggest that Ugolino ate his children, see D'Ovidio, *Nuovi studii danteschi*, pp. 63–116. Singleton's note for *Inf.* XXXIII, 75, in Dante, *Divine Comedy*, vol. I, pt. 2, p. 617, follows D'Ovidio's argument.

23. See J. B. Allen and Moritz, *Distinction of Stories*, pp. 10–11. The conviction that irony is a form of allegory and hence "not a denial of meaning but an affirmation of it" (p. 11) informs the Chaucers of Robertson and his students, and to a lesser extent, Jordan, in *Shape of Creation*. It seems to me a just description of irony in the *Commedia*, for Dante supplies the affirmations within the poem; but I have serious reservations about assuming that, because affirmative irony was a medieval intellectual habit, therefore Chaucer's irony is like infernal irony. This view seems to me another example of reading all fourteenth-century literature through the lens of Dante's work.

24. For the analogy between God's Book, bound with love, and Dante's book, by now also bound into one volume, see Ahern, "Binding the Book."

25. See, for example, the address to the reader at *Purg.* IX, 70–72, and indeed all the addresses to the "lettor," reader.

26. Hollander, in "Dante *Theologus-Poeta*," conclusively proves the uniqueness of this claim, which flies in the face of the scholastic

contempt for literature as lies, and far exceeds the defensive literary apologies of the fourteenth-century humanists.

27. See L. Benson's discussion of romance authentication in *Art and Tradition*, pp. 1–10.

28. On the renewal of "olde bokes," see Payne, *Key of Remembrance*, p. 175: "For the double vision which Donaldson describes [in Chaucer, *Chaucer's Poetry*, pp. 965–80] is exactly the aim of poetry in the rhetorical definition: the double validation of truth by finding it in the past and making it live in the present."

29. Whiting, *Chaucer's Use of Proverbs*, p. 49.

30. Ibid., pp. 48–75; and Lumiansky, "Proverbial Monitory Elements." See also Muscatine's discussion of the clash of styles, in *Chaucer and the French Tradition*, esp. pp. 142–45. Muscatine puts quotation marks around "characterization," but discusses the style characteristic of the narrator frequently and of Pandarus nearly always as full of sententious learning; this deflates the style characteristic of Troilus, the high courtly idiom. Proverbs are an important part of Pandarus's "turbulent, colloquial, energetic" natural realism, "full of the direct, concrete, colorful references that we find in the bourgeois idiom" (p. 142).

31. Kirshenblatt-Gimblett, "Toward a Theory," p. 821.

32. Isidore of Seville, *Etymologiarum*, 1.37.22.

33. Epistola X.vii, in Dante, *Opere latine*, ed. Giuliani, vol. 2, p. 42. Trans. mine.

34. Dante, *Convivio*, II.i.2–4; see Singleton, *Dante's 'Commedia,'* pp. 84–98.

35. Hollander, "Dante *Theologus-Poeta*," pp. 92–100; Hollander's hypothesis makes it clear that such an assumption was polemical in the context of the fourteenth-century debate he traces, and while not directly relevant to the *Convivio*, it was certainly crucial to the *Vita nuova* and the *Commedia*.

36. Augustine, *Confessions*, XI.xxvi–xxviii; ed. Watts, vol. 2, pp. 266–79. Attempting to find an analogue for the eternal present, Augustine gives the example of reciting a familiar psalm. The psalm is known in expectation before the speaker begins, and he holds this knowledge as he recites it, syllable by syllable, until the whole psalm is lodged in memory at the end. The meaning of the psalm is present in each syllable for the speaker, although for a listener who doesn't

know the psalm, meaning is not complete until the last syllable ceases.

37. Such translation applies to the allegoresis in the mythographic tradition interpreting the fable of Ulysses and the sirens, for example. The distinction between imposed and unimposed allegory is Tuve's, in *Allegorical Imagery*.

38. Barley, "Structural Approach," p. 737.

39. Ibid., p. 741, suggests that the entire proverb can be translated onto another level of diction, as for example, "birds of a feather flock together" and "fowl of similar plumage congregate together." Nonetheless, it seems to me that such change considerably weakens the proverb's power, here by eliminating the poetic, pointed language of the original. See, however, the Holstein cow below.

40. See de Saussure, *General Linguistics*, pp. 124–25, on fixed articulations such as idioms and clichés, which have passed into the system of language and do not issue from an individual speaker's combinative freedom. See also Barthes, *Elements of Semiology*, p. 19.

41. Barley, "Structural Approach," pp. 739–40.

42. Advertisers have learned to take advantage of proverbial authority while literalizing the metaphors. On the salt box, the slogan "When it rains it pours" accompanies a picture of a girl in a shower; clearly "rain" is precipitation. But the second "it" refers not to weather, but to the salt; equally literal, this term nonetheless works by making the "audience" (should I say "customer"?) shift its interpretation *within* the proverb. I thank Marie Borroff for this example.

43. We could also express our disapproval with the maxim "cleanliness is next to godliness," a sententia that typifies the tendency of fixed utterances to retain their "shape" at some level of analysis, even when this conservatism results in transformed meaning. In Middle English, "clene" could mean "pure," as of gold, conscience, or body; see, for instance, the Pearl-Poet's *Cleanness*. The word clearly had nothing to do with neatness, but referred instead to spiritual purity, as in the three grades of chastity, which placed virginity highest, next to God. The maxim has retained its sound even while the word migrated in meaning. In the eighteenth century, the Methodist John Wesley used "cleanliness is next to godliness" to typify the domestic, practical kind of religion he advocated; he meant bodily cleanliness. Perhaps because of its new and powerful Methodist associations, the saying fell into disuse until, in the early twentieth century, Pear's

Soap chose it as an advertising slogan. Again, an advertiser recognized the power of a traditional saying. I thank Thomas D. Hill and Gordon Turnbull for this example.

44. Jolles provides a fine example of a *Spruch* (a maxim in this case) that, with identical wording, reverses its meaning when applied to antithetical contexts: "man muß Glück haben" (one must have luck) applied to both a case of misfortune and a case of audacious seizing of the moment. See *Einfache Formen*, p. 157.

45. Payne, *Key of Remembrance*, p. 211, compares Pandaric proverbs to Criseyde; like Criseyde, they are "slydyng of corage."

46. Ibid., p. 175.

47. Dante uses these proverbs as well; see *Purg.* XXXI, 70–72, and *Par.* XXVI, 85–87.

48. Cf., for instance, Ovid, *Metamorphoses* IV.365. For examples of the image of the tree and the vine as lovers, see Young, *Origin and Development*, p. 148; and David, *Strumpet Muse*, p. 34. The most apposite pair, since they are linked by the love-potion tradition as well, is Tristan and Isolde in Marie de France's *Chevrefoil*.

49. Payne, *Key of Remembrance*, p. 207, discusses how the narrator seems to succumb "to the effectiveness of his own style" in Book III, so that the current of his sympathies flows counter to the main moral drift of his poem.

50. See Whiting, *Proverbs, Sentences*, B71–73, p. 24; and P377, p. 471. Bayard is usually alliteratively "blynde" or "bolde."

51. For more thorough discussions of the religious language of love, see Lewis, *Allegory of Love*, pp. 18–22; Lewis, "What Chaucer Really Did," pp. 66–74; and Meech, *Design*, pp. 262–70.

52. See Dunning, "God and Man," p. 174; Dunning characterizes the paganness of the poem's world as a time in which the lover has no choice but to deify his human beloved, since pagan gods were so human.

53. Eliason, *Language of Chaucer's Poetry*, pp. 126–34.

54. Schibanoff, in "Argus and Argive," p. 657, writes: "In his *Troilus*, a poem which consists much more of words than of action, Chaucer seems preoccupied with the conventional aspects of language, and with the attempts of the two lovers to probe the realities behind the words which had, by common usage and agreement, become the highly codified language of love. That words fail miserably to communicate realities, or that the people of *Troilus* fail miserably

to detect the truths they represent, is poignantly symbolized in the lover's realization that Criseyde's absence will be permanent: Troilus accepts the fact that Criseyde's 'name of trouthe / Is now fordon' (v. 1686–87) not because of Cassandra's words, but because of the undeniable implications of a material object—Criseyde's brooch torn from Diomede's cloak."

55. Dunning, "God and Man," p. 181, argues that Troilus's tragic error lies in "overcharging [human love] beyond the limits of human nature." Kean, *Chaucer*, vol. 1, pp. 121–24; apRoberts, "Central Episode"; and David, *Strumpet Muse*, pp. 31–32, all see Troilus's tragedy as his inability to relinquish vain expectations of permanence in merely human love. I emphasize here the role of courtly language in creating Troilus's expectations.

56. I am indebted to Stephen A. Barney for this suggestion.

57. See Wetherbee's excellent discussion of Cassandra's prophecy in *Chaucer and the Poets*, pp. 128–34.

58. Speirs, *Chaucer the Maker*, p. 79, calls the second courtship "an inferior and degraded replica" of the first; Muscatine, *Chaucer and the French Tradition*, pp. 163–64, notes that Diomede resembles Pandarus in his pragmatic powers of speech and action, tempered with a trace of Troilus—presumably for pragmatic rather than sentimental reasons. But see also I. Gordon, *Double Sorrow*, pp. 123–24, who finds the two courtships far more similar than different, and argues that Criseyde's "long resistance" to Troilus is far less comprehensible than her swifter acceptance of Diomede (pp. 110–11).

59. As, for instance, I. Gordon, *Double Sorrow*, pp. 110–24. Arguing against the psychological development of Criseyde's character, Mizener, "Character and Action," writes that her character remains stable and that she merely responds to changing circumstances. Donaldson, "Criseide and Her Narrator," p. 72, comments, of the reader's awakened sense of distrust, that "we are being encouraged to search [for signs of things to be realized in the future], though I do not think we are invited to find."

60. Muscatine, *Chaucer and the French Tradition*, p. 163.

61. Howard, *Three Temptations*, p. 120, makes a similar point about Troilus's combination of human and divine love, but without the link to Dante.

62. Cf. Wetherbee's argument, *Chaucer and the Poets*, pp. 27, 166–78, that Troilus is a "Dante-pilgrim" figure in the poem. The

qualification I would like to introduce stresses the difference in the *Troilus* between language and the experience it purports to describe.

63. Ripheus (along with Trajan, the traditional case of a virtuous pagan who gained salvation) is one of the saved pagans in the Heaven of Justice, *Par.* XX, 67–69. See *Aeneid* II, 426–27. Ripheus appears in the *Troilus* at IV.53, but only as a name; Troilus himself seems to replace the just "Riphëo Troiano."

64. On Troilus's ideal qualities, see David, "Hero of the *Troilus*"; Kean, *Chaucer*, vol. I, pp. 130–31; and Utley, "Troilus' Love." For arguments undercutting Troilus's ideal qualities, see Reiss, "Troilus"; and Lockhart, "Degeneration," which asserts that Troilus's love lacks the quality of selflessness.

65. See J. B. Allen and Moritz, *Distinction of Stories*, p. 11. I do not wish to argue that the *Troilus* affirms nothing, only that we need to distinguish degrees of affirmation if this concept of medieval irony is to be any more useful than the concepts Allen and Moritz criticize.

66. Bloomfield, "Authenticating Realism," pp. 178, 181–82.

67. Thus Chaucer exhibits a nominalist turn of mind; the only realities are particulars, and analogies are part of reason and language rather than substantial categories of being. For late-fourteenth-century reactions against the analogical habit of mind, see Delany, "Undoing Substantial Connection"; see also Boucher, "Nominalism."

Chapter 5

1. Bloomfield, "Distance and Predestination," p. 26.

2. See *Inf.* II, 32: "Io non Enëa, io non Paulo sono" (I am not Aeneas, I am not Paul), an instance of false modesty in which Dante implies exactly the correspondence he seems to deny. Dante echoes Paul when he wonders whether his flight is in body or in soul (*Par.* I, 73–75), and refers to Paul's visionary blindness on the road to Damascus (presumably the occasion of the *raptus*) at *Par.* XXVI, 12. Exegetical tradition granted Paul unsurpassed authority in the vision of God in this life, and Augustine thought that Paul saw God as the blessed will see him after death (*De Genesi ad litteram*, XII.27.55); but Gregory the Great decided that he did not see God face-to-face, because no one can. For references, see Mazzeo, *Structure and Thought*, p. 196 n. 7. In addition, pseudo-Dionysius the Areopagite, whose

hierarchy of angelic orders Dante uses, was thought in the Middle Ages to have been a disciple of Paul and to have learned all his angel lore from him.

3. Augustine, *De Genesi ad litteram*, XII.27.55. The lower levels of vision are corporeal, exemplified by Moses' sight of the burning bush; and imaginative, exemplified by John's apocalyptic vision. See Newman, "St. Augustine's Three Visions."

4. Richard's ladder of vision substitutes an affirmative system of *analogia*, the capacity of creatures to receive the powers God intended for them, for Dionysius's *via negativa*, which asserts that God can be known only indirectly through negation and dissimilitude. The habit of starting with the lowest and moving up by analogies to the most exalted, as the human eye divests itself of the veil of original sin (*revelatio*), is characteristic of Victorine thought. It is also present in the contemplative works of Bernard and of Bonaventure, whose *Itinerarium mentis in Deum* Richard directly influenced. See Kirchberger, "Introduction," pp. 47–56.

5. Epistola X.28; in *Dantis Allegherii epistolae*, ed. Toynbee, pp. 208–9. Dante refers here to Richard, Bernard, and Augustine.

6. Richard of St. Victor, *Benjamin minor*, LXXIV–LXXXII; trans. Zinn, pp. 131–41. The failures of sense, memory, and reason are in LXXXII, p. 141.

7. Ibid., LXXXVI–LXXXVII; trans. Zinn, pp. 145–47. Cf. also *Par.* XIV, 124–26, where Dante hears the hymn but cannot discern tune or words.

8. Boethius, *Consolation*, V.pr.6, 1–80; ed. Stewart et al., pp. 422–27.

9. Augustine, *Confessions*, XI.xxvi–xxvii; ed. Watts, vol. 2, pp. 266–75.

10. Ibid., I.vii; ed. Watts, vol. 1, pp. 24–27.

11. Dante's rebirth contrasts with his preconfessional state, in which Beatrice makes her accusation more pointed by associating it with adulthood (*Purg.* XXXI, 74–75). Dante's beard signifies not only his adulthood, but also his lapse. After his confession, he is finally prepared for the spiritual regeneration suggested by the child similes of the *Paradiso*. On the purely figurative status of Dante's beard, see Auerbach, *Dante*, p. 152.

12. Tables 1 and 2 give breakdowns of the verb forms in Bernard's prayer and in *Par.* XXXIII as a whole.

TABLE I   Verb Forms in Bernard's Prayer

Tense	1st Person	2d Person	3d Person	Total
Future	0	0	0	0
Present	4	8[a]	10[b]	22
Passato prossimo	0	0	2	2
Imperfetto	0	0	0	0
Passato remoto	1	1	2	4

[a] Plus two dependent present subjunctives.
[b] Plus three dependent present subjunctives.

TABLE 2   Verb Forms in *Paradiso* XXXIII

Tense	1st Person	2d Person	3d Person	Total
Future	0	0	2	2
Present	11	15[a]	46[b]	72[c]
Passato prossimo	0	0	2	2
Imperfetto	6[d]	1	17[e]	24
Passato remoto	10[f]	1	12	23

[a] Plus two dependent subjunctives.
[b] Plus four dependent subjunctives.
[c] In addition, there are five present participles.
[d] Plus one dependent subjunctive.
[e] Plus one dependent subjunctive.
[f] Plus two dependent subjunctives.

13. Donaldson, "Ending," p. 95, remarks: "This is the modesty convention again, but transmuted, I believe, into something close to arrogance."

14. Statius, *Thebaid*, XII.816–17; ed. and trans. Mozley, vol. 2, pp. 504–5. See Wetherbee's suggestion that Chaucer's reading of Statius came to him filtered through Dante's Statius in the *Commedia*, in *Chaucer and the Poets*, esp. pp. 111–44.

15. Most critics now agree that Troilus has attained a higher form of wisdom—even the highest degree—than he has exhibited hitherto. See Bloomfield, "Distance and Predestination," p. 25: "Troilus gets as close to Chaucer (and us) as is possible in observing events in their proper perspective—*sub specie aeternitatis*." Bloomfield also limits Troilus's understanding to "what peace can be found in a pagan heaven" (p. 26). See also David, "Hero of the *Troilus*," p. 570, who says that Troilus's laugh is the laugh of wisdom. Dronke, in "Con-

clusion," p. 48, writes: "Troilus' love and desire, and his truly regal nobility, have found their fulfillment in the eighth sphere." Dronke associates this highest fulfillment with divine love. In a different vein, Wetherbee, *Chaucer and the Poets*, pp. 224–43, after finding in Troilus's soul journey "a confirmation of the purity and depth of his intuition of the meaning of love" (p. 234), then focuses on the narrator, who is "finally liberated from the darkness of his long and excessive involvement with the story of Troilus" (p. 235) and who, in Dantean fashion, emerges at the end as the poet. Reiss, in his polemical essay "Troilus," goes much further: he considers Troilus's final attitude a bitterly disappointed *contemptus mundi*, which the narrator in no way shares; Chaucer directs a great deal of irony at Troilus to undermine the validity of his final understanding. I too think there is a failure of understanding, but it is not Troilus's.

16. For instance, Steadman, in *Disembodied Laughter*, p. 143, writes: "The poet as commentator (it would appear) is engaged in a running debate with himself as narrator. Each is endeavoring to speak the last word. Chaucer seems to be chasing his own tail."

17. The general approach I suggest here is not new; Donaldson, "Ending," attempts to resolve the internal contradictions of tone as Chaucer's depiction of the "narrator's internal warfare—a kind of nervous breakdown in poetry" (p. 91). See also Markland, *"Troilus and Criseyde,"* p. 158: "It is easier to visualize a fumbling narrator than a fumbling Chaucer, a fumbling narrator whose story has a force he cannot control rather than a fumbling Chaucer grown inept in closing his major completed poem." As will be apparent, my concentration on narrative rendering does not depend on such a sharp separation between poet and narrator. Rather, I agree with Howard, *Three Temptations*, p. 144, and Jordan, *Shape of Creation*, pp. 103–5, that Chaucer's pose is nearly "straight," in propria persona as a poet. The roles he plays are those any poet must assume to narrate a story.

The other difficulty of the ending, of course, is how to reconcile its view of love with the poem that precedes it. The ending has been roundly criticized as a "sudden and arbitrary," tacked-on moral by Tatlock, "Epilogue," p. 636. Perhaps the most extreme proponent of this view is Curry, "Destiny," esp. pp. 294–98. I think most critics now seek motivation for the ending in earlier parts of the poem; as does Muscatine through style and perspective, in *Chaucer and the*

French Tradition, pp. 161–65. See also Jordan, *Shape of Creation*, pp. 95–110. Donaldson, "Ending," pp. 99–101; David, "Hero of the *Troilus*," pp. 580–81; and Howard, *Three Temptations*, pp. 154–60, argue very persuasively that there *is* a contradiction between the two views of love, but that both are equally serious, and that the paradox results from the contradictory nature of medieval attitudes toward love and the world in general. More recently, Wetherbee, *Chaucer and the Poets*, pp. 224–43, argues that the narrator here joins the poet, having learned through the difficult experience of the poem what the poet knew from the beginning. He writes, "Though he seems utterly at the mercy of the cumulative effect of his long-standing delusions, there is in fact no moment in the poem at which he is closer to Dante and the poets of the past. To understand the conclusion of the *Troilus* it is necessary first of all to recognize the effect of the providential instinct that guides the narrator through this crucial transition" (pp. 224–25). My own reading is meant partly as a response to this account.

18. I follow Bloomfield here, "Eighth Sphere"; both Boccaccio, *Teseida*, XI.1–3, the major source, and Dante, *Par.* XXII, 100–154, Boccaccio's source, have the eighth sphere rather than the seventh, as most of the MSS of the *Troilus* have it. Boccaccio's eighth sphere is the sphere of the moon, but Dante's is that of the fixed stars. Chaucer seems to follow Dante in making Venus the third sphere, so this is probably also the Dantean eighth sphere of the fixed stars; see also Cope, " 'Seventh Spere.' " The sphere of the fixed stars is the ogdoad, the resting place for pagan souls related to the paradisal Elysium.

19. Steadman, who has collated the literary backgrounds for Troilus's soul journey, concludes that "the celestial flight is associated with cognition, with knowledge of the truth or vision of the highest Good" (*Disembodied Laughter*, p. 165).

20. Boccaccio, *Teseida*, XI.2; all references are from Branca's edition. The translations here and following are mine.

21. Cf. Reiss, "Troilus," p. 138.

22. Bloomfield, "Distance and Predestination," p. 26.

23. See Wetherbee, *Chaucer and the Poets*, p. 234; and Reiss, "Troilus," p. 142. Howard, *Three Temptations*, p. 145, also notes the vagueness of Troilus's final resting place. When Chaucer adapts the *Teseida* for the Knight's Tale, he leaves out the posthumous flight but

retains the indeterminacy of Arcite's end, substituting in this case blank protestations of ignorance about the state of souls after death (*CT*, I.2809–15).

24. Howard suggests in *Three Temptations*, pp. 150–51, that this gap led to more modern concepts of tragedy; in Shakespeare's tragedies, we do not know for certain whether the hero is saved or damned. But, as J. B. Allen argues, most recently in *Ethical Poetic*, the medieval concept of tragedy was not Aristotelian and cathartic. Derived only indirectly from the *Poetics* through Averroes (and Hermann the German's 1256 Latin translation of Averroes), tragedy was *ars laudandi*, and it was necessary to know to what extent the hero was praiseworthy. See esp. pp. 19–30.

25. Muscatine, *Chaucer and the French Tradition*, summing up a half century of commentary, still says it best: "She is as the world is and goes as the world goes. If between Troilus and Pandarus the mixed style produces an irony turning on the human incapacity to see, within Criseyde it produces an ambiguity turning on the human inability to be" (p. 154); and "Her ambiguity is her meaning" (p. 164).

26. Donaldson, in "Four Women of Style," pp. 53–59, discusses the unknowability of Criseyde in the narrator's descriptive portraits of her.

27. On the moral process of suggestion-delectation-consent, see Robertson, *Preface to Chaucer*, pp. 477–97; and Howard, *Three Temptations*, pp. 121–35. Robertson emphasizes the morality conveyed by this language, Howard the psychological realism.

28. Howard, "Experience," p. 190. See also Corsa, "Dreams," pp. 57–58, who writes that the dream shows Criseyde deeply desiring ravishment but at no cost of pain or disturbance.

29. As a color, "bon" usually means "ivory." But, as in the reference to ivory dice in the Pardoner's Tale ("This fruyt cometh of the bicched bones two"; *CT*, VI.656), the word can have an ominous resonance. Here, the violence of the eagle's action tends to stress the literal meaning of "bon" (bone) as well as the metaphorical color (ivory).

30. The problem, as Howard correctly insists in "Experience," p. 173, is not so much here as in the distanced report of Criseyde's second courtship.

31. For Troilus on determinism, see Curry, "Destiny"; Patch,

"Troilus on Determinism"; and Bloomfield, "Distance and Predestination," pp. 23–24.

32. Bloomfield, "Distance and Predestination," p. 26.

33. Robertson, *Preface to Chaucer*, pp. 500–501, equates Troilus's final understanding with Chaucer's. I find this confusingly inconsistent with his interpretation of Troilus as an idolator whose sin is misdirected love (p. 498), even softened as this argument is from his statement in "Chaucerian Tragedy," p. 118, that "the tragedy of Troilus is, in an extreme form, the tragedy of every mortal sinner." Why then would he be rewarded with the same insights as the Christian poet? I agree with Reiss, "Troilus," p. 144, that the two perspectives are different, but not, as will be apparent, because Troilus's final understanding is so bitter or futile. Steadman, *Disembodied Laughter*, p. 149, also equates Troilus's perspective with both the narrator's in the "Swich fyn" stanza and "the poet's final addresses *in propria persona*."

34. Donaldson, "Ending," p. 98, remarks on the "sweetness" of this stanza. See also Muscatine, *Chaucer and the French Tradition*, p. 165; and Howard, *Three Temptations*, p. 157, who use the same lines to illustrate the same point. Muscatine writes: "Were the world not fair, it would not have its deep and tragic attractiveness; were it not mutable and passing, it would not be the world." Howard places the attitude expressed here within the context of general medieval ideas of the world.

35. Dante's subject in the *Commedia*, according to the Letter to Can Grande (Epistola x.viii).

36. David, *Strumpet Muse*, pp. 23–35.

37. The best treatment I know of Dante's reconciliation of pagan and Christian history and literature is Mazzotta, *Dante*.

38. See *Inf.* XVI, 128, and *Inf.* XXI, 2; and see Barolini, *Dante's Poets*, esp. pp. 211–28.

39. Payne, *Key of Remembrance*, p. 232; and David, *Strumpet Muse*, p. 29, both conclude that the *Troilus* is about the earthly conditions and difficulties of making moral choices.

40. Auerbach, *Dante*. Howard, *Idea of the Canterbury Tales*, pp. 42–44, makes exactly this point about Chaucer in the *CT*. I hope that my discussion above, of the only place in Chaucer where eschatological matters are raised, subsumes the ending of the *Troilus* as well under the model of Chaucer, Poet of the Secular World.

41. For the Dantean echoes of the proem, see Schless, *Chaucer and Dante*, pp. 102–5; Schless's evaluation of them is cautious in the extreme. In addition to the ascriptions he discusses, "But ye loveres, that bathen in gladnesse, / If any drope of pyte in yow be, / Remembreth you on passed hevynesse / That ye han felt" (1.22–25) may echo *Inf.* v, 121–23, as well as Boethius (*Consolation*, II.pr.4, 3–6) and Boccaccio. Boccaccio does not link pity to "passed hevynesse," as do Boethius, Dante, and Chaucer. Chaucer's version also differs from Boccaccio's in the object of pity; Boccaccio's narrator asks his audience to have pity on *him* (*Filostrato*, 1.5); Chaucer asks his audience to have pity on "the adversite / Of othere folk" (1.25–26). Francesca too states the sententia in a more general case than does Boccaccio: "Nessun maggior dolore / che ricordarsi del tempo felice / ne la miseria; e ciò sa 'l tuo dottore" ("There is no greater sorrow than to recall, in wretchedness, the happy time; and this your teacher knows"; *Inf.* v, 121–23). When the correspondences between Dante and Chaucer are as thick as they are in the proem—even if the thoughts are commonplaces or available from other sources—it seems perverse not to consider the pattern that emerges. Chaucer returns to the magnifying effect of this contrast between joy and sorrow as a leitmotif; see, e.g., III.1219–20 and IV.482–83.

42. See *Inf.* v, 72, 93, and 140, and *Inf.* VI, 2; see also "pio" at *Inf.* v, 117. Robertson, *Preface to Chaucer*, p. 475, reads distance rather than involvement in Chaucer's proem. See Wetherbee, *Chaucer and the Poets*, pp. 37–44, for the link between the "pietà" of *Inf.* v and the narrator's "intuitive human sympathy" (p. 42) in the proem; he cites Dante's discussion of "pietà" in *Convivio*, II.x.6 (p. 43 n. 10). Wetherbee also connects "Thise woful vers, that wepen as I write" (*TC*, 1.7) to Francesca's "dirò come colui che piange e dice" ("I will tell as one who weeps and tells"; *Inf.* v, 126), thus associating Chaucer's narrator both with Dante's pilgrim and with Francesca. For Wetherbee, the connection shows the limitations of Chaucer's narrator, who, committed in the beginning to romance ideology, must be educated out of this delusion and toward a full understanding of the providential point of view also available, though mainly in retrospect, in the proem. Thus Wetherbee's understanding of the link between "pietà" and "compassioun" depends on his account of the narrator as evolving toward full knowledge and a Dantean unity with the poet at the end; see above, p. 85 and p. 236 n. 9. My own account

of the role of the providential point of view and its relation to "compassioun" differs, as will be seen below.

43. For the role of Virgilian *pietas* in defining the danger of "pietà" in *Inf.* V, see Mazzotta, *Dante*, pp. 168–69. For the suggestion that both Dante and Chaucer "evoke the contexts of classical epic as a way of suggesting levels of more profound meaning which their narrators, committed as they are to a 'romance' view of their material, can appreciate only dimly," see Wetherbee, *Chaucer and the Poets*, p. 41.

44. See Auerbach, "Figura," esp. pp. 80–81 in *Gesammelte Aufsätze*, and pp. 58–60 in Manheim's translation; and Freccero, "Introduction," p. 5. For the relations of narrative time and the view from the end in the *Troilus*, see Ganim, "Time and Tone."

45. See Davis et al., *Chaucer Glossary*, p. 47.

46. Singleton's commentary in Dante, *Divine Comedy*, vol. 1, pt. 2, p. 84. Boccaccio's full account of their ill-fated affair derives from the *Commedia* itself; see *Comento alla Divina Commedia*, ed. Guerra, vol. 2, pp. 137–39, lecture 20. Moreover, Boccaccio clearly presents the main point of Dante's story, the mediation of the book, as a fiction (p. 145).

47. For instance, Branca Doria (*Inf.* XXXIII, 129–41); although he did not die until ca. 1325, Dante puts his soul in the tenth circle. Examples of people still alive in 1300, but dead at the writing of the poem, are more common; in the same canto, see Fra Alberigo and Michel Zanche. Boniface VIII, though not physically present, is clearly destined for the *bolgia* of the simonists, as shown when Nicholas III mistakenly recognizes his papal successor in Dante (*Inf.* XIX, 52–57).

48. See Pézard, *Dante sous la Pluie de Feu*, pp. 77–108; and Nevin, "Ser Brunetto's Immortality," p. 23.

49. See Bloomfield, "Distance and Predestination," pp. 15, 18–19. For Criseyde before Chaucer, see Mieszkowski, "Reputation of Criseyde." On Chaucer's later explorations of the exemplary form, see Middleton, "*Physician's Tale*," esp. pp. 27–31. She writes of the reception of the *Troilus* as a cautionary exemplum: "What could the poet do, if an attentive and devoted audience could regard the complex narrative stance of the *Troilus* as tantamount to an Ovidian complaint about a faithless woman, and the tragedy as consisting in her rebellion against a current fashion in love? Chaucer's answer to the

problems posed by complexity was more complexity: if men insist that stories prove something, then that stubborn conviction would itself be subjected to scrutiny in fiction" (p. 30). I believe Chaucer was already wrestling with the problem of exemplary fiction in the *Troilus*, and that he calls attention to the inadequacy of the form as traditionally conceived by introducing such difficulties as the "moral" at V.1785: "Beth war of men, and herkneth what I seye!" This is intentionally jarring, and intended rhetorically to provoke thought.

50. See Trimpi, "Quality of Fiction," for the theory that fiction is ethical analysis derived from classical rhetoric. See also J. B. Allen, *Ethical Poetic*, which elaborates this theory on the basis of medieval commentaries.

51. This is the second theory of "legal fiction," from Jolles, *Einfache Formen*. The *Troilus* resembles literature derived from the "simple form" *Kasus*, discussed on pp. 171–99.

52. Howard, "Chaucer the Man," p. 343; and *Idea of the Canterbury Tales*, p. 125.

References

In the References, primary works are listed under the author's name rather than that of an editor or translator; anonymous works are listed by title. In every case, the short forms in the Notes will lead to the alphabetized entry in the References.

The following abbreviations are used:

ChR *Chaucer Review*
CL *Comparative Literature*
ELH *English Literary History*
JEGP *Journal of English and Germanic Philology*
MLN *Modern Language Notes*
PL J.-P. Migne, *Patrologiae cursus completus, series latina* (Paris, 1844–64)
PMLA *Publications of the Modern Language Association of America*

Ahern, John. "Binding the Book: Hermeneutics and Manuscript Production in *Paradiso* 33." *PMLA*, 97 (1982): 800–809.

Allen, Don Cameron. "Marlowe's *Dido* and the Tradition." In Richard Hosley, ed., *Essays in Shakespeare and Elizabethan Drama in Honor of Hardin Craig*. Columbia, Mo., 1962. Pp. 55–68.

Allen, Judson Boyce. *The Ethical Poetic of the Later Middle Ages*. Toronto, 1982.

———. "Hermann the German's Averroistic Aristotle and Medieval Poetic Theory." *Mosaic*, 9 (1976): 67–81.

Allen, Judson Boyce, and Theresa Anne Moritz. *A Distinction of Stories: The Medieval Unity of Chaucer's Fair Chain of Narratives for Canterbury*. Columbus, Ohio, 1981.

Allen, Robert J. "A Recurring Motif in Chaucer's *House of Fame*." *JEGP*, 55 (1956): 393–405.

apRoberts, Robert P. "The Central Episode in Chaucer's *Troilus*." *PMLA*, 77 (1962): 373–85.

————. "Love in the *Filostrato*." *ChR*, 7 (1972): 1–26.

Aristotle. *Politics*. Ed. and trans. H. Rackham. Loeb Classical Library. Cambridge, Mass., 1967.

————. *The Rhetoric and the Poetics of Aristotle*. Ed. Friedrich Solmsen, trans. W. Rhys Roberts and Ingram Bywater. Modern Library. New York, 1954.

Auerbach, Erich. *Dante, Poet of the Secular World*. Trans. Ralph Manheim. Chicago, 1961.

————. "Dante's Addresses to the Reader." *Romance Philology*, 7 (1954): 268–78.

————. "Figura." In Auerbach, *Gesammelte Aufsätze zur romanischen Philologie*. Bern, 1967. Pp. 55–92.

————. "Figura." In Auerbach, *Scenes from the Drama of European Literature*. Trans. Ralph Manheim. Theory and History of Literature, vol. 9. Minneapolis, Minn., 1984. Pp. 11–76.

Augustine. *Confessiones*. PL 32, cols. 659–868.

————. *Confessions*. Ed. and trans. W. Watts. 2 vols. Loeb Classical Library. Cambridge, Mass., 1977.

————. *De civitate Dei*. Ed. Emanuel Hoffman. 2 vols. In *Corpus scriptorum ecclesiasticorum latinorum*, vol. 40, sec. 5, pts. 1–2. Vienna, 1899–1900.

————. *De doctrina christiana libri quattuor*. Ed. William McAllen Green. In *Corpus scriptorum ecclesiasticorum latinorum*, vol. 80, sec. 6, pt. 6. Vienna, 1963.

————. *De Genesi ad litteram libri duodecim*. Ed. Iosephus Zycha. In Augustine, *Sancti Aureli Augustini opera*, vol. 28, sec. 3, pt. 1. Prague, 1894.

————. *In Ioannis Evangelium tractatus CXXIV*. PL 35, cols. 1379–1976.

————. *On Christian Doctrine*. Trans. D. W. Robertson, Jr. Indianapolis, Ind., 1958.

————. *The Soliloquies of St. Augustine*. Ed. and trans. Thomas F. Gilligan. New York, 1943.

————. *Soliloquiorum*. PL 32, cols. 869–904.

Averroes. *Middle Commentary on the Poetics of Aristotle*. Ed. and trans. O. B. Hardison, Jr. In Alex Preminger, O. B. Hardison, Jr., and Kevin Kerrane, eds., *Classical and Medieval Literary Criticism: Translations and Interpretations*. New York, 1974. Pp. 349–82.

Banfield, Ann. *Unspeakable Sentences: Narration and Representation in the Language of Fiction*. Boston, 1982.

Barley, Nigel. "A Structural Approach to the Proverb and Maxim, with Special Reference to the Anglo-Saxon Corpus." *Proverbium*, 20 (1972): 737–49.

Barolini, Teodolinda. *Dante's Poets: Textuality and Truth in the 'Comedy.'* Princeton, N.J., 1984.

Barthes, Roland. "L'Effet de réel." *Communications*, 11 (1968): 84–89.

————. *Elements of Semiology*. Trans. Annette Lavers and Colin Smith. New York, 1977; orig. pub. 1967.

————. "Introduction à l'analyse structurale des récits: A propos d'Actes 10–11." *Recherches des sciences religieuses*, 58 (1970): 17–38.

Battaglia, Salvatore, ed. *Grande dizionario della lingua italiana*. 13 vols. Turin, (1962–).

Bauer, Gero. *Studien zum System und Gebrauch der 'Tempora' in der Sprache Chaucers und Gowers*. Wiener Beiträge zur Englischen Philologie, vol. 73. Vienna, 1970.

Bennett, J. A. W. *Chaucer's Book of Fame: An Exposition of "The House of Fame."* Oxford, 1968.

Bennett, Josephine Waters. *The Rediscovery of Sir John Mandeville*. New York, 1971; orig. pub. 1954.

Benoît de Sainte-Maure. *Roman de Troie*. Ed. Leopold Constans. 6 vols. Societé des Anciens Textes Français, 58. Paris, 1904–12.

————. *Roman de Troie*. Trans. (in excerpt) Robert K. Gordon. In Gordon, *The Story of Troilus*. New York, 1964. Pp. 1–24.

Benson, C. David. "'O Nyce World': What Chaucer Really Found in Guido delle Colonne's History of Troy." *ChR*, 13 (1979): 308–15.

Benson, Larry D. *Art and Tradition in Sir Gawain and the Green Knight*. New Brunswick, N.J., 1965.

————. "The 'Love-Tydynges' in Chaucer's *House of Fame*." In Julian Wasserman and Robert J. Branch, eds., *Chaucer in the Eighties*. Syracuse, N.Y., 1986. Pp. 3–22.

Benveniste, Emile. *Problèmes de linguistique générale*. Paris, 1966.

Bersuire, Pierre. *Metamorphosis Ovidiana moraliter*. Paris, 1515.

Bethel, J. P. "The Influence of Dante on Chaucer's Thought and Expression." Ph.D. diss., Harvard University, 1927.

Bethurum, Dorothy. "Chaucer's Point of View as Narrator in the Love Poems." *PMLA*, 74 (1959): 511–20. Rpt. in Richard J. Schoeck and Jerome Taylor, eds., *Chaucer Criticism, Volume II: Troilus and Criseyde and the Minor Poems*. Notre Dame, Ind., 1961. Pp. 211–31.

Biblia sacra iuxta vulgatam Clementinam. 6th ed. Madrid, 1977.

Bloomfield, Morton W. "Authenticating Realism and the Realism of Chaucer." *Thought*, 39 (1964): 335–58. Rpt. in Bloomfield, *Essays and Explorations: Studies in Ideas, Language, and Literature*. Cambridge, Mass., 1970. Pp. 174–98.

———. "Chaucer's Sense of History." *JEGP*, 6 (1952): 301–13. Rpt. in Bloomfield, *Essays and Explorations: Studies in Ideas, Language, and Literature*. Cambridge, Mass., 1970. Pp. 13–26.

———. "Distance and Predestination in *Troilus and Criseyde*." *PMLA*, 72 (1957): 14–26.

———. "The Eighth Sphere: A Note on Chaucer's *Troilus and Criseyde*." *Modern Language Review*, 53 (1958): 408–10.

Boccaccio, Giovanni. *Il comento alla Divina Commedia*. Ed. Domenico Guerra. 3 vols. Bari, 1918.

———. *Il decamerone*. Ed. Vittore Branca. Vol. 4 of Boccaccio, *Tutte le opere di Giovanni Boccaccio*.

———. *De genealogie deorum gentilium*. Vols. 10–11 of Boccaccio, *Opere*. Ed. Vincenzo Romano. Bari, 1951.

———. *De mulieribus claris*. Ed. Vittorio Zaccaria. Vol. 10 of Boccaccio, *Tutte le opere di Giovanni Boccaccio*.

———. *Il Filostrato*. Ed. Vittore Branca. In Boccaccio, *Tutte le opere di Giovanni Boccaccio*. Vol. 2, pp. 1–228.

———. *Il Teseida*. Ed. Vittore Branca. In Boccaccio, *Tutte le opere di Giovanni Boccaccio*. Vol. 2, pp. 229–664.

———. *Tutte le opere di Giovanni Boccaccio*. Ed. Vittore Branca. 12 vols. Milan, 1964–76.

Boethius. *Tractates, De consolatione philosophiae*. Ed. and trans. H. F. Stewart, E. K. Rand, and S. J. Tester. Loeb Classical Library. Cambridge, Mass., 1978.

Boitani, Piero. *Chaucer and the Imaginary World of Fame*. Chaucer Studies, 10. Cambridge, 1984.

———. "Chaucer's Labyrinth: Fourteenth-Century Literature and Language." *ChR*, 17 (1983): 197–220.

————. *English Medieval Narrative in the Thirteenth and Fourteenth Centuries*. Trans. Joan Krakover Hall. Cambridge, 1982.

————. "What Dante Meant to Chaucer." In Boitani, ed., *Chaucer and the Italian Trecento*. Cambridge, 1983. Pp. 115–39.

Bonaventure. *Collocationes in Evangelium Joannis*. Vol. 6 of Bonaventure, *Opera omnia*, ed. Collegii a S. Bonaventura. 10 vols. Quaracchi, 1882–1902.

————. *Itinerarium mentis in Deum*. Vol. 5 of Bonaventure, *Opera omnia*, ed. Collegii a S. Bonaventura. 10 vols. Quaracchi, 1882–1902.

Booth, Wayne C. *The Rhetoric of Fiction*. Chicago, 1961.

Boucher, Holly Wallace. "Nominalism: The Difference Between Chaucer and Boccaccio." *ChR*, 20 (1986): 213–20.

Boughner, Daniel C. "Elements of Epic Grandeur in the *Troilus*." *ELH*, 6 (1939): 200–210.

Braswell, Mary Flowers. "Architectural Portraiture in Chaucer's *House of Fame*." *Journal of Medieval and Renaissance Studies*, 11 (1981): 101–12.

Bronson, Bertrand H. *In Search of Chaucer*. Toronto, 1960.

Brusendorff, Aage. *The Chaucer Tradition*. Oxford, 1967; orig. pub. 1925.

Bühler, Karl. *Sprachtheorie: Die Darstellung der Sprache*. Jena, 1934.

Bundy, Murray Wright. *The Theory of Imagination in Classical and Medieval Thought*. University of Illinois Studies in Language and Literature, 12. Urbana, Ill., 1927. Pp. 183–471.

Burnley, David. *A Guide to Chaucer's Language*. Norman, Okla., 1983.

Carruthers, Mary J. "Italy, *Ars Memorativa*, and Fame's House." *Studies in the Age of Chaucer, Proceedings*, ser. 2 (1987): 179–88.

Cerisola, Pier Luigi. "Il 'disdegno' di Guido Cavalcanti (*Inf.* X, 61–63)." *Ævum*, 52 (1978): 195–217.

Charity, A. C. *Events and Their Afterlife: Dialectics of Christian Typology in the Bible and Dante*. Cambridge, 1966.

Chaucer, Geoffrey. *The Book of Troilus and Criseyde*. Ed. R. K. Root. Princeton, N.J., 1954; orig. pub. 1926.

————. *Chaucer's Poetry: An Anthology for the Modern Reader*. 2d ed. Ed. E. T. Donaldson. New York, 1975.

————. *The Complete Works of Geoffrey Chaucer*. 2d ed. Ed. F. N. Robinson. Boston, 1957.

————. *The Riverside Chaucer*. 3d rev. ed. Ed. Larry D. Benson et al. Boston, 1987. Based on *The Complete Works of Geoffrey Chaucer*, ed. F. N. Robinson.

————. *Troilus and Criseyde: A New Edition of Chaucer's 'The Book of Troilus.'* Ed. Barry Windeatt. New York, 1984.

Chiampi, James T. *Shadowy Prefaces: Conversion and Writing in the "Divine Comedy."* Ravenna, 1981.

Chiarenza, Marguerite Mills. "The Imageless Vision and Dante's *Paradiso.*" *Dante Studies*, 90 (1972): 77–90.

Cicero. *De finibus bonorum et malorum*. Ed. and trans. H. Rackham. London, 1931.

Clanchy, M. T. *From Memory to Written Record: England, 1066–1307*. Cambridge, Mass., 1979.

Cleanness. In Malcolm Andrew and Ronald Waldron, eds., *The Poems of the Pearl Manuscript*. Berkeley, Calif., 1978. Pp. 207–300.

Clemens, Wolfgang. *Chaucer's Early Poetry*. Rev. ed. Trans. C. A. M. Sym. New York, 1964.

Coghill, Nevill. *The Poet Chaucer*. London, 1949.

Colish, Marcia L. *The Mirror of Language: A Study in the Medieval Theory of Knowledge*. Rev. ed. Lincoln, Nebr., 1983.

Contini, Gianfranco, ed. *Poeti del duecento*. 2 vols. Milan, 1960.

Cook, Robert G. "Chaucer's Pandarus and the Medieval Ideal of Friendship." *JEGP*, 69 (1970): 407–24.

Cook, W. R., and R. B. Herzman. "*Inferno* XXXIII: The Past and the Present in Dante's Imagery of Betrayal." *Italica*, 56 (1979): 377–83.

Cooper, Helen. "The Girl with Two Lovers: Four Canterbury Tales." In P. L. Heyworth and Dan Davin, eds., *Medieval Studies for J. A. W. Bennett, Aetatis Suae LXX*. Oxford, 1981. Pp. 65–79.

Cope, Jackson I. "Chaucer, Venus, and the 'Seventh Spere.'" *MLN*, 67 (1952): 245–46.

Corsa, Helen Storm. *Chaucer: Poet of Mirth and Morality*. Notre Dame, Ind., 1964.

————. "Dreams in *Troilus and Criseyde*." *American Imago*, 27 (1970): 52–65.

Coulthard, Malcolm. *Introduction to Discourse Analysis*. London, 1977.

Culler, Jonathan. *Structuralist Poetics: Structuralism, Linguistics, and the Study of Literature*. Ithaca, N.Y., 1976.

Curry, Walter Clyde. "Destiny in *Troilus and Criseyde.*" In Curry, *Chaucer and the Medieval Sciences.* 2d ed. New York, 1960. Pp. 241–98.

Curtius, E. R. *European Literature and the Latin Middle Ages.* Trans. Willard R. Trask. Bollingen Series 36. Princeton, N. J., 1973.

Dane, Joseph A. "Chaucer's *House of Fame* and the *Rota Virgilii.*" *Classical and Modern Literature,* 1 (1980): 57–75.

Dante Alighieri. *Convivio.* Ed. Ernesto Giacomo Parodi and Flaminio Pellegrini. In Dante, *Le opere di Dante: Testo critico della Società Dantesca Italiana.* Pp. 143–294.

———. *The Convivio of Dante Alighieri.* Trans. Philip Wicksteed. The Temple Classics. London, 1903.

———. *Dantis Allegherii epistolae: The Letters of Dante.* Ed. and trans. Paget Toynbee. Oxford, 1920.

———. *De vulgari eloquentia.* Ed. Pio Rajna. In Dante, *Le opere di Dante: Testo critico della Società Dantesca Italiana.* Pp. 295–327.

———. *La Divina Commedia di Dante Alighieri.* Rev. ed. Ed. M. Porena and M. Pazzaglia. 3 vols. Bologna, 1965–66.

———. *The Divine Comedy.* Ed. and trans. with a commentary by Charles S. Singleton. 3 vols., 6 pts. Bollingen Series 80. Princeton, N.J., 1970–75.

———. *Le opere di Dante: Testo critico della Società Dantesca Italiana.* Ed. Michele Barbi et al. 2d ed. Florence, 1960.

———. *Le opere latine di Dante Allighieri.* Ed. Giambattista Giuliani. Vol. 2: *Epistolae.* Florence, 1882.

———. *Rime.* Ed. Michele Barbi. In Dante, *Le opere di Dante: Testo critico della Società Dantesca Italiana.* Pp. 51–142.

———. *Vita nuova.* Ed. Michele Barbi. In Dante, *Le opere di Dante: Testo critico della Società Dantesca Italiana.* Pp. 1–49.

David, Alfred. "Chaucerian Comedy and Criseyde." In Mary Salu, ed., *Essays on Troilus and Criseyde.* Chaucer Studies, 3. Cambridge, 1979. Pp. 90–104.

———. "The Hero of the *Troilus.*" *Speculum,* 37 (1962): 566–81.

———. "Literary Satire in the *House of Fame.*" *PMLA,* 75 (1960): 333–39.

———. *The Strumpet Muse: Art and Morals in Chaucer's Poetry.* Bloomington, Ind., 1976.

Davis, Norman, Douglas Gray, Patricia Ingham, and Anne Wallace-Hadrill. *A Chaucer Glossary.* Oxford, 1979.

Delany, Sheila. *Chaucer's House of Fame: The Poetics of Skeptical Fideism.* Chicago, 1972.

―――. "Undoing Substantial Connection: The Late Medieval Attack on Analogical Thought." *Mosaic*, 5 (1972): 31–52.

de Man, Paul. "The Rhetoric of Temporality." In Charles S. Singleton, ed., *Interpretation: Theory and Practice.* Baltimore, Md., 1969. Pp. 173–209.

De Sanctis, Francesco. *Nuovi saggi critici.* 31st ed. Naples, 1921.

de Saussure, Ferdinand. *Course in General Linguistics.* Ed. Charles Bally and Albert Sechehaye, in collaboration with Albert Riedlinger. Trans. Wade Baskin. New York, 1966.

Disce mori (in excerpt). Ed. Lee W. Patterson. In Patterson, "Ambiguity and Interpretation: A Fifteenth-Century Reading of *Troilus and Criseyde.*" *Speculum*, 54 (1979): 297–330.

Donaldson, E. T. "Briseis, Briseida, Criseide, Cresseid, Cressid: Progress of a Heroine." In Edward Vasta and Zacharias P. Thundy, eds., *Chaucerian Problems and Perspectives: Essays Presented to Paul E. Beichner, C.S.C.* Notre Dame, Ind., 1979. Pp. 3–12.

―――. "Chaucer's Three 'P's': Pandarus, Pardoner, and Poet." *Michigan Quarterly Review*, 14 (1975): 282–301.

―――. "Chaucer the Pilgrim." *PMLA*, 69 (1954): 928–36. Rpt. in Donaldson, *Speaking of Chaucer.* Pp. 1–12.

―――. "Criseide and Her Narrator." In Donaldson, *Speaking of Chaucer.* Pp. 65–83.

―――. "The Ending of Chaucer's 'Troilus.'" In Arthur Brown and Peter Foote, eds., *Early English and Old Norse Studies Presented to Hugh Smith.* London, 1963. Pp. 26–45. Rpt. as "The Ending of Troilus" in Donaldson, *Speaking of Chaucer.* Pp. 84–101.

―――. "The Masculine Narrator and Four Women of Style." In Donaldson, *Speaking of Chaucer.* Pp. 46–64.

―――. *Speaking of Chaucer.* London, 1970.

D'Ovidio, Francesco. *Nuovi studii danteschi.* Milan, 1907.

Dronke, Peter. "The Conclusion of *Troilus and Criseyde.*" *Medium Ævum*, 33 (1964): 47–52.

―――. "Francesca and Héloïse." *CL*, 27 (1975): 113–35.

Dunning, T. P. "God and Man in *Troilus and Criseyde.*" In Norman Davis and C. L. Wrenn, eds., *English and Medieval Studies Presented to J. R. R. Tolkien.* London, 1962. Pp. 164–82.

Eliason, Norman E. *The Language of Chaucer's Poetry: An Appraisal of the Verse, Style, and Structure.* Anglistica 17. Copenhagen, 1972.

Eneas: A Twelfth-Century French Romance. Trans. John A. Yunck. Records of Civilization, 93. New York, 1974.

Erzgräber, Willi. "Tragik und Komik in Chaucers *Troilus and Criseyde.*" In Dieter Riesner and Helmut Gneuss, eds., *Festschrift für Walter Hübner.* Berlin, 1964. Pp. 139–63.

Ferrucci, Franco. *The Poetics of Disguise: The Autobiography of the Work in Homer, Dante, and Shakespeare.* Trans. Ann Dunnigan. Ithaca, N.Y., 1980.

Festus. *De verborum significatu.* Ed. W. M. Lindsay. Leipzig, 1913.

Fillmore, Charles J. *Santa Cruz Lectures on Deixis.* Available from Indiana University Linguistics Club. Bloomington, 1971.

Freccero, John. "Bestial Sign and Bread of Angels (*Inferno* 32–33)." *Yale Italian Studies,* 6 (1977): 53–66. Rpt. in Freccero, *Dante: The Poetics of Conversion.* Pp. 152–66.

———. "Casella's Song (*Purg.* ii, 112)." *Dante Studies,* 91 (1973): 73–80. Rpt. in Freccero, *Dante: The Poetics of Conversion.* Pp. 186–94.

———. *Dante: The Poetics of Conversion.* Ed. Rachel Jacoff. Cambridge, Mass., 1986.

———. "Dante's Prologue Scene. (I. The Region of Unlikeness. II. The Wings of Ulysses)." *Dante Studies,* 84 (1966): 1–25. Rpt. in Freccero, *Dante: The Poetics of Conversion.* Pp. 1–28.

———. "Infernal Irony: The Gates of Hell." *MLN,* 98 (1983): 769–86. Rpt. in Freccero, *Dante: The Poetics of Conversion.* Pp. 93–109.

———. "Introduction." In Freccero, ed., *Dante: A Collection of Critical Essays.* Englewood Cliffs, N.J., 1965. Pp. 1–7.

———. "Manfred's Wounds and the Poetics of *Purgatorio.*" In E. Cook et al., eds., *Center and Labyrinth: Essays in Honor of Northrop Frye.* Toronto, 1983. Pp. 69–82. Rpt. in Freccero, *Dante: The Poetics of Conversion.* Pp. 195–208.

———. "Medusa: The Letter and the Spirit." *Yale Italian Studies,* 1 (1972): 1–18. Rpt. in Freccero, *Dante: The Poetics of Conversion.* Pp. 119–35.

———. "The River of Death: *Inferno* ii, 108." In J. A. Molinaro and S. B. Chandler, eds., *The World of Dante: Six Studies in Language and Thought.* Toronto, 1966. Pp. 25–42. Rpt. in Freccero, *Dante: The Poetics of Conversion.* Pp. 55–69.

Freiwald, Leah R. "Swich Love of Frendes: Pandarus and Troilus." *ChR,* 6 (1971): 120–29.

Friedman, Norman. "Point of View in Fiction." *PMLA*, 70 (1955): 1160–84.

Fulgentius. *Opera*. Ed. R. Helm. Leipzig, 1898.

Fulgentius the Mythographer. Trans. Leslie George Whitbread. Columbus, Ohio, 1971.

Fyler, John M. *Chaucer and Ovid*. New Haven, Conn., 1979.

———. "The Fabrications of Pandarus." *Modern Language Quarterly*, 41 (1980): 115–30.

Galway, Margaret. "The *Troilus* Frontispiece." *Modern Language Review*, 44 (1949): 161–77.

Ganim, John M. "Time and Tone in Chaucer's *Troilus*." *ELH*, 43 (1976): 141–53.

Gardner, Edmund G. "Notes on the 'Matière de Bretagne' in Italy." *Proceedings of the British Academy*, 15. London, n.d.

Gaylord, Alan. "Friendship in Chaucer's *Troilus*." *ChR*, 3 (1969): 239–64.

Gellrich, Jesse M. *The Idea of the Book in the Middle Ages: Language Theory, Mythology, and Fiction*. Ithaca, N.Y., 1985.

Genette, Gérard. *Narrative Discourse: An Essay in Method*. Trans. Jane E. Lewin. Ithaca, N.Y., 1980.

Geoffrey of Vinsauf. *The New Poetics*. Trans. Jane Baltzell Kopp. In James J. Murphy, ed., *Three Medieval Rhetorical Arts*. Berkeley, Calif., 1971. Pp. 27–108.

———. *Poetria nova*. In Edmund Faral, ed., *Les Arts poétiques du XIIe et du XIIIe siècle*. Bibliothèque de l'Ecole des Hautes Etudes, 238. Paris, 1924. Pp. 197–262.

Gilson, Etienne. *Dante and Philosophy*. Trans. David Moore. New York, 1963.

———. *La Philosophie de saint Bonaventure*. Paris, 1924.

Girard, René. "The Mimetic Desire of Paolo and Francesca." In Girard, *"To Double Business Bound": Essays on Literature, Mimesis, and Anthropology*. Baltimore, Md., 1978. Pp. 1–8.

Gmelin, Hermann. "Die Anreden an den Leser in Dantes *Komödie*." *Deutsches Dante-Jahrbuch*, 29–30 (1951): 260–70.

Gordon, Ida L. *The Double Sorrow of Troilus: A Study in Ambiguities in Troilus and Criseyde*. Oxford, 1970.

Gordon, Robert K. *The Story of Troilus*. New York, 1964.

Green, Eugene. "The Voices of the Pilgrims in the General Prologue to *The Canterbury Tales*." *Style*, 9 (1975): 55–81.

Gregory the Great. *In expositionem Beati Job moralia, seu moralium libri*.

PL 75, col. 509, through 76, col. 782. Trans. as *The Morals on the Book of Job*, Members of the English Church. Oxford, 1850.

Guido delle Colonne. *Historia destructionis Troiae*. Trans. Mary Elizabeth Meek. Bloomington, Ind., 1974.

Guillaume de Lorris and Jean de Meun. *Roman de la rose*. Ed. Ernest Langlois. 5 vols. Paris, 1914–22.

Hamburger, Käte. *The Logic of Literature*. Trans. Marilynn J. Rose. Bloomington, Ind., 1973.

Hammond, Eleanor P. *Chaucer: A Bibliographical Manual*. New York, 1908.

Hanning, Robert W. "Chaucer's First Ovid: Metamorphosis and Poetic Tradition in the *Book of the Duchess* and the *House of Fame*." In Leigh A. Arrathoon, ed., *Chaucer and the Craft of Fiction*. Rochester, Mich., 1986. Pp. 121–63.

Hardison, O. B., Jr. "The Place of Averroes' Commentary on the *Poetics* in the History of Medieval Criticism." In vol. 4 of *Medieval and Renaissance Studies: Proceedings of the Southeastern Institute of Medieval and Renaissance Studies, Summer 1968*, ed. John L. Lievsay. Durham, N.C., 1970. Pp. 57–81.

Hatcher, Anna, and Mark Musa. "The Kiss: *Inferno* V and the Old French Prose *Lancelot*." *CL*, 10 (1968): 97–109.

Helterman, Jeffrey. "The Masks of Love in *Troilus and Criseyde*." *CL*, 26 (1974): 14–31.

Henryson, Robert. *The Testament of Cresseid*. In Henryson, *The Complete Works of Robert Henryson*, ed. Denton Fox. Oxford, 1981. Pp. 111–31.

Hollander, Robert. *Allegory in Dante's Commedia*. Princeton, N.J., 1966.

———. "Dante *Theologus-Poeta*." *Dante Studies*, 94 (1976): 91–136.

Holy Bible, Translated from the Latin Vulgate. Trans. the English College at Rheims, 1582–1609. New York, 1844.

Horace. *Satires, Epistles, Ars Poetica*. Ed. and trans. H. Rushton Fairclough. Loeb Classical Library. Cambridge, Mass., 1966.

Howard, Donald R. "Chaucer's Idea of an Idea." *Essays and Studies*, n.s. 29 (1976): 39–55.

———. "Chaucer the Man." *PMLA*, 80 (1965): 337–43.

———. "Experience, Language, and Consciousness: *Troilus and Criseyde*, II, 596–931." In Jerome Mandel and Bruce Rosenberg, eds., *Medieval Literature and Folklore Studies in Honor of Francis Lee Utley*. New Brunswick, N.J., 1970. Pp. 173–92.

————. "Fiction and Religion in Boccaccio and Chaucer." *Journal of the American Academy of Religion*, 47 (1979): 308–28.

————. "Flying Through Space: Chaucer and Milton." In Joseph Anthony Wittreich, ed., *Milton and the Line of Vision*. Madison, Wisc., 1975. Pp. 3–23.

————. *The Idea of the Canterbury Tales*. Berkeley, Calif., 1976.

————. "Literature and Sexuality: Book III of Chaucer's *Troilus*." *Massachusetts Review*, 8 (1967): 442–56.

————. "The World of *Mandeville's Travels*." *Yearbook of English Studies*, 1 (1971): 1–17.

Irvine, Martin. "Medieval Grammatical Theory and Chaucer's *House of Fame*." *Speculum*, 60 (1985): 850–76.

Isidore of Seville. *Etymologiarum sive originum libri xx*. Ed. W. M. Lindsay. 2 vols. Oxford, 1957.

Jakobson, Roman. "Shifters, Verbal Categories, and the Russian Verb." In Jakobson, *Selected Writing*. The Hague, 1957. Vol. 2, pp. 130–47.

James, Henry. *The Art of the Novel*. Ed. R. P. Blackmur. New York, 1934.

Jauss, H. R. "The Alterity and Modernity of Medieval Literature." *New Literary History*, 10 (1979): 181–227.

Jerome. *Libri duo adversus Iovinianum*. PL 23, cols. 211–336.

John of Salisbury. *Metalogicon*. Ed. Clemens C. I. Webb. Oxford, 1929.

————. *Polycraticus*. Ed. Clemens C. I. Webb. Oxford, 1909.

Jolles, André. *Einfache Formen*. Tübingen, 1974; orig. pub. 1930.

Jordan, Robert M. *Chaucer and the Shape of Creation: The Aesthetic Possibilities of Inorganic Form*. Cambridge, Mass., 1967.

————. "Lost in the Funhouse of Fame: Chaucer and Postmodernism." *ChR*, 18 (1983): 100–115.

————. "The Narrator in Chaucer's *Troilus*." *ELH*, 25 (1958): 237–57.

Kaminsky, Alice R. *Chaucer's Troilus and Criseyde and the Critics*. Athens, Ohio; 1980.

Kean, P. M. *Chaucer and the Making of English Poetry*. 2 vols. London, 1972.

Kellogg, Alfred L. "An Augustinian Interpretation of Chaucer's Pardoner." *Speculum*, 26 (1951): 465–81.

Kendrick, Laura. "Chaucer's *House of Fame* and the French Palais de Justice." *Studies in the Age of Chaucer*, 6 (1984): 121–33.

Kermode, Frank. "Secrets and Narrative Sequence." *Critical Inquiry*, 7 (1980): 83–101.

Kirby, Thomas A. *Chaucer's Troilus: A Study in Courtly Love*. Gloucester, Mass., 1958.

Kirchberger, Clare. "Introduction." In Kirchberger, ed. and trans., *Richard of St. Victor: Selected Writings on Contemplation*. London, 1957. Pp. 15–56.

Kirkpatrick, Robin. "The Wake of the *Commedia*: Chaucer's *Canterbury Tales* and Boccaccio's *Decameron*." In Piero Boitani, ed., *Chaucer and the Italian Trecento*. Cambridge, 1983. Pp. 201–30.

Kirshenblatt-Gimblett, Barbara. "Toward a Theory of Proverb Meaning." *Proverbium*, 22 (1974): 821–27.

Kittredge, George Lyman. *Chaucer and His Poetry*. Cambridge, Mass., 1915.

Koonce, B. G. *Chaucer and the Tradition of Fame: Symbolism in the House of Fame*. Princeton, N.J., 1966.

Lansing, Richard H. *From Image to Idea*. Ravenna, 1977.

Leicester, H. Marshall, Jr. "A General Prologue to the *Canterbury Tales*." *PMLA*, 95 (1980): 213–24.

Leo, Ulrich. "The Unfinished *Convivio* and Dante's Rereading of the *Aeneid*." *Medieval Studies*, 13 (1951): 41–64.

Lewis, C. S. *The Allegory of Love: A Study in Medieval Tradition*. New York, 1958.

———. *The Discarded Image*. Cambridge, 1964.

———. "What Chaucer Really Did to *Il Filostrato*." *Essays and Studies*, 17 (1932): 56–75.

Leyerle, John. "Chaucer's Windy Eagle." *University of Toronto Quarterly*, 40 (1971): 247–65.

Lockhart, Adrienne R. "Semantic, Moral, and Aesthetic Degeneration in *Troilus and Criseyde*." *ChR*, 8 (1973): 100–118.

Lowes, J. L. "Chaucer and Dante." *Modern Philology*, 14 (1916–17): 705–35.

Lubbock, Percy. *The Craft of Fiction*. New York, 1957.

Lumiansky, R. M. "The Function of Proverbial Monitory Elements in Chaucer's *Troilus and Criseyde*." *Tulane Studies in English*, 2 (1950): 5–48.

———. "The Story of Troilus and Briseida According to Benoît and Guido." *Speculum*, 29 (1954): 727–33.

Lydgate, John. *The Fall of Princes*. Ed. Henry Bergen. Early English Text Society, e.s. 121. London, 1924.

McAlpine, Monica E. *The Genre of Troilus and Criseyde*. Ithaca, N.Y., 1978.

McCall, John P. "The Trojan Scene in Chaucer's *Troilus*." *ELH*, 29 (1962): 263–75.

McGerr, Rosemarie Potz. "Retraction and Memory: Retrospective Structure in the *Canterbury Tales*." *CL*, 37 (1985): 97–113.

Mandeville's Travels. Ed. M. C. Seymour. London, 1968.

Mann, Jill. "Troilus' Swoon." *ChR*, 14 (1980): 319–35.

Marie de France. *Chevrefoil*. In Marie de France, *Marie de France: Lais*, ed. Alfred Ewert. Oxford, 1976. Pp. 123–26.

Markland, Murray F. "*Troilus and Criseyde*: The Inviolability of the Ending." *Modern Language Quarterly*, 31 (1970): 147–59.

Mazzeo, J. A. *Medieval Cultural Tradition in Dante's Comedy*. Ithaca, N.Y., 1960.

———. *Structure and Thought in the Paradiso*. Ithaca, N.Y., 1958.

Mazzotta, Giuseppe. *Dante, Poet of the Desert: History and Allegory in the Divine Comedy*. Princeton, N.J., 1979.

Meech, Sanford B. *Design in Chaucer's Troilus*. Syracuse, N.Y., 1959.

Mehl, Dieter. "The Audience of Chaucer's 'Troilus and Criseyde.'" In Beryl Rowland, ed., *Chaucer and Middle English Studies in Honour of Rossell Hope Robbins*. London, 1974. Pp. 173–89.

Meyer-Lübke, Wilhelm. *Romanisches etymologisches Wörterbuch*. 4th ed. Heidelberg, 1968.

Middleton, Anne. "Chaucer's 'New Men' and the Good of Literature in the *Canterbury Tales*." In Edward W. Said, ed., *Literature and Society*. Selected Papers from the English Institute, n.s. 3. Baltimore, Md., 1980. Pp. 15–56.

———. "The *Physician's Tale* and Love's Martyrs: 'Ensaumples Mo Than Ten' as a Method in the *Canterbury Tales*." *ChR*, 9 (1973): 9–32.

Mieszkowski, Gretchen. "The Reputation of Criseyde, 1155–1500." *Transactions of the Connecticut Academy of Arts and Sciences*, 43 (1971): 71–153.

Miller, Jacqueline T. "The Writing on the Wall: Authority and Authorship in Chaucer's *House of Fame*." *ChR*, 17 (1982): 95–115.

Minnis, A. J. *Chaucer and Pagan Antiquity*. Chaucer Studies, 8. Cambridge, 1982.

———. *Medieval Theory of Authorship: Scholastic Literary Attitudes in the Later Middle Ages*. London, 1984.

Mizener, Arthur. "Character and Action in the Case of Criseyde." *PMLA*, 54 (1939): 65–81.

Murphy, James J. *Rhetoric in the Middle Ages: A History of Rhetorical Theory from St. Augustine to the Renaissance*. Berkeley, Calif., 1974.

Muscatine, Charles. *Chaucer and the French Tradition*. Berkeley, Calif., 1957.

Nardi, Bruno. *Dante e la cultura medioevale*. 2d rev. ed. Bari, 1949.

————. *Saggi di filosofia dantesca*. Florence, 1967.

Nevin, Thomas. "Ser Brunetto's Immortality: *Inferno* XV." *Dante Studies*, 96 (1978): 21–37.

Newman, F. X. "St. Augustine's Three Visions and the Structure of the *Commedia*." *MLN*, 72 (1967): 56–78.

Nolan, Barbara. "'A Poet Ther Was': Chaucer's Voices in the General Prologue to *The Canterbury Tales*." *PMLA*, 101 (1986): 154–69.

Nykrog, Per. "The Rise of Literary Fiction." In Robert L. Benson and Giles Constable, eds., with Carol D. Lanham, *Renaissance and Renewal in the Twelfth Century*. Cambridge, Mass., 1982. Pp. 593–612.

Ong, Walter. "The Writer's Audience Is Always a Fiction." *PMLA*, 90 (1975): 337–43.

Ovid. *Heroides*. 2d ed. Ed. and trans. Grant Showerman, rev. by G. P. Goold. Cambridge, Mass., 1977.

————. *Metamorphoses*. Ed. and trans. Frank Justus Miller. 2 vols. Loeb Classical Library. Cambridge, Mass., 1976–77.

Ovide moralisé. Ed. C. de Boer. 3 vols. Verhandelingen der Koninklijke Akademie van Wetenschappen te Amsterdam, Nieuwe Reeks, 21. Wiesbaden, 1966.

Padoan, Giorgio. "Ulisse 'fandi fictor' e le vie della sapienza." *Studi danteschi*, 37 (1960): 21–61.

Patch, Howard R. "Troilus on Determinism." *Speculum*, 6 (1929): 225–43. Rpt. in Richard J. Schoeck and Jerome Taylor, eds., *Chaucer Criticism, Volume II: Troilus and Criseyde and the Minor Poems*. Notre Dame, Ind., 1961. Pp. 71–85.

Patterson, Lee W. "Ambiguity and Interpretation: A Fifteenth-Century Reading of *Troilus and Criseyde*." *Speculum*, 54 (1979): 297–330.

————. "'Rapt with Pleasaunce': Vision and Narration in the Epic." *ELH*, 48 (1981): 455–75.

Payne, Robert O. *The Key of Remembrance*. New Haven, Conn., 1963.

Pearsall, Derek. "The *Troilus* Frontispiece and Chaucer's Audience." *Yearbook of English Studies*, 7 (1977): 68–74.

Pézard, André. *Dante sous la Pluie de Feu*. Paris, 1950.

Poggioli, Renato. "Tragedy or Romance? A Reading of the Paolo and Francesca Episode in Dante's *Inferno*." *PMLA*, 72 (1957): 313–58.

Pratt, Robert A. "Chaucer and *Le Roman de Troyle et de Criseida*." *Studies in Philology*, 53 (1956): 509–39.

———. "A Note on Chaucer's Lollius." *MLN*, 65 (1950): 183–87.

Reiss, Edmund. "Chaucer and His Audience." *ChR*, 14 (1980): 390–402.

———. "Troilus and the Failure of Understanding." *Modern Language Quarterly*, 29 (1968): 131–44.

Richard of St. Victor. *Benjamin minor*. In *Richard of St. Victor: The Twelve Patriarchs, The Mystical Ark, Book Three of the Trinity*. Ed. and trans. Grover A. Zinn. New York, 1979. Pp. 51–147.

Robertson, D. W., Jr. "Chaucerian Tragedy." *ELH*, 19 (1952): 1–37. Rpt. in Richard J. Schoeck and Jerome Taylor, eds., *Chaucer Criticism, Volume II: Troilus and Criseyde and the Minor Poems*. Notre Dame, Ind., 1961. Pp. 86–121.

———. *A Preface to Chaucer: Studies in Medieval Perspectives*. Princeton, N.J., 1962.

Rohlfs, Gerhard. *Grammatica storica della lingua italiana e dei suoi dialetti*. Trans. Temistocle Franceschi and Maria Caciagli Fancelli. 3 vols. Turin, 1969.

Roman de la rose. See Guillaume de Lorris and Jean de Meun.

Roman d'Eneas. Ed. J. J. Salverda de Grave. 2 vols. Paris, 1925–29.

Romberg, Bertil. *Studies in the Narrative Technique of the First Person Novel*. Trans. Michael Taylor and Harold H. Borland. Stockholm, 1962.

Ronconi, A. "Aoristi e perfetti in Dante." *Lingua nostra*, 8 (1947): 3–6.

Root, R. K. *The Poetry of Chaucer*. 2d rev. ed. Boston, 1922.

Rowe, Donald W. *O Love O Charite: Contraries Harmonized in Chaucer's Troilus*. Carbondale, Ill., 1976.

Rowland, Beryl. "Bishop Bradwardine, the Artificial Memory, and the *House of Fame*." In Rossell Hope Robbins, ed., *Chaucer at Albany*. New York, 1975. Pp. 41–62.

Ruggiers, Paul G. "The Unity of Chaucer's *House of Fame*." *Studies in*

Philology, 50 (1953): 16–29. Rpt. in Richard J. Schoeck and Jerome Taylor, eds., *Chaucer Criticism: Volume II, Troilus and Criseyde and the Minor Poems*. Notre Dame, Ind., 1961. Pp. 261–74.

―――. "Words into Images in Chaucer's *House of Fame*: A Third Suggestion." *MLN*, 69 (1954): 34–37.

Santoro, Domenico. "Due acrostici nella 'Divina Commedia.'" *Giornale dantesco*, 12 (1904): 21–24.

Schibanoff, Susan. "Argus and Argive: Etymology and Characterization in Chaucer's *Troilus*." *Speculum*, 51 (1976): 647–58.

Schless, Howard H. "Chaucer and Dante." In Dorothy Bethurum, ed., *Critical Approaches to Medieval Literature*. New York, 1960. Pp. 130–54.

―――. "Chaucer and Dante: A Reevaluation." Ph.D. diss., University of Pennsylvania, 1956.

―――. *Chaucer and Dante: A Reevaluation*. Norman, Okla., 1984.

―――. "Transformations: Chaucer's Use of Italian." In D. S. Brewer, ed., *Geoffrey Chaucer: Writers and Their Background*. Athens, Ohio, 1975. Pp. 184–223.

Scriptores rerum mythicarum Latini tres Romae nuper riperti. Ed. G. H. Bode. Hildesheim, 1968.

Shoaf, R. A. "'Auri sacra fames' and the Age of Gold (*Purg.* XXII, 40–41 and 148–150)." *Dante Studies*, 96 (1978): 195–99.

―――. *Dante, Chaucer, and the Currency of the Word: Money, Images, and Reference in Late Medieval Poetry*. Norman, Okla., 1983.

―――. "Dante's *Commedia* and Chaucer's Theory of Mediation: A Preliminary Sketch." In Donald Rose, ed., *New Perspectives in Chaucer Criticism*. Norman, Okla., 1982. Pp. 83–103.

Shook, Laurence K. "The *House of Fame*." In Beryl Rowland, ed., *Companion to Chaucer Studies*. Rev. ed. Oxford, 1979. Pp. 341–54.

Simonelli, Maria Sampoli. "Il canto X del *Purgatorio*." *Studi danteschi*, 33 (1955–56): 121–45.

Singleton, Charles S. *Dante's 'Commedia': Elements of Structure*. Baltimore, Md., 1977; orig. pub. 1954.

―――. "In exitu Israel de Egypto." *Dante Studies*, 78 (1960): 1–24.

―――. "Inferno X: Guido's Disdain." *Dante Studies*, 77 (1962): 49–65.

―――. *Journey to Beatrice*. Baltimore, Md., 1977; orig. pub. 1958.

Slaughter, Eugene E. "Chaucer's Pandarus: Virtuous Uncle and Friend." *JEGP*, 48 (1949): 186–95.

Speirs, John. *Chaucer the Maker*. London, 1951.

Spenser, Edmund. *The Faerie Queene*. In Spenser, *Spenser: Poetical Works*, ed. J. C. Smith and E. de Selincourt. Oxford, 1977; orig. pub. 1912. Pp. 1–406.

Spitzer, Leo. "The Addresses to the Reader in the *Commedia*." In Spitzer, *Romanische Literaturstudien 1936–56*. Tübingen, 1959. Pp. 574–95.

————. "A Note on the Poetic and Empirical 'I' in Medieval Authors." *Traditio*, 4 (1946): 414–22.

————. "Speech and Language in *Inferno* XIII." In Spitzer, *Romanische Literaturstudien 1936–56*. Tübingen, 1959. Pp. 544–68.

————. "Zum Stil Marcel Prousts." In Spitzer, *Stilstudien*. 2 vols. Munich, 1961; orig. pub. 1928. Vol. 2, pp. 465–97.

Stammerjohann, Harro. "Strukturen der Rede: Beobachtungen an der Umgangssprache von Florenz." *Studi di filologia italiana*, 28 (1970): 295–397.

Stanzel, F. K. *Narrative Situations in the Novel*. Trans. J. P. Pusak. Bloomington, Ind., 1971.

Statius. *Thebaid*. Ed. and trans. J. H. Mozley. 2 vols. Loeb Classical Library. Cambridge, Mass., 1982.

Steadman, John M. *Disembodied Laughter: Troilus and the Apotheosis Tradition: A Reexamination of Narrative and Thematic Contexts*. Berkeley, Calif., 1972.

Stevenson, Kay. "The Endings of Chaucer's *House of Fame*." *English Studies*, 59 (1978): 10–26.

Strohm, Paul. "Chaucer's Audiences: Fictional, Implied, Intended, Actual." *ChR*, 18 (1983): 137–45.

Swing, T. K. *The Fragile Leaves of the Sybil*. Westminster, Md., 1962.

Tatlock, J. S. P. "Chaucer and Dante." *Modern Philology*, 3 (1905–6): 367–72.

————. "The Epilog of Chaucer's *Troilus*." *Modern Philology*, 18 (1920–21): 625–59.

Taylor, John. *The 'Universal Chronicle' of Ranulf Higden*. Oxford, 1966.

Taylor, Karla. "Chaucer Reads the *Divine Comedy*." Ph.D. diss., Stanford University, 1983.

————. "From *superbo Iliön* to *umile Italia*: The Acrostic of *Paradiso* XIX." *Stanford Italian Review*, 7 (1987): 47–66.

————. "Proverbs and the Authentication of Convention in *Troilus and Criseyde."* In Stephen A. Barney, ed., *Chaucer's Troilus: Essays in Criticism.* Hamden, Conn., 1980. Pp. 277–96.

———. "A Text and Its Afterlife: Dante and Chaucer." *CL,* 35 (1983): 1–20.

Thomas Aquinas. *S. Thomae Aquinatis in Metaphysicam Aristotelis commentaria.* 2d ed. Ed. M. R. Cathala. Turin, 1926.

Thompson, David. "Dante's Ulysses and the Allegorical Journey." *Dante Studies,* 85 (1967): 33–59.

Toynbee, Paget. "Dante and the Lancelot Romance." In Toynbee, *Dante Studies and Researches.* London, 1920. Pp. 1–37.

———. *A Dictionary of Proper Names and Notable Matters in the Works of Dante.* Oxford, 1898.

Traugott, Elizabeth Closs, and Mary Louise Pratt. *Linguistics for Students of Literature.* New York, 1980.

"A Tretys of Miraclis Pleyinge." In W. C. Hazlitt, ed., *The English Drama and Stage.* Roxburghe Library. New York, 1869. Pp. 73–95.

Trimpi, Wesley. "The Quality of Fiction." *Traditio,* 30 (1974): 1–118.

Tuve, Rosamund. *Allegorical Imagery: Some Medieval Books and Their Posterity.* Princeton, N.J., 1966.

Utley, Francis Lee. "Troilus' Love and St. Paul's Charity." In Beryl Rowland, ed., *Chaucer and Middle English Studies in Honour of Rossell Hope Robbins.* London, 1974. Pp. 272–87.

Valli, Luigi. "Il canto XIX nel *Paradiso.*" In Valli, *La struttura morale dell' universo dantesco.* Rome, 1935. Pp. 113–30.

Vance, Eugene. "Augustine's *Confessions* and the Grammar of Selfhood." *Genre,* 6 (1973): 1–28.

Virgil. *Eclogues, Georgics, Aeneid.* Ed. and trans. H. R. Fairclough. 2 vols. Loeb Classical Library. Cambridge, Mass., 1968.

Vitz, E. B. "The 'I' of the *Roman de la rose.*" *Genre,* 6 (1973): 49–75.

Wallace, David. "Chaucer and Boccaccio's Early Writings." In Piero Boitani, ed., *Chaucer and the Italian Trecento.* Cambridge, 1985; orig. pub. 1983. Pp. 141–62.

———. *Chaucer and the Early Writings of Boccaccio.* Chaucer Studies, 12. Cambridge, 1985.

Weinrich, Harald. *Tempus: Besprochene Welt und Erzählte Welt.* 2d rev. ed. Stuttgart, 1971.

Wetherbee, Winthrop. *Chaucer and the Poets: An Essay on "Troilus and Criseyde."* Ithaca, N.Y., 1984.

———. "The Descent from Bliss: 'Troilus' III.1310–1582." In Stephen A. Barney, ed., *Chaucer's Troilus: Essays in Criticism.* Hamden, Conn., 1980. Pp. 297–317.

———. *Platonism and Poetry in the Twelfth Century.* Princeton, N.J., 1972.

Whiting, B. J. *Chaucer's Use of Proverbs.* Harvard Studies in Comparative Literature, 11. Cambridge, Mass., 1934.

———. *Proverbs, Sentences, and Proverbial Phrases from English Writings Mainly Before 1500.* Cambridge, Mass., 1968.

Williams, George. "The *Troilus* Frontispiece Again." *Modern Language Review*, 57 (1962): 173–78.

Windeatt, Barry. "Chaucer and the *Filostrato*." In Piero Boitani, ed., *Chaucer and the Italian Trecento.* Cambridge, 1985; orig. pub. 1983. Pp. 163–83.

Yates, Frances. *The Art of Memory.* London, 1966.

Young, Karl. "Chaucer's *Troilus and Criseyde* as Romance." *PMLA*, 53 (1938): 38–63.

———. *The Origin and Development of the Story of Troilus and Criseyde.* New York, 1968; orig. pub. 1908.

Zimbardo, Rose A. "Creator and Created: The Generic Perspective of Chaucer's *Troilus and Criseyde*." *ChR*, 11 (1977): 283–98.

Index

Library of Congress Cataloging-in-Publication Data

Taylor, Karla, 1952–
Chaucer reads "The divine comedy" / Karla Taylor.
   p.   cm.
Bibliography: p.
Includes index.
ISBN 0-8047-1544-0
   1. Chaucer, Geoffrey, d. 1400. Troilus and Criseyde.   2. Chaucer, Geoffrey, d.
1400—Knowledge—Literature.   3. Dante Alighieri, 1265–1321—Influence—
Chaucer.   4. Dante Alighieri, 1265–1321. Divina commedia.   I. Title.
PR1896.T39 1989   89-4424
821'.1—dc19   CIP